A MOST DIPLOMATIC GENERAL

THE LIFE OF GENERAL LORD ROBERTSON OF OAKRIDGE

Also from Brassey's:

McGEOCH
The Princely Sailor: Mountbatten of Burma

KINVIG
Scapegoat: General Percival of Singapore

FOLCHER/HILL
Marching to Captivity: The War Diaries of a French Peasant, 1939–45

FARNDALE
THE HISTORY OF THE ROYAL ARTILLERY
The Years of Defeat: Europe and North Africa, 1939–41

A MOST DIPLOMATIC GENERAL

THE LIFE OF GENERAL LORD ROBERTSON
OF OAKRIDGE BT
GCB GBE KCMG KCVO DSO MC
1896–1974

———————

DAVID WILLIAMSON

BRASSEY'S
London • Washington

First English Edition 1996

UK editorial offices: Brassey's, 33 John Street, London WC1N 2AT
UK orders: Marston Book Services, PO Box 269, Abingdon, OX14 4SD

North American orders: Brassey's Inc., PO Box 960,
Herndon, VA 22070, USA

David Williamson has asserted his moral right to be identified as
the author of this work.

Library of Congress Cataloging in Publication Data
available

British Library Cataloguing in Publication Data
A catalogue record for this book is available from the British Library

ISBN 1 85753 180 9 Hardcover

Typeset by M Rules
Printed in Great Britain by Redwood Books, Trowbridge

To my Family and Friends

CONTENTS

LIST OF MAPS

LIST OF PLATES

11. Brian Robertson and Sholto Douglas (second and third from right) with other members of the Allied Control Council and Co-ordinating Committee, 1946–47.

12. Bizonal Conference at Frankfurt, 7 January 1948. Left–right Mr C Adcock and Generals Clay, Robertson and Macready. *(US National Archives III-SC-296087)*

13. Easter 1948. Brian Robertson gathering wood for a barbecue at Ostenwalde.

14. Brian Robertson appears to be decidedly unimpressed by an officer during his tour of the Rhine Army in March 1948. *(Crown Copyright/MoD)*

15. Brian Robertson and the Prime Minister, Clement Attlee, in Berlin on 10 March 1949. *(Crown Copyright/MoD)*

16. Brian Robertson's 'and spouses' invitation to Red Army Day celebrations on 23 February 1948.

17. Brian Robertson and Clay (second and third from right) at Villa Hügel, Essen, October 1948.

18. Brian Robertson arriving in the Canal Zone on 24 July 1950. *(Crown Copyright/MoD)*

19. A cartoon from the Egyptian paper *Akhbar El Yom*, 5 December 1953, referring to the recent victory of the pro-Egyptian parties in the Sudan. The caption below the cartoon runs:

> (The London press said that the war dance was the reason for the British defeat in the Sudan)
> Churchill: 'From now on, I want neither diplomacy, nor talks . . . I want you to dance like this man.'

Brian Robertson is top left, Eden top right and Churchill bottom right. *(Akhbar El Yom)*

20. The cartoonist of the News Chronicle (19 January 1955) depicts Brian Robertson's 'military style organisation' at the BTC.

21. Brian Robertson returning home after breaking his leg in a skiing accident in January 1959. *(Daily Express, 8 January 1959)*

FOREWORD

by

Lord Longford, KG, PC

Brian Robertson was an unforgettable man. With his military bearing he was every inch a soldier among professors. With his precise, scholarly way of speech, a professor among soldiers. The servant of political masters, he was able to hold his own with any of them.

I was closely associated with him for one year only 1947–1948, but I became friends with him later in the House of Lords and came to know and admire his remarkable life story. In the year when I worked with him I was Minister for the British Zone of Germany, responsible under the Foreign Secretary for the treatment of the subject population and for the 6,000 members of the Control Commission. He was the Executive Head of the Commission resident in Germany which I visited 26 times in the year.

Our relationship at that time was not and could not be an easy one. I came out from England filled with a passionate message of forgiveness for the Germans. It was his official duty to carry out the harsh policy of Potsdam which was only abandoned under the threat to the West from Russia. Looking back, I can easily see that he was of far more assistance to the German people than I was. The population of the Ruhr was horribly under-nourished. When Brian Robertson wrote a Memorandum summed up in the words 'without food nothing can happen', food supplies began to pour in almost at once.

It was Brian Robertson who brought out to Germany as Head of the Educational Service Robert Birley, former Headmaster of Charterhouse and later Headmaster of Eton. No man contributed more than Robert Birley to the democratic regeneration of Germany.

Two years after I had ceased to be Minister for the British zone I visited Germany as Minister of Civil Aviation and called on Dr. Adenauer, by then Chancellor of Western Germany. I had come to know him quite well when I was Minister. Adenauer was not a man who readily showed his emotions. But there was a break in his voice when he told me how much he would miss Brian Robertson, then the departing High Commissioner. He had found him a true friend of Germany.

Brian Robertson was a man of brilliant mind and incorruptible character.

PREFACE

It is History's loss that Brian Robertson was one of the few Second World War generals not to publish his memoirs in retirement. Neither, unfortunately, did he keep a diary or a large personal archive, which would have facilitated the writing of his biography. Consequently his achievements have latterly been largely unsung, except in a brief essay by a distinguished German archivist, Dr. Ulrich Reusch and a perceptive but essentially politically motivated article by Jack Straw. This biography is thus an overdue attempt to fill the gap.

Brian Robertson was not a fighting general like Patton or Montgomery, who caught the public's imagination with great miltary victories. He was primarily a gifted staff officer, who played an important and at times even pivotal role in his country's history during the middle two decades of the Twentieth Century. During the campaigns in North Africa and Italy he rapidly gained the reputation of an administrator of genius who could keep the troops supplied with everything from Christmas puddings to ammunition. It was however in Germany where first as Deputy Military Governor, then as Military Governor and finally as British High Commissioner he became, particularly during the Soviet blockade of western Berlin, a figure of international significance. Through strength of personality and sheer administrative excellence, he maintained British influence in Germany despite the precipitate post-war decline in British power. He was one of the midwives – perhaps indeed the senior midwife – who assisted at the birth of the German Federal Republic in 1948–49. In 1950, he moved on to become the Commander-in-Chief of the (British) Middle East Land Forces. The challenge facing him there was to reach an agreement with Egypt which would allow British forces to return rapidly to the great base on the Suez Canal in time of war. In arduous and lengthy negotiations in 1953 he laid the foundations for an agreement with Nasser, which almost reconciled the demands of Egyptian nationalism with Britain's need for a wartime base. Alas, this achievement was to be shattered in 1956 with the outbreak of the brief Suez war. His last eight years as a public servant were spent wrestling with the Sisyphean task of modernising and making profitable British Railways, which was ultimately beyond even his legendary skills.

To those who did not know him well Brian Robertson was a taciturn, even frightening figure. In a profession where accuracy, diligence and intelligence were essential to save lives and win battles, he could not tolerate fools or wastrels. Yet once he was convinced of the ability and good will of a subordinate, he would trust him and give him considerable license. When dealing with such pressing matters as the supply of armies or the populations of occupied territories, he was capable of making tough decisions, yet he also realised that the essence of politics was compromise and that half a loaf was often so much better than no loaf at all.

Above all, he was a convinced Christian, who genuinely tried to see the good in his fellow men. In the Second World War, where the pressure of events called for quick decisions and the ruthless subordination of the individual to the efficient machinery of command, this was not always evident, but later in Germany he showed a real understanding for the predicament of the defeated and demoralised Germans. In Egypt, too, he was able to establish a genuine rapport with Nasser and appreciate what he was trying to do for his countrymen. As Chairman of the British Transport Commission, he was far from a military autocrat. In fact, within the organisation he was often accused of compromising too much! Finally, in retirement during those perplexing and often infuriating years of the 1960s, he did not condemn modern youth. On the contrary, he remained an optimist convinced of its potential for good. As was abundantly clear from his speeches in the Lords and his work for the Gloucestershire Association of Boys Clubs and the Salters' Company, he moved with the times and surveyed the world with a shrewd, principled and essentially benign eye.

ACKNOWLEDGEMENTS

Without the kindness, encouragement and assistance of Major the Lord Robertson of Oakridge, the Hon. Mrs. Christine Cuming, the Hon. Mrs. Fiona Chapman and the late Mrs. Anne Handley-Derry this book would never have been written. I am also particularly grateful to the staff of the Public Records Office at Kew and of the Imperial War Museum, where I have done the bulk of my research. They unfailingly produced the files I needed. On my shorter visits to the Cabinet Office Historical Section, National Army Museum, the Liddell Hart Centre for Military Archives, The British Railways Board Record Centre, the British Newspaper Library, the Modern Records Centre, Warwick, the Salters' Company and the Royal Engineers Library and Archives, Chatham, I experienced the same efficiency and helpfulness. I also received invaluable advice, help and information from the following : The late Mr. A. Albu, Lord Aldington, Mr. S. Anderson, Mrs. Bardsley, Mrs. T Barnett, Mr. G. Behrend, Mr. M. Bonavia, Mr. C. Booker, Brigadier Browne, Mr. J. Brownjohn, Mr. I. Calvocoressi, Mr. D. Campbell, Sir Rupert Clarke, Mr. H. Collins, Sir James Colyer-Ferguson, Major T. Coverdale, Brigadier A. Cowgill, the late Lieutenant General Sir John Cowley, Lt. Col. H. Cuming, the late Sir Patrick Dean, Sir Alistaire Down, Sir Anthony Reay Geddes, Mr. D. Goodhead of Dunlop's, S. Africa, Mr. I.L. Gray-Jones, Lord Harding of Petherton, Lady Doris Humphreys, Mr. W. Hunt, General Sir William Jackson, the late Sir Ian Jacob, Dr. G. Jones of Reading University, Mr. A.G. Kentridge, Viscount Knutsford, Mr. Larkworthy, Mr. Lederer, Lord Longford, Major-General Sir James Lunt, Mr. J. Mackeurtan, Mr. A. Marecco, Mr. E. Merrill, Mr. J. Morris, Mr. P. Murray, Dame Alison Munro, Mr. H. Naylor, Mrs. L. Orde, General Sir Douglas Packard, Mr. E. Page, Mr. B. Parker, Sir Edward Playfair, the late General Sir Charles Richardson, Sir Frank Roberts, Miss P. Rumbold, Mr. I. Sconce, Mr. D.L. Stewart, Prof. N.M. Temperley, Mr. J. Thomas, Count N. Tolstoy, Lady Helen Vincent, Mrs. Wansborough-Jones, Mr. B. Weeks, Sir Reginald Wilson, Mr. B. Windsor, Mr. R.J. Wood and Mr. G. Wright.

Without a generous grant from the British Academy in 1994 I would not have been able to proceed so quickly with the archive work necessary for this biography.

I would like to thank the following for granting me permission to use copyright material within their possession: Mrs. D. Bagnall Oakley; British Railways Board; the Librarian and Archivist of Charterhouse School; Mr. M. Cornwall Jones; the family of Major General Sir George Erskine; Earl Haig; Mrs. R.M. Harris; the Trustees of the Imperial War Museum; the Trustees of the Liddell Hart Centre for Military Archives, King's College London; Viscount Knutsford; the Modern Record Centre, Warwick; the National Army Museum; the National Museum of the History of Labour; Mrs. Lavinia Orde; the Fellows of Queens' College, Cambridge; The Royal Institute of International Affairs; Major the Lord Robertson of Oakridge; and Major N. C. Wimberley. Crown Copyright material in the Lymer Papers and the quotation on p.87 from the *British Zone Review* are reproduced with the permission of the controller of HMSO. In some cases copyright owners have been elusive despite every effort to track them down.

1

CHILDHOOD AND YOUTH

When, in middle age, Brian Robertson was Military Governor of the British Zone in Germany, he appeared to many of his German 'subjects' to be a caricature of a high ranking British officer. Not only was he a baronet but his immaculate dress and confident bearing seemed to indicate that here was a man whose family had long provided officers, ministers and colonial governors for the Crown. On his father's side, at any rate, this impression was far from the truth. His father, Field Marshal Sir William Robertson, had certainly reached the very top of the British Army, but his achievement was all the more remarkable because he had risen to this eminence from the ranks of the Victorian Army[1].

William Robertson, or 'Wully' as he was later called in the Army, grew up in the small Lincolnshire village of Welbourne where his father was both tailor and postmaster. Wully attended the local village school, where his ability was such that it attracted the patronage of the local rector. However, in the absence of a scholarship system that would have enabled him to progress to a grammar school and ultimately to university, he had to give up his studies at the early age of 13. For the next four years he was in service with a succession of employers, the most prestigious of whom was the Earl of Cardigan of Deene Park in Northamptonshire.

In 1877, despite his mother's implacable opposition, Wully joined the 16th Lancers. After ten years in the ranks, by which time he had become Troop Sergeant Major, he took advantage of a new scheme introduced as part of the Cardwell reforms to take a commission in the Third Dragoon Guards, then stationed in India. To enter the moneyed and caste-conscious world of the officers mess of a cavalry regiment in the late nineteenth century was a brave step for him to take, but despite spells of considerable personal loneliness, he exploited his chances to the full – even to the extent of having lessons in Hindustani in the heat of an Indian afternoon. His intellect and meticulous grasp of detail were soon noticed by General Sir Henry Brackenbury, who was in the process of modernising the Intelligence organisation of the Indian Army. In 1892, he joined the Staff at Simla and it was here that he met and then married two years later Mildred Palin, the daughter of a Lieutenant Colonel in the Bombay Staff Corps. Her family were privately appalled at the marriage of their daughter to somebody whom they regarded as little more than a

1

Lincolnshire yokel. Nevertheless, as Wully's biographer drily observed, it was not to be so long before 'they were only too happy to bask in the warmth and glory of later successes'.

The marriage, too, was a real success and was to provide a stable and loving environment for their four children. Initially, life was far from easy. Not only did Wully have to swot hard for the all-important entrance exam into the Staff College at Camberley, but their first child, Hubert, died in infancy. Fortunately on 22 July, 1896, a second son was born. In September he was duly baptised Brian Hubert in Christ Church at Simla. That Autumn, Wully gained the crucial place at the Staff College and so the family returned home to England in December.

Two years later, Wully graduated from Staff College, second in his year, and was promptly given a War Office appointment. While he commuted daily to London, his family lived in Horsell near Woking. His son Brian was only three when he first experienced the abrupt separation and disruption to family life that a military career can cause. At the outbreak of the Boer War, his father was transferred to Lord Roberts' Staff in Cape Town. His mother was deeply upset by her husband's departure. Her unhappiness comes vividly alive in her first letter to Wully when she told him:

> You shall never go away again without me if I can possibly help it. No one knows what it was to see you standing so desolate on that boat and feel you being carried further and further away[2].

She found some consolation in her small son's company. Understandably, his father's dramatic departure and the apparently ever-present threat to him from a mysterious enemy called the Boers made a deep impression on Brian. In that first letter to Wully, Mildred enclosed a short but remarkably neat note in which Brian begged 'darling Dadda to take care of [himself]' and his bed time prayers were full of imprecations called down upon his father's enemies. In another letter, Mildred informed Wully that 'the boy prays for your safety at night in bed and tonight he added on his own a comment: "and kill all the Boers" '. A month later he was still begging the Almighty not to let the Boers be 'enemeing after Dadda'.

Although the adult military world of his father, with all its menacing unpredictability, had momentarily cast a shadow over Brian's life, as far as one can judge from his mother's letters it did not seriously impinge upon all those intriguing but inconsequential pursuits which so delight a small child. He developed, for instance, a great interest in stray dogs. He enjoyed chasing after them in friends' gardens and he speculated intensely upon the fate of one particular unfortunate creature he had observed in the Basingstoke Canal. Later that summer he was also given what was then the princely sum of 6d to spend at a bazaar, and in due course his fourth birthday was celebrated by a party to which all his friends, and presumably fellow dog chasers, were invited.

From South Africa, Wully closely followed his wife's reports on 'the boy's' progress. With the death of their first son still fresh in his memory, he naturally wanted to be reassured of Brian's good health and that Mildred was taking good care of him. There is no doubt that he was already deeply attached to his son, but the more he loved him, the more anxious he was that he should grow up a devout Christian aware of his responsibilities. Later these were to involve working hard at school and then becoming a good officer, but initially it was on his son's duties to his mother that he concentrated. Wully had been devoted to his own mother, who had died in 1893. In a long letter written specially in capitals so that Brian would be able to read it himself, and timed to reach England for his fourth birthday, Wully carefully tempered paternal affection with advice:

> I hope you will spend a very happy day and I am sure your dear mother will try to make it a happy one for you. . . . I am sure that you will remember to be a good boy both today and when you grow a big man. Boys who are kind to their mother are always loved by everybody, besides boys must remember how very kind their mothers are to them and they ought to do all they are told because mothers tell them to do what is best and right[3].

In the autumn of 1900, Wully returned to the War Office, where, promoted somewhat tardily by the authorities to the rank of Brevet Lieutenant. Colonel, he was put in charge of the vital section dealing with Foreign Military Intelligence. With a salary of only £800 per annum, which in 1907, when the War Office briefly put him on half pay, sank to a mere £300, family life was inevitably circumscribed by rigorous economies and treats had to be on a small scale. Nearly sixty years later, Brian Robertson reminisced to his father's biographer about the family's picnics at Wisley, and bicycle rides around the Surrey country-side 'with stops at inns to munch their sandwiches and drink an occasional glass of beer or ginger pop'. Sometimes on Sundays, Brian would be taken off alone by his father to visit a church in one of the outlying villages where the vicar had a good reputation for preaching 'a sound Broad Church service'.

For Brian personally, the main consequence of his family's straitened financial circumstances was that it was essential for him to win a scholarship to a public school as his parents would otherwise be unable to afford the full fees, which at that time were about £115 per year. Thus, like his father, he came to understand that hard work was a vital requirement for a man without a hereditary position and private means. Grasping this essential truth so early put him on the same wavelength as his father. It helped him to appreciate the extraordinary efforts his father had made to rise out of the ranks and made him receptive of his advice and anxious not to disappoint him. Had he grown up at a later date, when the family's finances were secure and Wully a figure of national importance, he might well have been more relaxed and extrovert, but at the same time, like many sons, more sceptical of their fathers' exhortations to work hard. Looking back in 1991 on their childhood, his sister Helen reflected that 'Brian was brought up quite differently from the way we were. He had to live up to his father's expectations and above all work for a scholarship to a public school'[4]. The fact that father and son shared the same values ensured that their relationship was one of mutual love and trust, which lasted until Wully's death in 1933. For the rest of his own life, Brian Robertson remained fiercely loyal to his father's memory and strongly reacted to the mildest criticism of him or even the slightest risqué joke at his expense[5].

By 1909, Wully and Mildred had four children. After Brian, first Rosamund was born in 1901, then Helen in 1905 and finally John in 1909. Brian, as his eldest, and for a long time only son, was regarded by Wully as the deputy head of the family. In August 1905, when Wully was in Canada and his family holidaying in Colwyn Bay, Brian was sent a letter reminding him firmly

> 'to look very well after your mother. I mean by looking after you should be very careful to do all she asks you to do, and that you should also try to do such things as you feel she would like you to do although she may not ask you to do them. I should explain to you that the history of the world shows that all good men, and so far as I know, all great men have always been good sons of their mothers'[6].

Wully was fortunate that he had a son who could live up to the exacting standards he had set. At home, Brian was a paragon of virtue. For instance, years later, one of the servants in the Robertson household recalled how when she suddenly had to return home because her mother was dangerously ill, Brian 'fetched her bicycle and brought it to the door to hasten her departure'.

In January, 1905, he was sent off to Tanllwyfan, a preparatory school buried deep in the Welsh countryside. On the whole, he enjoyed school life even if there were times when he disliked playing football in the driving rain. In his weekly letters home, after giving his parents the vital details of his test results and position in class, he regaled them with descriptions of the more amusing side of school life: masters who made funny remarks, riotous assemblies and, after he had been there for a year or so, the short comings of the unfortunate new boys.

Despite the occasional lapse in concentration, his academic record was excellent. A surviving report from the Summer Term of 1905 shows him coming first in his form in several key subjects, including Arithmetic, French and Latin[7]. In 1908, his intellectual progress was sufficiently impressive for his father to transfer him to Pinewood in Hampshire, which was one of the main feeder schools for Winchester College. His ability was quickly recognised by one of the senior masters, G.T. Atkinson, who did much to stimulate his formidable intellect. Indeed Atkinson remained in touch with him long afterwards and continued to encourage his studies from afar. As late as Christmas 1939, he ordered a copy of H.A.L. Fisher's *History of Western Europe* for Brian from Harrod's. In the summer of 1910, however, he failed to win an award at Winchester, but he did win a foundation scholarship at Charterhouse worth £39 per annum and tenable until he was sixteen 'or until election to a senior scholarship'.

In 1910, Charterhouse was not a place for sensitive adolescents. Even if Robert Graves' notorious description of the school as a hotbed of bullying and homosexuality was somewhat exaggerated, other contemporaries of Brian Robertson, such as the writer G.D. Martineau, who was in the same house – Saunderites – confirm that it was a school where only the robust could survive. Unlike Winchester and Eton, the scholars were not a respected élite. Indeed, according to Graves, 'unless good at games and able to pretend that they hated their work . . ., they always had a bad time'[8]. Like most contemporary public schools, outside the classroom discipline at Charterhouse was in the hands of the senior boys. This would have become very clear to Brian Robertson and his fellow 'new bugs' when they had to undergo the dreaded ordeal of the Saunderites 'new bug exam', which according to Martineau:

> . . . made no pretence of being anything but an occasion on which candidates were systematically 'failed' and required to sing in the long room before the assembled House[9].

For Brian Robertson, who in late middle age used to try to escape his wife's attempts to involve him in a choral group, or 'catawalling' as he called it, by taking the dogs for a walk, this must indeed have been a daunting experience. However, essentially, Charterhouse would not have been too great a culture shock for him. After all, it was a boisterous male community not unlike the Army about which he already knew a lot. Since 1907, the family had lived first near Britain's major garrison city, Aldershot, when Wully became Chief of Staff of Aldershot Command, and then in the Commandant's house in Camberley, when he was appointed Commandant of the Staff College. By the end of his last term, in December, 1913, he was convinced that the school had done him 'remarkably well' and that his house 'Saunderites' was 'the best' as it was 'not ruled by a crowd of unintelligent athletes . . . and yet is capable of great feats in the field'. Not surprisingly he was in due course to send his own son to Charterhouse[10].

Brian Robertson, unfashionably and stubbornly, made academic work an over-riding priority. Both to enhance his own future prospects and, of course, to lighten the financial burden on his father, it was vital for him to win a senior scholarship in the summer of 1912, which in cash terms was worth nearly three times the junior award. Unlike many of his contemporaries, he had therefore to work hard from the very start. The markbooks in the Charterhouse School archives indicate that apart from some initial teething problems in Maths and Science, he was a fine scholar, who usually came second or third in his class in most subjects. In the summer of 1912, his efforts were rewarded when he won a senior scholarship 'valid so long as the holder remains in the school'. In the Autumn he moved on into the Army Division of the 6th form and began to prepare for the entrance exam into the Royal Military Academy, Woolwich.

His persistence and single-minded determination inevitably cut him off – initially at least – from his contemporaries, one of whom as a nonagenarian in 1992, still remembered him as 'a very austere type of boy. . . who had the reputation of never saying anything or joking around'[11]. He was not, however, a person to be trifled with, as he took up boxing in a very 'hard hitting and unscientific way' as one of his opponents later recalled. In a letter home Brian described in detail the extraordinary two rounds of a fight that became legendary[12].

> I was drawn against another new boy about my own age but a good deal taller, and everybody, myself included, thought I should lose. My match was held almost last, the other boxing had been rather dull, so I intended to make my match lively even though I lost it. The first round was in my favour because I never let my opponent have time to breathe, so that the second round I was to [sic] blown to do very much and he got me a terrible one on the nose, then the umpire said the match must stop in my opponent's favour because there was to [sic] much blood all over me.

Outside the classroom, Brian Robertson's main interests were the Rifle Corps, which he joined in the autumn of 1911, and the school debating society. There must have been few, if any, boys at Charterhouse for whom the worlds of school and home so overlapped in the Rifle Corps. Not only were the Corp's field days supervised and umpired by familiar figures like Wully's friend, Brigadier General Haking, who was also to be his future Corps Commander on the Western Front, and on another occasion even by his father himself, but they often took place on familiar terrain where, as a younger child, he had picnicked with his family. As part of the efforts to modernise and expand the British Army, which were pushed forward by the energetic Liberal Minister of War, Viscount Haldane, in the years immediately before 1914, public school cadet forces were taken seriously by the War Office as a means for giving the élite of British youth elementary military training. Field days were organised on a large scale and involved the participation of several schools and units of the Regular Army, and were reported on in the pages of *The Daily Telegraph.*

A good record in the school Rifle Corps and a sound pass in the 'Cert. A' test were an essential preliminary for a successful military career. Not surprisingly therefore Brian showed the same tenaciousness in his drill and marksmanship as he did in his boxing and academic studies. In February 1912, for instance, he told his father:

> About a week ago I went down to the rifle range and shot so poorly that I only got 40 instead of 60 which passes. The next day I went down and passed and several days later I got 97, thus becoming a marksman[13].

However, it was in the school debating society that Brian Robertson came out of his shell and most obviously enjoyed himself. The society, which was the focus of intellectual life at Charterhouse, met every Saturday evening. It was patronised by all the 6th Formers who had any intellectual or cultural pretensions and the more modern-minded masters like George Mallory, the mountaineer, or Guy Kendall, the poet, who both tried to break through the entrenched traditions of hostility at Charterhouse between teacher and pupil[14]. On 15 February 1913, Robertson made his maiden speech on a motion that was to have painful relevance for his generation, namely 'That modern warfare does not pay the victor'. The gist of his argument, as reported in the school magazine, the *Carthusian,* was that:

> . . . the chief evils of war were an influx of jingoism, super-patriotism and excessive confidence. Thus Russia, the conqueror of Turkey, had succumbed to Japan. War had ruined finance: our Consols had been low ever since the Boer War[15].

Until he left Charterhouse in December, he spoke regularly in the Saturday debates, which covered a whole range of motions from the pros and cons of the Channel tunnel to euthanasia and cremation. The climax to his debating career came on the evening of Saturday 22 November 1913 just after he had sat the second day of the entrance exams for the Royal Military Academy at Woolwich. The society had invited P.F. Warner of the National Service League down to propose a motion approving the introduction of compulsory National Service. This was seconded by

Brian, who in essence employed the same arguments as he was to use in the House of Lords in 1969 when debating the Soviet threat to the West:

> . . . the very fact that Lord Haldane had embodied the territorials at all showed that he considered a force set apart for home defence necessary. His scheme had failed, and something else must be substituted. Compulsory service was the only alternative. The voluntary impulse of individuals could never be made an efficient substitute for the genuine national method[16].

His speech greatly impressed Warner who wrote the following day to Lord Roberts, the founder of the League, that:

> You will no doubt be glad to hear that the motion in favour of National Service was carried by 104 to 15 – a majority of 89. Robertson, a son of General Robertson, seconded the motion and spoke very well[17].

Although Brian Robertson spoke confidently in the debate, he had a nagging fear that he had not performed well in the Woolwich entrance exam. However, his pessimism was confounded when he heard in January that he had passed in tenth on the Woolwich list. His father was delighted and immediately wrote to him:

> You have done well. I felt certain all would be well and in any case, all would be for our best. I hope you did not forget your prayers last night[18].

Why had his father advised him to apply for Woolwich rather than Sandhurst? Quite apart from the fact that life in the Engineers was considerably cheaper for a young subaltern than in the cavalry or one of the smarter infantry regiments, Wully was convinced that an engineer and signalling training provided the best chance for getting on in the modern Army. He emphasised to his son a year later that 'some of the finest characters in our military history had been engineers', and he could also have pointed out that on the outbreak of war in 1914 the two best known officers in Britain and France, Kitchener and Joffre, were both engineers.

For first year cadets, or 'snookers', life at Woolwich[19] was every bit as spartan as it had been in the public schools, from whence the overwhelming majority came. Brian Robertson had to share a sparsely furnished bedroom, rise at 6.15 in the morning and keep his uniform immaculately clean. The presence of even a speck of dust on a cadet's uniform unfailingly led to an extra parade as punishment. Initially the snookers' day consisted of lengthy periods of drill with a mere two hours of lectures. Gradually this balance changed and a more academic programme consisting of Military Law, History, Science, French and Maths was introduced. Sports, particularly riding, which was regarded as a vital accomplishment for gunner and sapper officers, played an important part in the curriculum. Riding was taught by the highly regarded but tyrannical Paul Rodzianco, who managed to instil in Brian Robertson such a fear of riding that it took several years for him properly to recover his nerve. The summer term of 1914 was dominated by inter-company competitions, matches against Sandhurst, dances and other entertainments, but the ultimate aim of their training was never lost sight of. On Public (or inspection) Day the Chief of the Imperial General Staff, Sir Charles Douglas, and Wully himself, in his new role as Director of Military Training, carried out an inspection of the Academy. Douglas, painfully aware of the Curragh 'mutiny' when, in March 1914, the officers of the Curragh garrison resigned rather than march against Ulster to enforce Home Rule, urged the cadets to 'remember that the Army was knit together by ties of comradeship, discipline and loyal obedience. If these ties were snapped by the younger generation then the Army would deteriorate and might crumble away in their hands'[20].

The following day, the summer vacation began. Brian had every reason to be pleased with himself. The Commandant had given him a good report concluding with the observation that he had 'work[ed] very well and is keen' and thus 'should do well'. He had been planning to visit Germany and meet up with a group of fellow snookers there. It was, however, fortunate for his career that when war broke out with Germany on 4 August, he was still in England, otherwise he would have spent, as four cadets and one of the French lecturers indeed did, the next four years in the internment camp at Ruheleben.

The immediate impact of the war on Woolwich was graphically summed up in the autumn edition of the Academy's magazine:

> Like everything else the 'Shop' has been revolutionized by the war. To begin with the holidays were shortened by nearly a month, and everyone came hurrying back on August 5 . . . Last term's 'Snookers' are now the senior term, and before this is in print another batch of new cadets will have joined . . . There is not much time for the hard worked cadet at the present moment to show his prowess in games; he gets plenty of gun drill with which to exercise his muscles without mentioning such gentle games as bridge building, digging and ordinary infantry drill.[21]

As a consequence of the War, Brian Robertson became an Under Officer in charge of a company of snookers, amongst whom was John Glubb, the future Glubb Pasha. On 17 November he passed out of Woolwich fourth in his year and was commissioned into the Royal Engineers. His father, who since the outbreak of war had been the Quarter Master General of the British Expeditionary Force in France, congratulated him warmly in a long letter in which he also gave his son important advice on life and the art of commanding men:

> I hope you will try to be a good officer and do your duty to your country. It is the most honourable and patriotic of all professions – the Army, but it carries great responsibilities. You must learn how to command men. Remember they are human and if properly treated they will always do their best for their officers. You must be very careful in your conduct to your superiors. Good manners and proper respect cost nothing and are essential to your equipment. Make up your mind to do your duty at all times, and do it well. Do not be misled by those who would lead you away from that path. There are such. Never get into debt . . . Never back a bill for anyone. Never drink more than you need . . . I have often drunk water at mess.'

On a more practical note, Wully informed his son that he would pay for his full dress uniform and give him an allowance of £40 per year. He ended his letter with a moving paternal blessing:

> And now, my dear boy, I leave you in God's firm hands. May you ever be a good and faithful soldier of Christ as well as a good soldier of the King[22].

Although the outbreak of war had abruptly curtailed Brian Robertson's studies at Woolwich, it had also given him the bonus of an early start to his chosen career.

2

MILITARY APPRENTICESHIP 1914–33

For the next 19 years Brian Robertson served as a regular officer and laid the foundations of a distinguished career. He lived up to his father's exacting standards but at the same time remained very much his own person.

THE FIRST WORLD WAR

After passing out from Woolwich in November 1914, the 18-year-old Second Lieutenant Robertson reported to the School of Military Engineering at Chatham on Sunday 29 November for a two month course in practical engineering. From France, Wully instructed Mildred to ensure that he set off immediately after lunch, so that he would have time to settle in before the end of the day. He anxiously enquired whether he had 'got good boots and a pair of warm gloves'. He was also worried about his son's financial situation and told Mildred to:

> See that Brian has plenty of money when he goes to Chatham. I feel rather ashamed putting him on £40 a year and giving him only half of it now. I want to make him realise the value of money, but I don't want him to be wretched. Better give him £5 for pocket money to start with.[1]

In February, 1915, Brian went on to Aldershot for a 12 week course at the reserve Signal Depot. When he had completed this at the end of April, it became very clear that, by virtue of being Wully's son, he had been born with the military equivalent of a silver spoon in his mouth. As he was still too young to be sent to the front, Wully, who was now Chief of Staff of the British Expeditionary Force in France, invited him to become his second ADC. Brian's main responsibility was to look after his father by ensuring that his frequent journeys to London or to Paris were accomplished as smoothly and rapidly as possible, and that his horses were always available whenever he needed them. He evidently performed these duties so effectively that he was mentioned in dispatches in January, 1916. He would also have had the opportunity to observe how his father ran the General Staff and have dined regularly in his small mess with men

11

of the calibre of Colonel Maurice, who had taught at the Staff College in Camberley and was one of the best staff officers in the British Army. Inevitably then, this was an invaluable introduction for Brian Robertson to the whole concept of military staff work.

When Wully was appointed Chief of the Imperial General Staff in December, 1915, Brian Robertson returned to the Royal Engineers and assumed that he would soon see active service. Haig, possibly as a gesture of friendship towards Wully, whose forthrightness and lack of a sophisticated veneer he did not always appreciate, invited his son to become one of his ADCs. The invitation was not entirely welcome to Brian as a second spell as an ADC merely put off the time he could begin his real career as a sapper. However, on reflection and probably with some prompting from his father, he did realise that the offer was much too good to refuse and in the end accepted. He returned to St. Omer where Haig had taken over from Sir John French as Commander-in-Chief of the British Expeditionary Force. He joined a team of four ADCs whose duties were primarily concerned with ensuring that Haig's private office and daily programme functioned as smoothly as possible. A particularly busy time for them was the move of the GHQ to Montreuil in March. In the early summer of 1916, as Brian Robertson rode around behind the lines in Haig's entourage, he would have witnessed first the gigantic build up for the Battle of the Somme and then the early stages of the battle itself. His spell at GHQ gave him a bird's eye view of the requirements and needs of a modern army, in which, as Haig observed, 'the workings of the railways, the upkeep of the roads, even the baking of bread and a thousand other industries go on in war as in peace[2]. This was an invaluable lesson for a future Chief Administrative Officer.

In mid-August, 1916 when the Somme was at its height, Brian Robertson was transferred to the headquarters of XI Corps, commanded by General Sir Richard Haking[3]. Here he was given an 'apprenticeship' in staff duties and in January, 1917, was appointed a GSO3 – General Staff Officer Grade 3. In retrospect this can be seen as one of the most decisive moves in his long military career. It ensured that his formative experience during the First World War was to be as a staff officer rather than as an active front line soldier. To go straight from being an ADC to Haking's staff was an unusual move. Most junior staff officers had initially spent a considerable time commanding troops on the front. His father, who had no inhibitions about helping his own son, almost certainly pulled strings to achieve this. Haking was a friend and had been Wully's contemporary at the Staff College and could be relied upon to keep an eye on his son.

XI Corps occupied what in 1916–17 was a relatively quite sector on the Western Front between Bethune and Loos. In many ways it was an ideal posting for a young officer beginning to pick up the rudiments of staff work. Haking encouraged a mutually supportive atmosphere amongst his staff. For instance he grouped his staff together in the same building 'so that any member of it, without any delay, can go and see another member of it in an adjoining room'[4]. Years later, when he was Deputy Military Governor of the British Zone in Germany, Brian Robertson followed this example at his own headquarters in Berlin. Haking's Chief of Staff, Brigadier Anderson, was described by Captain Tower, Brian Robertson's immediate superior, as 'one of the best staff officers ever produced in the war'[5]. Tower himself was an intelligent and outspoken young officer who was privately highly critical of Haking's military skills.

In Joan Littlewood's musical, *Oh What a Lovely War!*, staff officers are caricatured as a gilded, idle group of men living in luxury far behind the lines. It was, of course, quite true that Corps Headquarters was quite a way behind the front line, and that consequently staff officers were relatively safe. One brigadier calculated for instance that the life prospects for his newly appointed staff captain, who had previously been a bombing officer, had improved by 90 per cent. Nevertheless, it is a myth that staff officers did not visit the front. Haking, like any Commander, insisted that

> . . . Staff Officers should know all that is going on. In order to do this they must go about amongst the troops . . . to find out what difficulties are being met with and how these can be got over[6].

The work of a junior staff officer was unglamorous but responsible. Troops were constantly being moved in and out of the line 'in a recurrent pattern like some old fashioned square dance'[7]. In XI Corps, as its War Diaries record[8], it was often Brian Robertson's job to see that the complicated logistics for moving such large bodies of men worked. If they failed, it would be his responsibility and he would also have the added discomfort of realising that at the very least he had made the lives of exhausted front-line troops needlessly difficult. One of his contemporaries, involved in similar work, wrote years later:

> One of the most harrowing sights was an infantry battalion going out to rest. It would be a shadow of its former self. All ranks would be haggard and half dead with fatigue. They marched without taking any interest in anything. When I met them I always felt ashamed of my easy life, but there it was, nothing I could do would help them except protect them as far as possible from German attack[9].

During the winter of 1916–17, the main aim of XI Corps was to prepare for a spring offensive and, in the meantime, to make life as difficult as possible for the Germans. The Corps' War Diary, written up by Robertson, records that on Christmas Eve:

At noon we commenced a methodical bombardment of the enemy's
lines along the whole Corps front to continue till daybreak of 27
December, 1916. The objects of the bombardment were (a) to
destroy points of practical importance in the enemy's line and (b) to
prevent any attempt at fraternisation on the part of the enemy[10].

In early March, 1917, Brian, who had been promoted to Captain,
accompanied his father on a brief tour of the Italian front. When he
returned, he found that XI Corps had been assigned the task of diverting
German attention from the coming attack at Vimy. The Corps had to mis-
lead the Germans into thinking that operations were imminent along the
Aubers-Fromelles ridge, rather than further south at Vimy, by setting up
bogus ammunition dumps, acres of uninhabited tents and firing off a
prolonged artillery barrage which, by rapid fire, was to give the impression
that the Corps had many more guns than it really possessed. In all this frenetic activity, Brian Robertson's role was to draw up the 'march tables' for
the artillery batteries, which had constantly to be on the move to confuse
the Germans. For his meticulousness in this important but undramatic
task he was mentioned in dispatches in May, 1917[11].

In stark contrast to the hundreds of thousands of men involved in the
terrible slaughter of the Third Battle of Ypres, XI Corps had a relatively
quiet summer punctured only by desultory artillery bombardments and
trench raids. In the autumn, however, enemy activity increased, and it is
probably during this period that Brian Robertson won his military cross,
a medal given for gallantry in the field and which was awarded to him officially in the New Year Honours Lists in January, 1918[12]. Unfortunately,
the citation does not survive, but the War Diary records numerous incidents in any one of which, as a frequently peripatetic staff officer, he
could easily have become involved.

On 18 November, 1917, XI Corps was ordered urgently to northern
Italy where, in late October, the Austro-German forces had inflicted a
devastating defeat on the Italians at Caporetto and were poised to sweep
on southwards to Venice. Together with the French X Army, the Corp's
task was to stop the enemy crossing the River Piave. However, by the time
they reached Italy, the front had already been stabilised along the river by
the Italians themselves and the German 12th Division had been recalled
to Germany. For the rest of the winter, the war subsided into an artillery
duel between the opposing armies and XI Corps was fortunate to see little action. After the mud and desolation of northern France, the Italian
theatre was, in the words of the Official Historian, 'a very good war'.
Robertson shared a villa with a fellow staff officer and was able to keep
both a dog and a horse.

In the comparative peace of the Italian winter, he began to ponder his
own future. It was fast becoming time for him to move on from his present

appointment. Both his father and Haking urged him to accept promotion to Brigade Major, a post which entails being Chief of Staff of a brigade, but he had considerable reservations about this advice. He wrote to his father in January 1918:

> To sum up the whole thing, the way I look at it is: I must move on some-where: there are only two places I can move to (1) Brigade Major (2) a company. I don't think that I am sufficiently experienced for (1) yet, and I feel that if I became a Brigade Major I should not have confidence in myself . . ., and therefore the only alternative is (2). Furthermore if I go to a company now, I should be able to become a Brigade Major after some experience with a unit. I may say that I can see tremendous dis-advantages in the way of comfort, pay, rank and so on ahead when I join my unit, but I think that it is necessary to put up with them. I am sorry to fly in the face of advice given me by yourself and the C.[orps] C.[ommander] in this way, but have thought the whole thing out very carefully and cannot get away from the conclusion I have come to. The Corps Commander goes on leave tomorrow, and I am afraid that he may see you before you get this letter, but I hope not[13].

Yet when XI Corps returned to France in early March, Robertson did not take over a company. Instead he departed to Cambridge for a three month course at the staff school in Clare College. After his firm decision to gain practical experience on the battlefield, this move comes as a sur-prise. However, the course was primarily aimed at training staff captains and brigade majors and thus it would have been rash of him to have turned down a place on it, once it was offered to him, particularly if it was offered on the recommendation of Haking.

While Brian Robertson was reviewing his own future, his father's was being decided in London. Wully was locked into a bitter quarrel with the Prime Minister, Lloyd George, ostensibly over whether the proposed inter-Allied Military Supreme Council in Versailles or the CIGS in London would determine British military priorities. In reality, of course, the Prime Minister was using this issue to force Wully's resignation as CIGS, which he succeeded in doing on 17 February, 1918. Essentially, he disagreed with Wully's deeply held belief that only on the Western Front could the War be won.

In later life, Brian Robertson was highly critical of Lloyd George for the way he treated his father, but at the time he seems not to have appreciated the magnitude of Wully's humiliation. In a letter to his father shortly after his resignation, he was, as young men usually are, far more taken up with own affairs: his imminent transfer to Cambridge and his regret at 'losing sight' of his dog and horse in Italy. Nevertheless, for Wully his son's return to England was welcome news at a very difficult time. The carelessly affectionate way in which Brian concluded his letter must have brought a somewhat wry smile to his father's face: 'I must go now to have a bath; looking forward immensely to seeing you next month[14]'.

It is always possible that Haking pulled strings to ensure that Brian Robertson was given a place on the Cambridge course in order to spare Wully the added anguish of losing his son in battle.

At a time when the Ludendorff offensive on the Western Front was threatening to drive the British Army into the sea, the staff course in the idyllic setting of Clare College could not have provided a greater contrast to life in the front line. A contemporary of Brian's described his three months there in glowing terms: 'We aren't overworked, everyone is very pleasant, there is enough to do to fill up every moment, and all the time one is learning: what more could one want?'

***

Brian Robertson returned to France in July and became Brigade Major of 177 Brigade, which was part of XI Corps' 59 Division. This was not composed of crack fighting troops and was categorised by Haking as a 'B' Division. As Brigade Major, his main task was to assist the Brigadier in implementing operational instructions coming from divisional head-quarters and ultimately Haking himself. He joined the Brigade on 17 July when it was training behind the lines. It moved back up to the front a few days later and Robertson's first taste of action since his return to France came on 26 July when, for two hours, Brigade Headquarters at Bretencourt Château was shelled.

By the end of July, 1918, it was clear that the Ludendorff offensive had failed and the Germans were beginning to be pushed back on the defensive. In the subsequent Allied advance 177 Brigade was, of course, a very small but, in the end, a relatively efficient cog. Initially, the Brigadier and Brian Robertson were worried that their men were not 'filled with the proper spirit of aggression' and the battalion commanders were told that:

> Everything must be done to give the enemy a bad time. Enemy M[achine G'[un]s firing at night require special attention and they must be vigorously engaged by Lewis guns, rifles, grenades and rifle fire. By day, every man in the front line should fire a few rounds over the parapet[15].

By the time the Armistice was signed in November, 59 Division had pushed back the Germans on its sector of the front some 30 kilometres. This advance involved crossing several rivers and traversing areas where the whole drainage system had been smashed by earlier heavy fighting. Haking was so pleased with the Division's progress that he decreed that it should no longer be referred to as a 'B Division'[16]. When the Armistice was announced on 11 November, the Brigade was in the process of establishing a bridgehead across the Scheldt. In June, 1919, Brian Robertson's role in this impressive improvement in military efficiency was recognised by the award of a DSO in the Birthday Honours List[17].

With the ending of hostilities, the main priorities of the Brigade Staff switched from killing Germans to working out plans for occupying the time of what had become a bored and resentful civilian army, which wanted to be demobilised as quickly as possible. Robertson drew up a daily programme which involved a mixture of military training, general educational courses and the production of plays 'to amuse the men'. When on 30 January he was ordered 'to proceed to the UK for duty at Chatham', he must have been glad to leave the increasingly disorganised and semi-demobilised British forces in France for the more intellectual rigours of engineering and mathematical courses at the School of Military Engineering.

INDIA, 1920–25

Once back in the austere dignity of Brompton Barracks, Chatham, Brian Robertson resumed the engineering and technical studies, which the outbreak of war in 1914 had so abbreviated[18]. While he was immersed in a series of courses on constructional engineering, survey and field engineering, the Army went through an agonising metamorphosis from a mass conscript force to a small, compact organisation composed entirely of volunteers. The long-term implications of this for Brian Robertson's generation was that the days of accelerated promotion were now over and ahead lay the prospect of serving at least a decade as a captain and thereafter only very slow progress up the career ladder.

That, however, was more a problem for the future. In November, 1920, Brian Robertson was posted to the Indian Army for a five year tour of duty. He was attached to the King George V's Own Bengal Sappers and Miners, whose headquarters was at Rorkee, some hundred miles north of Delhi. After acclimatising himself, learning Hindustani and acquiring his polo ponies, for the first time in his career he had to undergo the acid test of commanding troops. In April he was put in command of No. 3 Field Company, which consisted of some 250 Indian Sepoys divided into Sikh, Muslim and Hindu platoons, each of which was led by a *Jemadar* or Viceroy's Commissioned Indian officer[19]. Initially Brian Robertson found the prospect of turning the raw recruits of his company, many of whom were tough Pathan tribesmen, into soldiers a daunting prospect, but he was greatly assisted by the first-class quality of his junior officers. His second in command was Lieutenant Ian Jacob, the son of General Sir Claud Jacob, the Chief of Staff of the Indian Army. In many ways, however, the key man in the Company was the senior Indian officer, the *Subedar*, Ram Rup Singh, who had fought in both France and Mesopotamia, and acted as an indispensible link between the Company Commander and his Indian troops. Although Brian Robertson was to spend most of his army career as a military staff officer and administrator, his record in India does suggest that he would have been an effective commander who would have taken good care of his men. In December 1921, after the annual inspection his company was awarded a 'fine report'[20], and Ian Jacob, who was later to become a key member of Winston Churchill's personal military staff throughout the Second World War and, later, Director General of the BBC, regarded him as a 'splendid man to work for' and an excellent officer whom the Indians 'liked and respected . . .'[21].

In April, 1921, No 3 Company moved up to Peshawar, a hill station on the North West Frontier which, in Wully's expressive words, was 'a torment in the Summer. Very hot and full of fever.' As Ian Jacob recalled, the weather inevitably enforced a somewhat leisurely pace on the local garrison:

> In the hot weather. i.e. March to September we had a parade at 5 am for drill or parade training till about 8, when we came back to mess for breakfast. Then work, either supervising the men at their training, or in the office, then lunch about 1.0. Then sleep until 4.30 when we either played polo, or tennis or games with the troops – Drink at the club, mess dinner, then bridge or billiards[22].

In the cooler season, the troops moved down to camp along the banks of the Indus to practise bridge building and field works.

In February, 1922, Wully visited India and in due course arrived in Peshawar. He must have been somewhat surprised when Brian discussed with him the possibility of leaving the Army for a career in business. Possibly he was finding the slow pace of peacetime soldiering in India stifling, although Ian Jacob cannot remember detecting any signs of boredom or disillusionment in him[23]. It is more likely that he was worried by the threat to his career prospects which the continuing contraction of the Army both in India and Britain presented. Around him in the messes in Rorkee and Peshawar there were elderly bachelor captains in abundance, whose fate was a grim warning to a young and ambitious officer. There may, too, have been a personal reason for his desire for a change. Before he sailed for India, he had already met, on a house party in Scotland, his future wife, Edith Macindoe, a cheeky, intelligent and pretty girl who was intrigued rather than alienated by his shyness and abruptness of manner.

Wully, who in retirement had joined the boards of several companies, inevitably had mixed feelings about the possibility of his son leaving the

Army. Yet once back in London, as he had promised, he sounded out his business contacts, particularly Dudley Docker and Sir Eric Geddes, the new chairman of Dunlop's. He also had Brian's curriculum vitae drawn up 'by a friend in the War Office', who presumably had access to his personal reports. Nevertheless, he remained distinctly uneasy about his son's plans. In May he wrote to him:

> I feel you could not wish to throw away what you now have without first seeing something reasonably assured in its place. I feel I can trust you. But you might keep me informed of how your mind works in response to this particular subject . . . It is very upsetting that you should care to think of changing at all and perhaps you may not have to do so. Military things may improve . . .; other wars will come; and soldiering will look up again[24].

Wully's tone obviously irritated his son and in July he went out of his way to re-assure Brian that he was not trying to force him to remain in the Army against his will. However, by September, probably swayed by his father's observation that 'the country is stuffed full of ex-Army and ex-Navy fellows who want to get into business of which, by the way, there is precious little for anybody', he decided, at least for the time being, to remain put.

Events in Waziristan on the North West Frontier also conspired to push these thoughts to the back of his mind and fill up his time with more exacting and dangerous work, involving the construction of the Waziristan circular road, which was the strategic key to the Raj's efforts to pacify Waziristan. In 1894, a joint Anglo-Afghan commission had demarcated the frontier between British India and Afghanistan. For 25 years the British did not bother to exercise effective control for some 60 miles south of this line, but in 1919, as a result of increasingly serious frontier incursions by the Mahsuds, not only was a punitive expedition despatched, but the Army managed to persuade the Viceroy to agree to a permanent garrison being stationed at Razmak. To do this, it was, however, necessary to build a metalled road some 20 feet wide through the most rugged and inhospitable country in India, to link up Razmak with the railhead in the south and the existing Tochi road in the north[25]. The road was started in July 1922, but it was not until November that Brian Robertson's company was ordered up to the engineers' base at Tal. By January, they had moved on to Razani and began to build the section running across the Ramzak plateau. Ian Jacob remembered how:

> . . . there was nothing whatever to do except work and play bridge in the evening – our individual little tents were dug into the ground so that one could stand up in them and the sand bag covered walls of the excavation

gave protection against snipers. We spent all day on the road we were building to Ramzak[26].

At night, one of Brian Robertson's main problems was to stop the Mahsuds stealing his Company's camels. Later he described how:

Partly for my own amusement in addition to putting up an apron fence round the evil smelling collection, I inserted in the fence a number of those devices, which Heath Robinson must surely have invented, classified in the old field works manual as 'Flares and Alarms'[27].

Needless to say, the camels continued to disappear!

Overall, despite the dangers and the gruelling work, the very fact that Robertson and his fellow sappers could measure the progress made in terms of miles of road built, brought its own satisfaction. When General Rawlinson inspected the road in October 1923, he sent a note back to Wully commenting on how his son 'was looking in the best of health and . . . [had] earned golden opinions'. A sapper officer needs the skills and temperament of a first-class staff officer or what the Chief Engineer of the Waziristan force called in Hindustani, *Bundobust*. This means in effect that not only has he to be meticulous in his organisation, but he must see 'everything everywhere, every moment'. It was thus not surprising that Brian Robertson proved to be a good road maker, even though he did lose a few camels in the process. He was mentioned twice in dispatches[28].

In late October 1923 No. 3 Company returned to Peshawar. Throughout the preceding year his father had been urging him as relentlessly as one of the steamrollers on the Circular Road to start preparing for the entrance examination to the Staff College at Camberley, attendance at which was essential for any ambitious officer. Robertson's best chance of gaining a place was by nomination by the Army Council on the basis of his previous record and current 'good service in the field' rather than by open competition. Yet to be eligible for this he still had to reach pass standard in three papers: *Training for War, Organisation and Administration* and *Imperial Organisation*. It was calculated in a much discussed article in *The Royal Engineers Journal* that a candidate needed to work some 20 to 30 hours a week for at least a year before the exam. Waziristan obviously did not provide the ideal background for such a formidable intellectual undertaking. Not surprisingly Wully fulminated against the 'incessant road making' and at times, to his son's evident embarrassment and irritation, attempted to pull strings at the War Office. Wully even managed to arrange for him to be given the option of transferring to a home command, so that he would have more time to study, but Brian did not accept this offer, probably because he was given seven months leave starting in April 1924.

Once back in the family home at 88, Westbourne Terrace, Bayswater, he did at last have the time to buy the recommended books at Messrs. Sifton Praed and Co. Ltd in St. James Street, use the library of the Royal United Services Institute and pick his father's brains, but his whole leave was not spent 'swotting'. He bought a car, saw something of Edith Macindoe, acted as best man at Ian Jacob's wedding and spent August in Sussex. By December he was back again with his company in Peshawar.

The crucial Staff College exams were timetabled to be sat in India at the end of February, 1925, but three weeks before this Robertson went into hospital with a very high fever. He was able to sit the exams, but inevitably did not acquit himself very well. Wully did not hide his disappointment:

> By now you will be having a rest and be recovering from your disappointment in not having done much better in your exam than you could have done or ought to have done. These post mortems are no good anyway and you must just stick it out and hope for the best – a rotten remark to make . . . I still hope you will squeak in and I don't at all like to think you will not be coming back till the end of next year.[29]

An indication that Wully's hopes that his son would 'squeak in' were not entirely misplaced was given when, at the end of March, Brian was unexpectedly promoted to Brevet-Major, and in April invited to become ADC to Sir Claud Jacob. In June, the news then came through that he had been awarded, after all, a nominated place to the Staff College. In late 1925, he set sail for home.

STAFF COLLEGE, 1926–27

By the time Brian had returned to Chatham in December 1925, the Army had recovered from its turbulent post-war period of contraction and had settled down to a 'humdrum routine of home security and Imperial policing'[30]. Ironically, his youthful observations in a school debate at Charterhouse (see page 7) on how military victory brought few rewards to the victor was amply borne out by the history of the British Army between the Wars. With the notable exception of a relatively few talented and dedicated officers, like Gort, Montgomery and Dill, the British Army, unlike the *Reichswehr*, made little effort to evaluate systematically the military lessons that could be learnt from the First World War, and it had to pay a heavy price for this in 1940.

Inevitably, the two year Staff College course reflected some of the weaknesses of the contemporary Army, of which, of course, it was a part. There was a tendency to re-fight the battles of the last war rather than explore the new tactics made possible by the tank and aeroplane and to give the students insufficient practice in the logistics of handling armies rather than divisions. One of Brian Robertson's contemporaries, Major General Hawes, was later to argue that 'all in all the great value I got from Camberley was how not to run a Staff College'. Nevertheless, despite all its faults, most students found it on balance a positive experience. One of the most valuable aspects of the course was that its participants met the best military brains of their generation either as fellow students or as instructors, who as Majors or Brevet Lieutenant Colonels were only a few years their senior. Two men in particular at Camberley, as will be seen later, were to have a profound influence on Brian Robertson's career: his fellow student, Alexander or Alex, and one of his instructors, Bernard Montgomery. For Brian the main value of the course was the opportunities it gave him to improve his skills as a staff officer by studying the varying staff duties within a division in great detail. To emphasise the need for team work, the students were divided into syndicates, which were each given specific problems to solve and had, rather like a jury, to come up with an agreed solution. Students were also expected frequently, and often at very short notice, to write individual papers. All this was interspersed with visits to various military installations and dockyards, exercises in the Welsh Hills aimed at simulating operations on the North West Frontier and the umpiring of manoeuvres in the summer. Above all, twice a week there was the drag hunt, which students, who were specifically given a 'charger' for this very purpose, were expected to attend. The hunt was rapidly becoming an anachronism, although it was true that in 1926 most British officers were still mounted.

In May 1926, this routine was dramatically interrupted by the General Strike. The students were encouraged to volunteer to help keep essential services running, and the great majority went up to London dressed in their oldest clothes to work as tube motormen, bus drivers, guards or stevedores but unfortunately there is no record of what Brian Robertson did during those ten days in May.

Probably the most enjoyable part of the course took place during Easter 1927. Small groups of students were given sufficient money to travel to France or Belgium and study a First World War battle of their own choice. An interesting light was shed on the more congenial aspects of this tour in an article in *La Vie Parisienne*:

> *Chaque soir vêtus d'impeccable smokings ils dînent ensemble et discutent tactique et stratégie . . . Les problèmes de stratégie sont multiplis, et les officiers anglais en soutenant leurs forces d'un peu de champagne et de brandy*[31]

Brian Robertson rapidly emerged as one of the ablest students in his division. This became clear when the Staff College was ordered by the

War Office to create a special high fliers set of about 12, which was to deal with more advanced staff and command problems. The College directing staff disliked such crude streaming and almost weekly changed the composition of the set, but significantly a hard core of some six students always remained, amongst whom were both Brian Robertson and Alexander. On one occasion Lieutenant Colonel Lindsell, the 'Q' teacher readily conceded that Brian Robertson's solution to a major administrative problem 'was probably better than the . . . directing staff's official answer'.

Brian Robertson showed the same determination to make the most of his chances as he had done at Charterhouse, but he was not, like a small band of officers, waging a private crusade to modernise the British Army. He was very much aware that there was more to life than soldiering. In August, 1926, he married Edith Macindoe. Their marriage turned out to be a genuinely successful and loving partnership. Although Edith was essentially a deeply conservative person, she loved to tease the serious minded and pompous. She was highly intelligent and had a great respect for her husband's ability and integrity, but he was not exempt from her teasing. Yet for all her banter, she was of the generation that was still attracted by the image of the strong, silent Englishman, which Brian Robertson personified. He, in his turn, appreciated her humour and the odd mixture of teasing, dependence and love which she showed towards him.

In the autumn of 1926, the Robertsons moved into a furnished cottage near the Staff College. For Edith it must have been a curious introduction to army life. Her husband attended formal dinners once a week at the Staff College in a scarlet mess jacket, only to return home in the small hours dishevelled and often with his shirt covered with blood after playing a particularly vigorous game of 'High Cock O'Lorum'[32]. At other times she might find her husband's syndicate closeted in their dining room for hours on end working on some strategic problem which had to be solved quickly. There were, of course, opportunities for more civilised socialising and dinner parties, but the College did claim a high proportion of its students' time and wives had to make their own social life and entertainments. In August, 1927, their marriage entered a new phase with the birth of their first child, Christine.

Brian Robertson finished the course at the Staff College in December and, after a few weeks leave, was transferred to the Quarter Master General's Department at the War Office.

THE WAR OFFICE AND GENEVA, 1928–33

War Office appointments were not popular with most officers as they involved desk work in Central London and little opportunity for an active life. Between the Wars, the War Office itself also had the reputation for being a stifling bureaucratic organisation out of touch with the real needs of the Army[33]. Nevertheless, Brian Robertson's tour of duty in London did have the advantage of enabling his family to lead, at least temporarily, a settled existence. He acquired a comfortable house near Beaconsfield and commuted daily to Whitehall. Unexpectedly, however, the pleasurable experience of setting up a new home with his wife and baby daughter was suddenly overshadowed by the death of his 18-year-old brother, John, from pneumonia in the South of France in March 1928. It was a blow from which Wully never fully recovered and naturally made him more appreciative of his remaining son's presence in Beaconsfield.

After spending a brief spell of three months on the Quarter Master General's staff, Brian Robertson was transferred to his father's old department, the DMO & I – the Directorate of Military Operations and Intelligence – where he served under Colonel Piggott in Section MI2a which specialised in analysing military intelligence from the Americas, Italy, the Far East and the Balkans. In this work, involving the piecing together of an intricate mosaic of information drawn from numerous sources, Robertson rapidly made a reputation for himself as an efficient intelligence officer. Piggott was particularly impressed that:

> . . . like his father, Brian had an unerring eye for the vital point of any problem; and he presented, and if necessary argued, his case with a smooth but firm manner, which I found very convincing.[34]

Although analysing the ebb and flow of the Chinese Civil War and the growth of Japan's military capabilities were the most pressing tasks of Piggott's department, much of Brian Robertson work was concerned with the Central and South American states. In the spring of 1929 he had a marvellous opportunity to escape the daily grind of paperwork in the War Office and go on a four month fact-finding tour of six South American states – Argentina, Bolivia, Chile, Ecuador, Peru and Uruguay. Primarily, he was required to assess the military situation and the condition of the armed forces there, but, as he argued in his report[35], this could hardly be divorced from an analysis of the political and economic background. He wrote dismissively about the comic opera armies of South America, but also noted that the armed forces in four key states, Argentina, Chile, Bolivia and Peru, were all being trained by German military missions. Although he believed that Germany was primarily aiming to open up the South American export market, he nevertheless warned that under certain circumstances the 'Germanisation of the armies of half South America might have considerable significance'.

The essential message of Brian Robertson's report was that whichever Power controlled South America economically would also be able to strengthen its industrial base enormously and so enhance its capacity to wage war. He pointed out how the United States had been investing heavily in South America, and if all went according to plan, 'will become the virtual possessor of a part of the world which contains perhaps more undeveloped resources than any other.' In many ways, for somebody who still had not excluded the possibility of a business career, this was a marvellous chance to examine in detail the shortcomings of British commerce in South America. He contrasted American success with Britain's own sluggish efforts. As a future managing director of a Dunlop factory in South Africa his comments are of particular interest:

> Firstly, we are not sending out our best men . . .; instead of clever, energetic young fellows, out to make their names and fortunes . . . one meets listless and half-educated individuals who pass their time consuming unnecessary drinks and grousing . . . Secondly, the reason for this is to be found in the parsimony of Directing Boards; the top executive posts are generally under-paid, and therefore the best service is not obtained . . . Thirdly, production and administrative methods suitable fifty years ago will not suffice today; in particular British firms must combine and cooperate in order to cut down overhead charges, and present a united front to their common rival . . .

He was equally forthright about the lack of assistance to British businessmen from their local Consular and Diplomatic representatives.

The Foreign Office found his comments on the political and diplomatic background 'very useful' and he was invited to lunch by one official to expand on his complaints about British diplomats in South America, but overall his report achieved relatively little. The Foreign Office certainly agreed with his main recommendation that more military attachés should be appointed, whose main work would be to secure orders for British industries but, like the War Office, it could make little headway against the parsimony of the Treasury[36]. All that Brian Robertson's report ultimately resulted in was that the British military attaché to the United States would in the future also be accredited to the capitals of Mexico and the independent central American and Caribbean states[37].

In the spring of 1930, perhaps inspired by the feeling that he could do better than many of the businessmen he had seen at work in South America, Robertson again approached Dunlop. This time he was successful, but the job offered him confronted him with a difficult dilemma. It was well paid but it involved a ten year posting to the steamy heat of Bombay. Wully succinctly summed up the problem:

> You are wanting to change so as to have a better personal future (in many other ways you stand to loose, society, etc) and you object to exile.[38]

In the end he turned it down, but continued to look around for a more suitable post. His father feared that news of this might come to 'the ears of [his] masters', but came to the conclusion that they too were 'subject to change'[39]. In this he was right. Colonel Piggott moved on to become Deputy Military Secretary and Brian Robertson, who became a substantive Major in January, 1930, was then attached to Brigadier Temperley, the War Office's representative on the League of Nations' permanent Advisory Commission on Disarmament. In 1927 the League had set up a new commission to draw up a draft convention on disarmament. When this was finished, in December 1930, it proposed that the long-awaited disarmament conference should open in Geneva in 1932 and use the draft convention as an initial basis for discussion. For most of 1931, Brian Robertson was busy analysing the implications of this plan for the War Office.

When the Conference opened in February 1932, Robertson, together with his colleagues Colonel Dawney and Brigadier Temperley, acted as advisers to the British Delegation. Working sometimes in London and sometimes in Geneva, he gained an invaluable insight into the overlap between the political and military worlds. In the War Office and Foreign Office files on the Conference it is possible to catch brief glimpses of his work. He was the secretary of an internal War Office 'Committee on the Abolition of Tanks'[40]. Then in November, 1932, he moved over permanently to Geneva to replace Dawney. There his main duties were to attend, with Temperley, the lengthy sessions of the Conference as a technical adviser to the British delegation and also to help keep Anthony Eden, the Minister without Portfolio for League of Nations Affairs, briefed on the thinking of the War Office.

In February, 1933, just as Brian Robertson was in the process of arranging for his family to join him in Geneva, his father died from a heart attack. As the only son and heir to the baronetcy, he had to hasten back to London and arrange both the funeral at the crematorium in Brookwood and the memorial service at Westminster Abbey, which, following Wully's firm instructions, was an entirely civilian ceremony without the slightest military pomp[41]. His return to Geneva was further delayed by the death of Edith's mother a few days later. Eventually he returned to Geneva, not only with Edith and the two children, Christine and Ronald, who had been born in December 1930, but also his mother and sister.

Meanwhile the Disarmament Conference had reached deadlock.

Hitler's appointment as Reich Chancellor on 30 January had sounded its death knell. In March, Ramsay MacDonald, the British Prime Minister, made a belated last effort to save the Conference by producing a complicated plan which, after allowing for a two year transitional period, then made provision for working out the exact number of troops each power should have. On Temperley and Robertson fell the burden of these calculations. They produced impressive tables marred only by their initial failure to include Turkey. Their labours were, alas, in vain as, on 14 October, Hitler announced Germany's withdrawal from the League.

In the days immediately before this fatal decision, Robertson sent back to London an account of an interesting discussion with Admiral von Freyberg, one of the technical advisers to the German Delegation. In places it reads like a prologue to a Greek tragedy:

> Admiral von Freyberg came to see me this morning in order, as he said, to pursue a conversation started at the dinner table last night. He came, he said, as a personal friend and not because he had received any kind of instruction to do so. He wished to tell me personally how very seriously he regarded the present crisis. It was quite possibly too late in any case to do anything . . . He traced the past history of the crisis to show how justifiable was Germany's position but he said that the justice or otherwise of her case was of little relative importance in comparison with the catastrophe for which we were now heading . . . I said that we in the Delegation fully appreciated the gravity of the situation and had done our best to discover some means by which it could be eased. The real difficulty lay in the fact that what might have been possible twelve months ago was not possible now . . .[42]

Ironically, just as the prospects for world peace began to recede, with all the advantages which that would ultimately bring to a military career, Brian Robertson was made a new and more tempting offer by Dunlop of a job in South Africa. Rather than go the Indian Army Staff College at Quetta as an instructor, where the War Office intended to send him, he retired on half pay and accepted Dunlop's offer. Ian Jacob remonstrated with him, but, as he recalled over sixty years later, Brian:

> was very definite about it. 'Well you see, it's like this: I suppose if I stay on in the Army and there's no war, I may become a Major General, whereas if I go to South Africa with Dunlop, I can stay on until I am 60, and if there's a war, I shall come back and become a general anyway[43].

After the Second World War, when Brian Robertson was Deputy Military Governor of the British Zone in Germany, this decision became legendary and was often quoted as an example of his decisiveness[44]. Yet it was not a decision that was quickly taken and he had been weighing up the pros and cons of quitting the Army for at least 12 years. It was perhaps finally made easier for him by his wife's reluctance to transplant two young children to India, but essentially he left the Army because it seemed to offer him so little in the way of long-term career prospects. Years later, he told Reay Geddes, then the Managing Director of Dunlop, that it was 'the boredom of regimental soldiering in peace' that prompted him to leave the Army in 1934[45].

He took particular care to break the news gently but firmly to his widowed mother:

> I am writing to Dunlop's by this post to accept their offer. Apart from intermittent flutterings of doubt, Edith is as strongly in favour of taking it as I am. South Africa is a long way off, and I shall hate leaving you and the family. But I see no reason why we should not see each other regularly and frequently. Apart from leaves, which will not occur too often, I shall hope that you will make a habit of coming out to us. Well the decision is taken. . . . We can only pray God that it will turn out for the best. Of one thing I feel quite confident – Dad would have approved of it.[46]

On one level, it is arguable that this was the best move that Brian Robertson ever made, as the officer who filled his post in Quetta was killed there in the catastrophic earthquake of May 1935.

THE DUNLOP INTERLUDE
1934–40

Brian Robertson's transfer to Dunlop marked a radical break in his career, yet in Germany such a move would have been seen as a logical step for a staff officer from the Engineers to take. The German Army had set up a special Economics Staff in 1924 and created a whole network of ex-officers in business and industry to liaise between the generals and the industrialists. In his assessment of economic trends in South America and then later in South Africa, Robertson certainly showed an awareness of the significance of economic potential in modern warfare. Arguably then, his years with Dunlop complemented his staff training and gave him some practical experience in what the Germans called the 'defence based economy'[1]. However, he joined Dunlop as an aspiring businessman, not as a staff officer in camouflage. As long as there was no war, his first loyalty was to Fort Dunlop, not to the War Office!

By 1934, Dunlop was one of the economic success stories of inter-war Britain. It had bought out many of its rivals in the home market and while continuing to make rubber tyres in increasing quantities, was also diversifying into such products as Dunlopillo (latex foam), Wellington boots and golf balls. It was, too, poised to set up manufacturing plants in Eire, India and South Africa. It was an 'establishment firm' which practised an enlightened welfare capitalism and had an *esprit de corps* not unlike a good British regiment[2].

Sir Eric Geddes intended Brian Robertson eventually to take over the post of managing director of the South African tyre producing plant which was about to be built in Durban. He spent his first year working in the company's overseas office in London, frequently travelling up to its main production plant at Fort Dunlop in Birmingham. In October, 1934, a team of 24 technicians and administrators were sent over to supervise the construction of the Durban plant. Brian followed in the New Year and his family joined him in April. Until 1937, he was officially 'the personal assistant' to Malcolm Irving, the sales manager in South Africa, but in practice, as a result of Irving's ill health, he ran the factory almost from the beginning[3].

Architecturally, the Dunlop plant was an ultra-modern showpiece set in a landscaped environment. According to the *Natal Mercury* 'even the boiler house chimney . . . achieves an aspect of some grace with its coat of aluminium paint and black tip'. Initially it employed a work force of 450, of whom slightly over 50 per cent were white. Being a factory of its time and place, the Indians and Africans inevitably did the bulk of the unskilled work. Nearly 30 years later, Robertson candidly recalled in the Lords that the Africans:

> . . . who worked in our factory had to live in petrol-tin shanties, in stinking barges in Durban Bay, just where they could get cover over their heads. When they were sick, which they frequently were, they were sent back to the kraals, because there was no hopitalisation of any consequence to look after them. When they died, my officers came to me asking that they should be buried at the firm's expense because otherwise they would not get a decent burial[4].

The factory was formally opened in a blaze of publicity on 13 August, 1935, by General Hertzog, the South African Prime Minister. Not only did the *Natal Mercury* publish a 13 page supplement in its honour, but the proceedings were recorded by a reporter with a 'wandering microphone' from the South African Radio. General Hertzog, who had been one of those very Boers whom the three year old Brian Robertson had fervently begged the Almighty to stop 'enemeing after dadda', sternly informed the Dunlop management team that his government would 'insist upon them paying proper attention to the comforts and care of the employees' – essentially, of course, he had only the European employees in mind. Irving hit the right note in his reply by emphasising that:

> We also recognize a responsibility as regards our selling policy. This policy I can put before you in a very few words: a fair price to the public, a fair profit to the trader and not more than a fair return to ourselves on our outlay[5].

In many ways, these events provide the clue as to why Geddes sent Brian Robertson to Durban. Dunlop did not need a ruthless, swashbuckling entrepreneur there, but rather an efficient administrator used to teamwork and consultation, who could liaise effectively with both businessmen and politicians as well as play a leading part in the local community. In the 1930s, the emphasis in big business was essentially on the creation of cartels and mutually advantageous cooperation. At the Durban factory, for instance, Dunlop also fabricated tyres for the American company Goodyear, which reciprocated by doing the same for Dunlop in Argentina. In September, 1935, Brian Robertson greeted the news that Firestone, another American company, was about to set up a rival plant in Port Elizabeth with near panic and was convinced that it would unleash a

price war and that 'probably neither they nor we shall make any money'[6].
Yet his fears were to prove exaggerated and he was to become a good
friend of Jack Cohill, the Managing Director of Firestone, who eventually
became godfather to his younger daughter Fiona.

There is no doubt that the Durban factory prospered under Brian
Robertson's management. In 1936, it was already making a 12.6 per cent
profit and a year later plans for further expansion were already in hand. In
April, 1938, Sir George Beharell, Dunlop's Chairman, gave the Annual
General Meeting a glowing account of the company's operations in South
Africa, which he saw as 'a complete justification of our policy of local
manufacture'[7]. It would be wrong to attribute this success solely to
Robertson's business acumen. The South African economy was buoyant,
largely as a consequence of the huge profits earnt by the gold mining
industry. This prosperity was reflected in the increasing number of
imported cars which arrived every month from America and Britain and
in the virtual absence of unemployment amongst the white population.
Arguably then, it would have been difficult for Dunlop not to have made
a profit in the prevailing economic climate. Nevertheless, this should not
detract from Brian Robertson's achievements. His workforce recognised
him as an efficient and conscientious manager in whose hands their liveli-
hood and future were safe. He earnt their respect rather than affection. He
was perceived – not surprisingly – as one former employee put it, to have
been '. . . very much influenced by his previous military career. Therefore
very precise and highly organised and motivated'[8]. The distinctive and
often rather abrupt Robertson style of management, which was to become
so familiar to British officials in Germany after 1945, was beginning to
emerge. Another employee from the Finance Department vividly recalls
the following incident, which in many ways also encapsulated his
approach to administration:

> I wrote a letter to him once . . . and gave it to him with the remark 'that
> the letter is short, terse and to the point and I hope it will be alright' To
> which Sir Brian replied: 'If it is short and makes the point satisfactorily
> it will be alright.'[9]

Robertson believed strongly in a clear chain of command and in ensuring that his employees knew exactly what their responsibilities were. He
conducted, for example, a furious correspondence with Reay Geddes,
who was his link man in London, until certain ambiguities in the relations
between Durban and the Head Office were clarified[10].

Within the wider business community, he rapidly became an influential
figure, who seemed to be a natural chairman or president. In 1936, for
instance, he became Chairman of the Rubber Growers' Association and
in November, 1938, he was elected President of the Natal Chamber of

Industries and spent the subsequent year dealing with the impact on local businesses of new company legislation, minimum wages acts and industrial conciliation bills.

All in all, Brian Robertson was a big fish in a small pool. He lived with his family in a comfortable two-storey house with a large garden and a marvellous view out to sea amongst the Durban business nabobs in the wealthy suburb of Berea. He was able to keep three polo ponies and play polo for Durban regularly on Sunday. He took the game very seriously. One year, for instance, when Durban was drawn to play against the superior up-country club of Karkloof, he was worried that some of his team would drink too much whisky at a cocktail party which Edith and he were planning to hold for all the players on the evening before the match. To prevent this they put to test the theory that after two glasses of whisky, a drinker cannot tell the difference between the hard stuff and cold tea. The experiment worked and the following day the Durban team won[11]!

The society columns of the *Natal Mercury* carried regular reports of the Robertsons at dinners, balls and parties, Edith invariably being described as 'exquisitely gowned'. Although a shy and reserved person, Brian quickly adapted to the pace of social life in Durban. In September 1935 he told his mother that:

> We were out every evening last week except Friday. It is really too much but I find it hard to refuse, partly for Edith's sake, partly because I enjoy a game of bridge myself.

That same month, he was also invited to speak on the South African Radio about the League of Nations[12].

The Robertsons were fortunate to live in Durban at a time which was a golden age for the British community in Natal. Their's was a world which had much in common with the stockbroker belts of Surrey and Buckinghamshire. The shops were full of British goods all priced in pounds, shillings and pence, while the *Natal Mercury* kept its readers fully in touch with events in Britain and the luxury liners brought over a stream of British visitors. In May, 1935, when the Robertsons were celebrating King George V's Silver Jubilee in the Marine Hotel, George Bernard Shaw himself was present, casting a sceptical eye over the proceedings.

Yet events in Europe inevitably cast a shadow over this happy and carefree life. Robertson made his own assessment of the international situation a few days after Chamberlain's first meeting with Hitler at Berchtesgarden in September 1938 in a letter to his mother:

> I sometimes consider if there was ever a period in European History when acute tensions and danger of war [have] lasted so long . . .

Hitler and Mussolini seem to exist on crises, and yet neither of them can possibly want war in his heart. I am afraid that things cannot go on for ever like this, and as they show no signs of getting better, I am beginning to fear that war will come one day, quite suddenly, when no one expects it and no one really means to have it. We need only one good 'incident' such as the accidental shooting of a German or Italian diplomat to blow everything up[13].

When Britain and France declared war on Nazi Germany on 3 September, Hertzog and the Nationalist Party went into opposition rather than support South Africa's entry into the War as a member of the Commonwealth, and remained implacably hostile to the new pro-British government headed by General Smuts. Robertson, as President of the Natal Chamber of Industries, threw himself into supporting the war effort. He exhorted its members to release the army reservists working in their factories or offices and persuaded them to pay their wages while they underwent military training. He was also influential in determining how the money raised by the South African Mayors' National Fund could best be spent on helping the Empire's war effort, and was appointed one of the fund's administrators. In his farewell address to the Natal Chamber of Industries, in November, 1939, Brian Robertson appealed for national unity and an end to political bickering between the Afrikaners and the British South Africans:

The worst thing that this war has done for us so far is to rekindle the embers of racial animosity. This fair land to-day is being sown with dragons' teeth and if the iniquitous work goes on unimpeded, we shall one day reap the inevitable whirlwind.

Significantly, he also looked forward to the end of the war and made some perceptive observations about the principles upon which a lasting peace would have to be built:

This war, so far at least, is very unlike the last. It is equally certain that the peace treaties, which have yet to be made, will be quite unlike those which ended the last war. Those treaties were failures because they were based upon fear and vindictiveness. The next treaties, if they are to give lasting peace, must be founded upon confidence and generosity, and they must strike at the root causes of international unrest. Chief among these causes is that economic nationalism which has grown up like a rank weed to stifle the national flow of trade between nations. Some very uncomfortable adjustments will have to be made in the economic life of many countries, and it may well be that South Africa will have to make an even bigger contribution to peace than she has made to war[14].

In November, 1939, he could hardly envisage that later, as Military Governor of the British Zone in Germany, he himself would be able to play a significant role in shaping the postwar settlement. At the end of November, 1939, he tried to rejoin the British Army. Contrary to his confident assumption of some five years earlier, the War Office refused to have him back on the grounds that, at 43, he was already too old. The only prospect of eventual employment it could offer him was of some dead end post such as Railway Transport Officer in Durban[15]. He therefore decided to bypass Whitehall and volunteer for service in the Union Defence Force, which was short of staff officers. He was accepted and given the rank of Lieutenant Colonel with effect from 1 February, 1940, but then almost immediately afterwards he suffered a severe attack of pneumonia which nearly killed him. By May, he had sufficiently recovered to attend a refresher course at the South African Staff College where he graduated first out of 23 students with the glowing report: 'Outstanding. Recommended for a major staff appointment in any capacity'[16]. On 16 June he embarked for Mombasa as part of the advanced headquarters' staff of the South African Expeditionary Force.

4

AN IRONMONGER OF GENIUS
1940–43

When Italy declared war on Britain on 9 June, 1940, Kenya was in a particularly vulnerable position. Two weak divisions, composed for the most part of African troops with very little motorised transport or technical back-up, had to defend the 750 mile frontier with the Italian territories of Abyssinia to the north and Italian Somaliland to the east. On paper at least, the Italians possessed an overwhelming superiority of over a quarter of a million troops well supported by artillery and air power. Smuts responded to urgent appeals from the British Government for reinforcements by sending firstly an infantry brigade in July 1940 and then in November a full division. The South Africans not only brought with them bomber and fighter squadrons but also motorised transport and the vital technical units necessary for waging modern warfare[1].

On his arrival in Nairobi, Brian Robertson joined the headquarters staff of the East African Force, commanded by Major General D P Dickinson, as Assistant Quarter Master General (AQMG), or 'ironmonger', under Colonel Duff, a gifted soldier-scholar, who had been his exact contemporary at Woolwich and Camberley. The work of the Q staff is often routine and undramatic and has nothing of the glamour and excitement that surround strategy and tactics. Yet, as General Wavell argued, 'administration' or logistics is 'the real crux of generalship'[2]. If the logistics of a campaign are faulty, no amount of tactical flair by the commander will compensate. This was obvious enough in the days of Marlborough and Wellington but by 1940, with the advent of mechanised armies, this had become even more of a truism. In Brian Robertson's words:

> When rations and forage ran short, men and horses could still struggle on and fight effectively. When lorries and tanks run short of petrol, they stop altogether and the force which they compose is at the mercy of its enemy[3].

In 1918, the British Army in France was easily supplied from the nearest railhead. Apart from ammunition the demands for a division remained fairly consistent and only a small balance of reserves was kept up in the forward area. By 1940, this had radically changed. Mechanisation enabled an army, especially under desert conditions, to advance rapidly, and its lines of communication might stretch over hundreds of miles, vulnerable to both the enemy and the vagaries of the elements. It therefore became necessary to keep supplies of petrol, food and ammunition well forward, as it was difficult to calculate at any one time the quantities needed by the advancing units. Consequently, as Brian Robertson was later to stress, a modern commander was very much in the hands of his administrative staff:

> Far more so than he is on the operational side. He can hope to have almost as good a grasp of the details of the operational plan as his chief of staff. He cannot have the same immediate knowledge of the administrative plan[4].

EAST AFRICA, JUNE, 1940–JUNE, 1941

Brian Robertson's first task was to organise the movement of the South African troops and their equipment from Mombasa to their training camps in the north of the colony. As a former British regular officer now serving with the Union Defence Force, he played an invaluable role as mediator between the fiercely independent South Africans and the senior British officers who wanted to integrate the South African staff fully into the East African Force Headquarters at Nairobi. South African national pride was appeased by a compromise whereby the domestic affairs of the Union's contingent were made exclusively Robertson's responsibility. Far from wanting to rejoin the British Army through the back door, he was 'rather proud of [his] association with the South Africans'[5] and was happy to wear his orange shoulder flash, which indicated that he had volunteered for overseas service, right up until he formally rejoined the British Army in October, 1945. While looking after the interests of the South African troops, he encountered few problems from the senior British officers on Dickinson's staff, 'though they were not completely free from the quiet conceit of the average Englishman', but

> . . . among the more junior staff officers there were a lot of men who had been given jobs in Kenya, reserve officers who had settled in the Colony. They were sometimes not very efficient and not very tactful.[6]

The task confronting the East African Force was to defend Kenya and then, when the Colony was secure, to attack the enemy in Abyssinia and Italian Somaliland. In the late summer of 1940, the Italians had seized the frontier posts of Moyale and El Wak in northern Kenya and occupied

British Somaliland. Nevertheless, by September the fundamental strategic weakness of their position in East Africa inevitably imposed a defensive policy upon them: the Royal Navy had severed their lines of communication and their grip on Abyssinia was threatened by internal unrest. The Italian Empire was a house of cards waiting to collapse. However, before an offensive could be launched from Kenya, the disparate units there had to be welded into an effective fighting force and, above all, the necessary supplies had to be accumulated. By November, some progress had been made but the base installations were only 50 per cent complete and the workshop and repair units were still in an embryonic stage of development. Not surprisingly, General Cunningham, who took over the command of the East African Force in November, initially decided to postpone operations until after the spring rains. Yet O'Connor's rapid advance against the Italian positions in North Africa and the brilliant success of the raid on the Italian outpost of El Wak persuaded Cunningham to risk an offensive in early February. In a two-pronged attack, the South African Division was to advance into southern Abyssinia, while the 11th and 12th African Divisions were to attack Italian Somaliland. As the success of the attack hinged on administrative preparations, immense responsibilities rested on the shoulders of the 'Q' Staff. Before the troops could advance, roads had to be constructed, water supplies located and dumps of food and petrol established as near to the frontiers as possible. Amongst Brian Robertson's main responsibilities were transport, ordnance services, canteens and lines of communication between the front and the rear supply dumps. In the weeks before the advance into Italian Somaliland and Abyssinia, his days were filled with frenetic activity involving the issue of movement orders to all kinds of military units, sorting out the zones of administration between operational commands, chairing meetings on the construction of the vital Sorota–Juba road link, which was to be the key to the invasion of Italian Somaliland, and fielding complaints about the inadequacy of the NAAFI canteens[7]. Long days of meetings and paperwork were interspersed with short tours where he could escape the office and see for himself how the supply situation was developing. On 10 January, for instance, he visited the 11th and 12th African Divisions for five days during which he had to investigate reasons for unloading delays at the Thika railhead, arrange for water supplies to be improved for the 24th Gold Coast Brigade at Mile 62 camp, survey possible camp sites for incoming units and inspect ammunition and supply dumps. On his travels he was particularly pleased to meet up with and stay the night with a South African road construction company, which was virtually identical to a group of men he had invited to lunch in Durban when, a few months earlier, they had been engaged on building the Durban–Johannesburg trunk road[8].

Shortly after returning from this tour, he wrote a revealing letter to his mother:

I have recently been on a trip lasting six days. I thoroughly enjoyed it. Only the fact that I can get out on these trips makes a job at headquarters bearable. I had one fellow on my staff in front of me yesterday with a request that he should be transferred to a unit in the forward area . . . I told him that as far as I know there isn't a man here who doesn't envy the chaps in the forward area, who live a free, open air life, go to bed at 8 pm and have no bigger worries than the arrival of the next mail and whether the canteens will produce strawberry jam or some other sort. In short he was to stay right here, where he is pulling the most weight in the troop[9].

On 2 February, Cunningham gave the order to advance into Italian Somaliland and seize the port of Kismayu. It fell on 13 February and, after a record-breaking advance of 250 miles in two and a half days by the 23 Nigerian Brigade, Mogadishu fell on 25 February. The speed of the advance fully tested the administrative plans made by Colonel Duff and Brian Robertson. On the whole, they worked. Cunningham's last minute decision to cut down the size of the invading force by two brigade groups ensured that there was just about enough transport to keep it supplied and mobile[10]. As the operation zones were pushed forward, new supply dumps were opened up and the roads, which were ploughed into deep furrows by the constant motor traffic, were kept open by bulldozers and grading machines. At times the number of lorries available was barely adequate. The only way that sufficient transport for personnel and water-carrying could be provided for the front line was by drastically pruning the number of lorries 'working third line from railheads forward'[11]. There were no reserves to replace any transport destroyed by enemy fire or put out of action by mechanical failure.

The opening up of the ports of Kismayu and Mogadishu eased the problems of supply. However, this gave only a temporary respite as, after the fall of Mogadishu, General Cunningham immediately decided to pursue the Italians across the frontier into Abyssinia. According to Brian Robertson:

This was a very different proposition. The distance from Mogadishu to Berbera [the next port in the Gulf of Aden] was 600 miles. A very fine tarmac road was marked on the Italian maps but did not in fact exist after a few miles out of Mogadishu[12].

The advance, which proceeded at about 14 miles a day, taxed the ingenuity of Cunningham's 'Q' staff to the utmost. Nevertheless, thanks to the South African transport companies, they just about managed to keep the flow of vital supplies going. The War Diaries of the 12th African Division show for instance that food supplies were adequate even though there

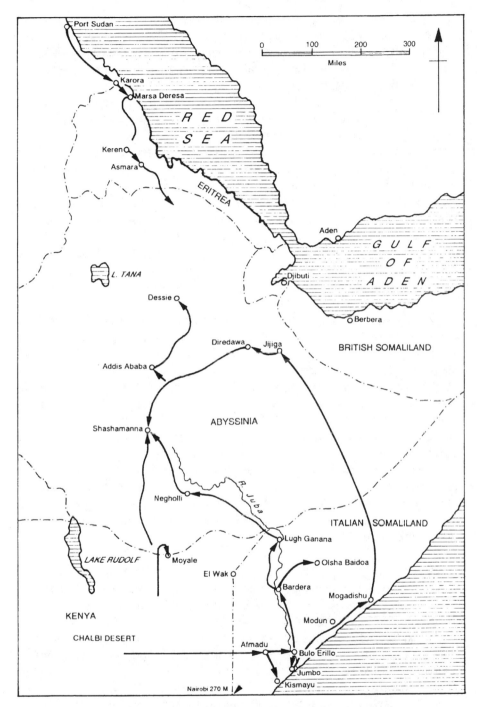

General Cunningham's Operations in East Africa, January–May 1941

were temporary shortages of sugar, milk, biscuits and rice. There were, however, times when petrol supplies all but dried up. In March, the 11th African Division used up all its reserves, while the 1st South African Brigade could only continue its advance thanks to the discovery of an Italian dump of 350,000 gallons[13].

Even with the fall of Addis Ababa on 5 April, the pressures on the Q staff were not for a moment relaxed. The two African divisions moved southwards to deal with a large pocket of Italian and colonial troops in the lakes region, while the 1st South African Brigade advanced northwards to link up with the Sudan force. On 12 April, Colonel Duff and Brian Robertson flew up to confer with the Q Staff of the the 11th and 12th African Divisions about lines of communication, the location of petrol dumps, the arrival of new equipment and medical arrangements. Once the advance was resumed, they were again bombarded incessantly with urgent requests for every conceivable item of supply varying from rice and *poshto* for the African troops to makeshift ambulance planes for flying out the wounded. Usually they managed to provide what was demanded, albeit at times with some delay.

On 3 July, the Italian forces surrendered after being defeated in the battle of the Lakes. Some two weeks earlier, Cunningham had sent Robertson down to Pretoria to discuss the administrative implications of the dispatch of South African troops to the Middle East. After snatching a brief weekend at home, he returned on 17 July to Mombasa by flying boat. At the end of August, he then flew on to Cairo to take over the Q duties of the South African Middle East Defence Force. He confided to his mother that while he wanted to go to Egypt, 'I am sure I shan't like it when I get there. Too hot in more ways than one'.

It was in the East African campaign that Brian Robertson really acquired his skills as 'ironmonger', which he was to practise even more successfully in North Africa over the next two years. He gained experience in operating over long lines of communication and in supplying a rapidly advancing force. Above all he learnt that:

> In administration there is an ever present temptation to provide for everything and to insure against every risk. This can easily lead to a piling up of administrative staffs, administrative units and of large reserves all of which in the early stages of an operation can only be provided at the expense of men and weapons with which the battle itself is fought . . . Administration in battle must ride in a Ford Utility and not a Rolls-Royce de Luxe[14].

In his despatches, Cunningham did not stint his praise for the crucial role played by Duff and Robertson in the administrative side of the operations:

I found them undaunted by the magnitude of the demands made on them. That throughout the vicissitudes of bad roads and ports without appliances, ample supplies were able to keep up with the troops, must be accounted a fine achievement by those two officers. . . .[15]

THE WESTERN DESERT, JULY, 1941–JANUARY, 1943

Initially. Brian Robertson found being the 'Administrative Chief of the South African Defence Force in the Middle East' a tolerably interesting and challenging post, but in the long term he realised that:

. . . it [would] be terribly routine work, plus what is worse, the handling of all the squalid business of appointments, promotions, etc . . . It would have meant living in Cairo always except for occasional visits to the troops[16].

He was, however saved this fate when General Cunningham, who had taken over command of the Western Desert Force or Eighth Army as it was re-named in September, invited him to become his AQMG. After the East African campaign Cunningham had the charisma of an apparently invincible commander and Brian Robertson leapt at the chance, even though it meant being demoted from Brigadier back to being a Lieutenant Colonel again. Cunningham accordingly sent:

. . . a personal telegram off to the CGS in Pretoria asking if he would allow me to go, and got a very prompt refusal! However the CGS sent his deputy up here a few days later to do some business with GHQ and Cunningham decided to have another go at it through him. He brought 'the Auk' [General Auchinleck, the Commander-in-Chief of the Middle East Forces] into it this time and the Deputy CGS went back to Pretoria with a personal request from both of the generals. A telegram arrived the night before last agreeing to my posting. . . . In a few days I shall be living in a hole in the desert instead of this great luxurious hotel, and I know that I am going to enjoy it a great deal more, I hate Cairo and I should always hate it.[17]

Without Cunningham's persistence, Brian Robertson's career would have been very different. He would have vegetated in Cairo for much of the war and would probably never have come to Montgomery's notice as an 'ironmonger' of genius with all the important consequences for his future which that was to have.

On 19 September, he was formally seconded to the Eighth Army to take the post of AQMG under Brigadier Miller, the DA & QMG, who rapidly found him 'a tower of strength'[18]. Robertson worked at the Rear Headquarters where he was allocated three assistants, one of whom was Oliver Poole, later to be chairman of the Conservative Party. With Miller, Robertson had overall responsibility for supply in all its multitudinous forms, maintenance and the movement of troops. At weekly, sometimes even at daily intervals, Miller and he had to assess the needs of the Eighth Army after consulting with the 'Q' staffs of its component parts, 13 and 30 Corps. These needs were then passed on to GHQ at Cairo, when it was decided to what extent they could be met. Once the resources reached the Eighth Army area, it was Miller and Robertson's responsibility to utilise them in the most effective way possible. The pattern of the desert war was succinctly summed up by Miller:

> The further the battle [moves] from the sources of supply the weaker must the army become. Conversely the shorter the L[ine] of C [ommunication], the quicker can reorganisation and reinforcement be achieved. Provided therefore one or other force is not totally destroyed in battle . . . the two opponents could manoeuvre backwards and forwards indefinitely.[19]

The challenge facing the 'Q' Staff was therefore to ensure that in any future advance this pattern would be broken and the attack sustained with adequate supplies.

Brian Robertson arrived in the desert as Cunningham and Auchinleck were working on the final details of CRUSADER, an operation aimed at rolling back the Axis forces from the Sollum-Sidi Omar line, lifting the siege of Tobruk and reoccupying Cyrenaica. In those optimistic weeks before CRUSADER was launched, when confidence in victory was still high, Robertson's life was a hectic rush to ensure that all the necessary administrative preparations were in place. Wherever he was – in tent, caravan or house – he always started his day, where possible, with the same routine. His driver and batman, Eric Page, remembered how:

> I would take him his cup of tea at 6.30 always and he would say, 'Good morning, Eric', and right away reach for his pen and note book and begin writing for at least half an hour . . .[20]

★★★

Brian and his assistants initially reconnoitred sites for forward bases and the new Field Maintenance Centres where there would be reserves of food, water, ammunition and medical supplies stored, and salvage facilities for armoured vehicles and prisoner of war 'cages' would be set up. They then fixed the dates for when these installations would become operational, confirmed with the Q Staff of the Corps the quantities of stores and ammunition to be dumped there and ensured that the necessary labour companies moved up in time. These plans were, of course, liable to be disrupted by enemy air raids. For instance on 12 October, when the Fuka railhead was bombed, not only were trucks carrying ammunition and aeroplane fuel destroyed and a large crater blown in the railway-line but, more seriously, vital water pumping machinery was wrecked[21]. Although the railway was rapidly repaired, detailed administrative schedules had to be re-written and new instructions issued to the sub-areas. An idea of the scale of the dumping programme can be gauged from the fact that 'the transport engaged upon it was consuming 180,000 gallons of petrol a day'[22].

CRUSADER was launched on 18 November but the storm which broke shortly before dawn, bringing torrential rains, created considerable problems for Brian Robertson, as no supply trains were able to reach the Desert railhead from Mohalfa. Until the track was fit for use again he had to exercise a tight control over the issue of rations and petrol from the Field Maintenance Centres. His 'Daily Reports on the Administrative Situation' plot the response of the Eighth Army's Q Staff to the course of the battle[23]. The demands of the forward bases were carefully monitored and, where possible, met even if this meant a last minute change of plan or improvisation. During the heavy fighting which lasted from 22–25 November, when the success of CRUSADER seemed to hang in the balance, and Cunningham lost his nerve and had to be replaced by Ritchie, the Q Staff continued methodically to organise the distribution of petrol arriving at the Misheifa railhead, keep the water flowing down the pipeline and the ammunition dumps topped up. The fact that Miller was so confident about the supply situation was one of the factors that persuaded Auchinleck to persevere with the battle[24]. Given the mobility of modern armies and the desert terrain, even the Q Staff at Rear Headquarters could get caught up in the fighting. On 24 November, for instance, when a powerful force of the Afrika Corps broke through the line at Sheferzen and seemed to be heading for the railhead at Misheifa, Brian Robertson was ordered to co-ordinate all available units to defend the Rear Headquarters area, and only narrowly avoided being taken prisoner himself[25]. Fortunately for him, the Germans then changed direction and swung north towards Bardia.

In early December, it was clear that Rommel was pulling back his forces and the Eighth Army was able to advance into Cyrenaica. By 21 January, 1942, the Guards Brigade had reached Agheila. It was now the turn of the British to be operating on long lines of communication 'stretched to breaking point'[26]. Auchinleck still hoped to continue the advance into Tripolitania, but before attacking Rommel's position at Agheila, he needed time for reorganisation and the accumulation of sufficient supplies. In consequence, opening up the ports of Tobruk, Derna and Bengasi became the overriding priority of the Q staff. How effectively ships could be unloaded there would determine whether or not the offensive could continue. As soon as Rommel decided to lift the siege of Tobruk on 4 December, work began on repairing the docks. However, by 8 January only 1,200 tons per day were being unloaded and in the meantime the Eighth Army was 'living from hand to mouth'[27]. Five days later, Brian Robertson went to Tobruk to expedite matters. There he came to the conclusion that the main causes for delay 'appear to be present lay-out of depots and drivers of vehicles wasting time between port and depot'. He consequently recommended re-organising the whole layout of the depots and 'tightening up on the drivers' as well[28]. As the advance continued, Benghazi rapidly became more important than Tobruk as a forward base, and, as he constantly reiterated, 'every ton put into Benghazi [was] of much greater value than the same amount at Tobruk'[29]. In mid-January, the Q staff drew up the administrative plan for supplying the Eighth Army in the event of a further advance. Essentially, it hinged on Benghazi becoming a fully operational port, yet this could by no means be guaranteed. After conferring with Brian Robertson, Miller recorded in his diary that:

> BR was quite helpful about Benghazi and there is no doubt that all that is required is fair weather and safe arrival of ships. Without this, progress must be slow and this is a bad season of the year with a port facing the wrong way[30].

While the Eighth Army was forced to mark time, Rommel's forces were not only much nearer to their main base at Tripoli, but thanks to some heavy losses inflicted on the Royal Navy in the Mediterranean by German U-boats and Italian 'human' torpedoes, Axis convoys carrying petrol and tanks had been able to berth there safely. On 22 January, Rommel launched a strong counter-attack and by 25 January Benghazi had to be evacuated. Now, for the first time in his career, Brian Robertson was forced to organise the logistics of a retreat: convoys had to be diverted to alternative destinations and the evacuation of both Advanced and Rear Headquarters arranged at great speed.

By the end of the first week in February, the front was stabilised and the fighting died down. There was an uneasy pause until Rommel renewed his offensive on 26 May. Temporarily, Robertson was given a respite in the nerve-wracking business of supplying a retreating army but, of course, the daily administrative routine continued with an unceasing round of paper work, inspections and conferences with the Q staffs of the two Corps. He

had, too, to deal with matters as diverse as the supply of summer clothes
to the troops and the provision of a cinema for the Tobruk garrison[31].
Increasing enemy air activity complicated his work. Thus he ordered that
trains between Misheifa and Capuzzo were to be run as far as possible
'during hours of complete darkness' and that tankers were only to steal
into Tobruk harbour on moonless nights[32].

Tobruk remained potentially a vital base for the Eighth Army, but as
the Germans were only 35 miles to the west of it, Miller and Robertson
were reluctant to store more than one week's reserves there in case they
fell into German hands and enabled Rommel to drive on to the Delta[33].
In the end, they were overruled by Cairo, and Tobruk was duly re-stocked
for the time when the Eighth Army would renew its offensive, but when it
fell to the Germans in June their fears were fully vindicated.

On 26 May, the German forces advanced and forced the Eighth Army
into a humiliating retreat from Gazala to El Alamein. A week later, Brian
Robertson was promoted to the rank of Brigadier and moved up to the
Headquarters of the 'Main (Eighth) Army' to take over the post of DA &
QMG from Miller. Like Montgomery a few months later, he quickly
ensured that he had a comfortable caravan free of flies and conducive to
calm, collected thought. According to his old friend, Major General
Wimberley, the GOC of the 51st Highland Division, he evidently thought
it tactful to keep his caravan 'well out of sight' of General Auchinleck, who
was notorious for the acute discomfort of his headquarters[34]. Brian's main
task was to keep the administrative structure of the Eighth Army intact,
while it retreated to the El Alamein Line. Although apparently without the
knowledge of either Ritchie or Auchinleck, the Q Staff had 'in complete
secrecy'[35], drawn up contingency plans for this retreat. Nevertheless, it was
a period of hectic improvisation, involving the constant rearrangement of
supply lines and rearward movement of headquarters. On the other hand,
provided that the retreat did not turn into a route, the actual process of
supplying the troops became easier. The further the British moved back
towards the Egyptian Delta, the shorter were their supply lines. In contrast,
those of the Germans grew longer and more vulnerable.

By the end of June, the Eighth Army had reached the Alamein Line.
After a brief pause to 'get the supply lines working well', Brian Robertson,
acting on Auchinleck's assessment that the Germans had outrun their
strength, ordered his staff to begin considering 'the arrangements necessary for an advance'. These arrangements duly enabled Auchinleck to
launch a series of counter-attacks, which, together with the German
riposte of 15–20 July, became known as the First Battle of Alamein.
Auchinleck did indeed succeed in stopping Rommel, but the Afrika Korps
was still very much in existence and continued to pose a threat to the
Delta. After the long retreat from Gazala, the morale of the Eighth Army
was at rock-bottom, and the average soldier had only bitter scorn for the

Commander-in-Chief and the Headquarters Staff. One sergeant, whose opinion would have been regarded at the time as a platitude, observed:

> Rommel thinks it all out and takes whatever he needs with him . . . Our lot! Christ, they couldn't organise a piss-up in a brewery![36]

As far as the Q Staff were concerned, this was demonstrably unfair. The necessary supplies of food, equipment and munitions did reach the fighting troops and in the rear areas, medical services, entertainment and hot baths were all provided in abundance. Brian Robertson's work was officially recognised when he was awarded a CBE in September, even though he cynically observed that it was 'like the measles: You've got to get it sometime'[37]. But of course the slump in the morale of the whole Army affected him and, as he confessed to his wife, he would have welcomed the chance to be posted away from the Middle East. His mood of growing disillusionment rapidly changed when Montgomery was appointed in August, 1942. He knew Montgomery, who had been one of his instructors at Camberley, but it was his professionalism in an army that suffered so much from amateurism that impressed him and in his opinion so abundantly compensated for the glaring faults in Montgomery's character. Three months later, after the Second Battle of Alamein, Brian Robertson wrote to his wife:

> What gave me confidence, more than anything else was Monty's attitudes and methods. To watch him on his job is like watching a test match played after watching just good club performance.[38]

All in all he found Montgomery a 'hellava a chap'[39].

At the end of August, Rommel made a final desperate attempt to smash through the British lines at Alam Halfa and reach the Delta. In the middle of the battle, Brian Robertson sent an interesting interim assessment of it to his wife:

> While it is therefore wise and necessary to be cautious and conservative, the fact remains that we have won a definite victory. The Boches have been quite severely hurt. Particularly his soft stuff (personnel and transport) has suffered. . . . Great credit must be given to Monty who not merely made skilful dispositions but far more important, breathed a fighting spirit into his troops. By the time this reaches you, the papers will have told you whether the battle has been continued and with what result. Writing tonight I can only say that so far the battle has gone quite definitely in our favour. It is well to recall that the Boche has not yet in this war launched a major offensive on any front without achieving some considerable measure of success. It will be a very big thing if this

proves to be the final occasion of that sort. I might add that he has with-out [fail] had the best of every armoured battle, yet in this battle there has been an armoured fight and he got the worst of it. That means a lot to us.[40]

Three days later he continued:

The Boche continues to go back. I went round yesterday over the ground he had left the previous day. There was gratifying evidence of the loss he had sustained in tanks, transport and men. For some odd reason, the BBC and press are trying to hush up what has in fact been a great victory . . . It is all a great tribute to Monty who by his tactical skill and personal influence has made the Eighth Army win a great victory.[41]

Despite some of Montgomery's more recent critics, Brian Robertson was right in his assessment of Alam Halfa. Montgomery's victory was in great measure due to his immediate recognition, on taking over the Eighth Army, of the tactical significance of the position and the steps he then took to ensure that he had enough forces, backed by ample fire power, to provide a fully adequate defence[42]. Needless to say, the logistic preparation for that battle had been extensive and Robertson and his staff had done a fine job.

Once Rommel had been effectively stonewalled, Montgomery began to plan his own offensive. Thanks to the domination of the sea routes by the Royal Navy and the almost total air superiority gained by the Allied Air Forces, regular ocean convoys ensured a steady delivery of everything needed for the coming offensive. The shortness of the lines of communi-cation, the good condition of the roads and rail links and an abundance of motor transport all added up to a quartermaster's dream. A major prob-lem facing the Q Staff was to hide from the Germans as long as possible the preparations for the offensive. This was done by the cunning use of camouflage and an elaborate deception plan involving dummy vehicles and guns, dumps and pipelines which misled them into thinking that the build-up of forces was merely a training exercise[43]. The quantities involved were considerable – 3,000 tons of ammunition, 2,000 tons of petrol, 600 tons of ordnance stores, 600 tons of miscellaneous items, 420 tons of engineer stores – all had to be dumped and concealed. In addition, a new 10-inch water pipe had to be laid from Alexandria. It was a major logistic operation, completed with absolute precision in order to ensure that the brilliantly conceived deception plan should not be breached. Small wonder that Montgomery formed a high opinion of Brian Robertson's professional skill, for the execution of that operation had been his responsibility.

On the very day that the Second Battle of El Alamein began Brian

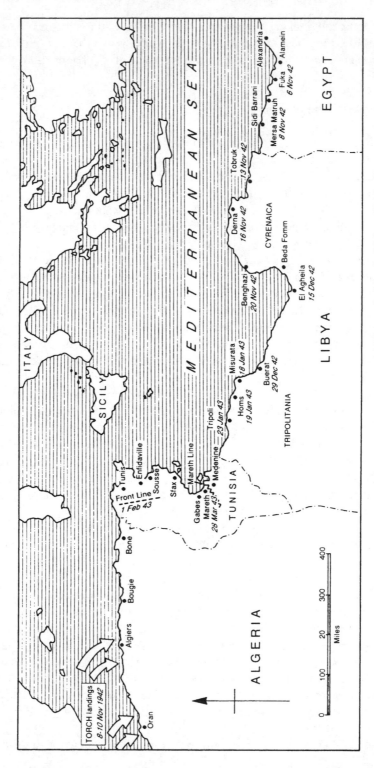

The Advance of the British and Commonwealth Forces in North Africa, 1942–43

Robertson was evacuated to hospital with pneumonia. He wrote despair-
ingly to Edith:

> I could cry with anger. Tomorrow morning when I should be red hot on
> the job, hearing every bit of news, adapting my plan to situation, etc., I
> shall be lying in Alex knowing nothing. I shall know now if Monty likes
> me or not because he can easily take advantage of this to get a new
> A/Q[44].

He also gave his wife an interesting commentary on the coming battle:

> It is an entirely different battle to any previous desert battle. There is no
> open flank. The enemy's left is on the sea, his right on the impassable
> Quattara Depression. Therefore we are compelled to make a frontal assault
> on a highly organised defensive position. No general does that for choice.

When Robertson left hospital on 26 October, the battle was at its height.
He spent the night at Rear Headquarters and the next day was plunged back
into the ceaseless round of Q duties, daily conferences and tours of inspection. By 4 November, the Eighth Army had broken through the German
lines and Rommel was in full retreat. On 23 November, the subsequent
advance had reached Agedabia, which was some 778 miles from the
Alamein line. Brian Robertson, elated by these successes, wrote to Edith:

> I think that my last letter to you was written . . . just before the attack
> which finally broke the Hun's resistance. There were not a few here who
> were shaking their heads in a grave and knowing manner. Casualties . . .
> rather stiff, though actually about 15% less than the estimate which I
> had given the doctors before the show started. . . . At all events we have
> galloped away since and returned to the line from which we were driven
> in June in less than half the time it took us to beat the retreat. Credit
> must be given to the Boches. For the speed at which he has beat it. My
> own department I am glad to say has kept the Army going at a pace
> which was not expected previously[45].

He then went on to describe with some amusement how General der
Panzertruppen Wilhelm Ritter von Thoma, who had been taken prisoner, coped with Montgomery's question about the impact of Alamein on
the strategic position of the Afrika Korps:

> . . . the General, a very decent fellow, with a sense of humour, said, 'Oh,
> nothing very much, I think. You may get Agheila . . . but, after all, you
> have been there before'.

To Brian Robertson, however, the crucial difference between the advance of November 1941 and the brilliant successes he was writing to his wife about was that 'we are commanded by a shrewd and determined man, who knows exactly what he is doing'[46]. Under Montgomery's leadership, Robertson became an administrator of genius, who ruthlessly overcame obstacles to the advance and who did not hesitate to eliminate troublemakers, 'however efficient'[47].

Inevitably, the ever-lengthening supply lines again presented the Q Staff with immense problems[48]. Water pipelines, coastal roads and railways had rapidly to be repaired, but the key to keeping the Eighth Army mobile was, of course, to open up the ports along the Libyan coast, of which Tobruk and Benghazi were the largest. Shortly before Alamein, Brian Robertson obtained Montgomery's agreement initially to use fighting troops rather than labour companies to work the newly captured railheads and ports. He argued convincingly that it was 'uneconomical even to feed a large force of labour when one is already feeding an equally large force of soldiers who are waiting for supplies before they can resume battle'. Apparently they could 'even be persuaded to enjoy it'![49]

Tobruk fell on 13 November. The following day, Brian Robertson visited it. He found it 'a filthy place now, swarming with flies. Most of the houses a heap of rubble, none intact'[50], but by 16 November ships were already being unloaded there. Benghazi was taken four days later. Since the last advance in December 1941, Robertson had developed a more streamlined technique for organising the newly occupied ports and railheads:

> . . . as we advanced from railhead to railhead or port to port, this same Area HQ went forward and created the organisation necessary to run that place. By using the same HQ and by keeping with it as far as possible the same various administrative Staffs and installations which it requires, we were able to develop these places quickly as it were by drill.[51]

Five days before Tobruk had fallen, the greatest seaborne invasion in history to date, Operation TORCH, had put General Eisenhower's Anglo-American force ashore between Casablanca and Algiers, and the whole face of the war in North Africa had been changed. Whilst the problems of supporting an advance even as far as Tripoli must have dominated Brian Robertson's every thought at that time, he was far too good a logistician not to recognise the significance of TORCH for the Eighth Army, even though the nearest point of contact with Eisenhower was nearly 2,500 miles away by air, let alone by the circuitous route that the Eighth Army would now have to follow over desert and mountain, to join hands with their comrades of the British First and American Fifth Armies. A long, hard, challenging advance lay ahead and the logistic problems were daunting.

The momentum of the advance came to stop just before the German defences at Agheila. The Eighth Army, as in January 1941, was now in danger of outrunning its supplies and of becoming vulnerable to a German counter-attack. This imposed an inevitable administrative delay until supplies were accumulated for the next phase of the attack, but Brian Robertson's staff managed to come up with a plan which met Montgomery's deadline of 12 December. The attack was to be mounted by 30 Corps only, which would be supplied by road from Tobruk with transport taken from 10 Corps.

Some two months later, Brian Robertson explained in detail to a distinguished military audience how such plans as this were evolved:

> The Army commander clearly is always looking ahead. He wants to know what he can do within the limits of the administrative possibilities, and he asks his DA & QMG. It would not be very satisfactory if that officer had to say on every occasion, 'I must go and consult Rear Army before I can tell you'. The DA & QMG must know sufficient of his administrative situation to be able to give an immediate answer in general terms and possibly subject to certain qualifications. It is most important that this immediate answer should be reasonably accurate. On it the General will frame his plan in more detail and give ideas as to the date and weight of the attack. Having said what he is going to do, a Commander must not cheat. He must not beat the pistol, nor wangle up additional troops, nor sneak his troops further forward than he said he would. A good administrative staff does not over-insure and cannot be cheated without unfortunate consequences. Some Generals have no morals. Fortunately, General Montgomery does not cheat – whether this is due to his innate honesty or to the fact that I watch him like a cat does not matter – and moreover he doesn't let other people cheat. The DA & QMG must then get into touch with his Rear Army and it is there that the problem is thrashed out in detail . . . Contact must also be made with the Corps who are then beginning to form their Corps plan. . . . Contact must also probably be made with GHQ in order that they may accelerate or modify their arrangements for supply by land and sea . . . After that the Army Administrative plan takes final shape . . .[52]

Once the Germans were pushed out of Agheila on 17 December, it was clear that they would next attempt to make a stand at Buerat, some 250 miles to the west. Montgomery was determined not only to take Buerat but 'to carry the momentum of attack right through to Tripoli'. In the longer term, the possession of this major port would quickly ease the maintenance problems of the Eighth Army, but in the short-term the logistics of the advance were going to be a nightmare for the Q staff. Cairo was more cautious than Montgomery. The Q Staff there initially estimated that it would take three months to prepare for the attack, although Lindsell, the Chief Administrative Officer, believed that it could be achieved in two months, but Brian Robertson and his staff were able to improve dramatically on this timetable and produce a plan enabling Tripoli to be taken by 21 January 1943[53]. Crucial to this plan was that at Benghazi, which the Middle East Planning Staff described as 'the corner-stone of the British maintenance framework' until Tripoli was secured[54], some 2,380 tons should be unloaded daily, of which 1,200 would be a bulk delivery of petrol. This was, however, a gamble. Initially the Navy was painfully slow in removing sunken ships from the harbour. General Sir Charles Richardson, who was then on Montgomery's staff, remem-bered vividly Brian Robertson trying to explain to Montgomery how the Navy seemed to be doing nothing and that ships were 'popping about like corks in the harbour'. He was sent off immediately 'to tell the Admiral from me . . . to get on with the job'[55]. This seems to have galvanised the Navy and by 20 December there was a marked improvement in the amount of tonnage off-loaded. For the next two weeks, the administrative preparations worked comparatively smoothly. On Christmas Day, after a conference, Brian Robertson was able to go to Church and then eat a lunch of turkey and pork at the mess, where not surprisingly, according to the War Diary, 'everybody was happy'. Thanks to the efforts of the Q Staff the same menu was available to the whole of the Eighth Army.

However, this atmosphere of palpable well-being was rudely shattered by the violent storms of 3–5 January. These not only blew two ships in Benghazi harbour loose from their moorings, but also made a 100 foot gap in the outer mole allowing heavy seas to wash right into the inner harbour and flood several administrative departments. Inevitably, as the Official History commented, 'this occurrence at a time when every day and every ton was being counted was almost a disaster'[56]. Montgomery then accepted an alternative plan put forward by his Q Staff: 10 Corps was again 'grounded' and its transport companies were to be used to supple-ment 'the road lift' from Tobruk. Later, Brian Robertson conceded that the divisions disliked being turned into 'a Carter Patersons organisation', but that it was only by 'ruthless use' of such transport that the Eighth Army had been able to reach Tripoli[57].

On 15 January, the attack on Buerat and the subsequent drive to Tripoli began. It was an epic gamble. If Tripoli had not been taken within 10 days, supplies would have run out and the Eighth Army would have been forced to retreat. Ultimately, success was achieved, not so much by Montgomery's tactical skill and the inspired improvisation by his Q staff as by Rommel's blunder in withdrawing his forces from what should have been an impregnable defensive position in the Tarhuna–Homs line to counter a weak threat to his flank by the New Zealand Division.

On the evening of 19 January, while waiting for the final break through to Tripoli, Robertson was momentarily able to turn his thoughts to family affairs in Durban and write to Edith about the price of storing furniture in Britain, his own post-war prospects in Dunlop and above all their children's education. Not surprisingly for somebody who had not seen his family for two years he was only too aware that:

> . . . one of my difficulties in writing to you on this subject is that I do not wish to appear obstinate or dogmatic. You are constantly with the children and have far better opportunity to study them and consider their future.[58]

The fall of Tripoli and the imperative need to make the port operational brought an abrupt but temporary halt to any further correspondence home.

'KING' OF TRIPOLITANIA, FEBRUARY–JULY, 1943

Once Tripoli was occupied on 23 January and its harbour cleared of block ships, the nature of Brian Robertson's responsibilities changed. Montgomery decided to set up a permanent base and a lines of communication centre in Tripoli from which the Eighth Army could be supplied as it advanced towards the Tunisian border, and Brian Robertson, promoted to the temporary rank of Major General, was put in command. He had mixed feelings about the appointment, as he confided to Edith:

> My long spell in my pleasant job is coming to an end. I am to be made 'King' of this country . . . I shall still be under Monty. I am being congratulated later . . . it will mean promotion, but I feel that it is a rather ambiguous rise. There is no better AQ job than my present one. . .[59]

Brian took some time to settle into his new job and to adapt to a new chain of command:

> . . . the most difficult part [of which] is that in a sense, I now come under Miles [Graham], formally my junior. As the senior administrative staff officer on Army HQ he naturally gives me my orders. As he is rather touchy and a bit sharp with his pen, I have to swallow my pride sometimes[60].

Nevertheless, the job did have some very solid advantages. After living in a tent just outside Tripoli, where one night he was nearly washed away by a storm, he was able to move into a palatial villa, which was 'hideously ugly inside, the rooms being lined for the most part with glazed doors'[61]. His office, which was 'larger than any room in Dunlop's', was situated near the harbour and was regularly exposed to German air attacks, but fortunately had 'a good basement to which we resort if we get caught by an enemy raid'[62]. He also felt 'very grand rolling around as a general with a smart red flag on [his] car', although he conceded that the novelty would rapidly wear off[63].

As Commander of the Tripolitania Base, Brian Robertson's responsibilities were wide ranging. Since the base was initially an operational headquarters, he delegated responsibility for the civilian population to Brigadier Lush, the Deputy Chief Civil Affairs Officer whom he regarded as his 'staff officer for civil affairs', and only interfered in this area when he felt that military interests were at stake. He did, however, firmly block the attempts by Lush's officials to take over *The Tripoli Times* which he insisted was an Eighth Army paper, although privately he was shocked by its racey contents. At one juncture he even wanted its editor sacked, but was curtly refused permission by Montgomery. He also displayed considerable skill in inter-Allied relations. He handled the Americans tactfully but firmly and managed to deflect their demands for a place on the Tripoli Supply Board by increasing the powers of the various committees on which the American Air Force was represented. He argued strongly that the Board should only deal with matters of policy, and that the fewer people who discussed policy the better.

He was above all anxious to dispel the idea that the war was nearly over and that Tripoli should become a glorified rest camp for the Eighth Army. Thus when approached by its Assistant Chaplain General on the need for making the troops comfortable, he agreed but with the following caveat:

> . . . I feel strongly that a frank and firm attitude must be taken towards those who imagine that this Army can now sit down and enjoy itself. It is useless to make statements to the effect that the troops have deserved a reward, or are entitled to leave or any other particular benefit. There are definite restrictions of geography and transport, which preclude large scale movement of men from one part of the world to another for the sake of leave. Moreover, and this is the most important point of all, we are confronted with a ruthless enemy who does not let up, and we shall only defeat him quickly if we deal with him relentlessly and without pausing for the sake of relaxation[64].

In marked contrast to his opinion in September 1942, when he had seemed to think that the war might well be over within a year, he had now become increasingly pessimistic about the chances of a speedy victory:

The big weakness, of course, is that our army in England and its leaders are inexperienced in the war and the Americans are quite untrained. Worse still they don't realize it and think they know everything. Dieppe and Tunis point this moral very forcibly. With such troops victory one feels, must be a costly and slow business[65].

Nevertheless, despite being acutely aware of the dangers of relaxation when so much fighting still remained to be done, he would have been inhuman if he had not enjoyed the fruits of victory and basking in the glory of being a key figure on Montgomery's staff. A flood of important visitors passed through Tripoli. On 3 and 4 February Winston Churchill, who was always delighted to see the son of his 'old friend Wully', was there[66]. Other visitors included a Turkish military mission, a brace of Chinese generals, the Cardinal Archbishop of New York and then, on 19 June, the King Emperor himself. Brian Robertson was understandably proud of his role as host to George VI. He later wrote to Edith:

The King's visit is just over – as far as I am concerned. I saw a lot of him, as I command more troops – in number – than any other individual commander. . . . My lads really excelled themselves. Both tea and lunch were perfect. The menu today was Hors d'oeuvres, diane soupe, saddle of lamb and peach melba.

He was also amused by how:

[d]riving in the car after lunch he [the King] went asleep on my shoulder. Unfortunately he woke up to catch me giving a very disloyal wink to General Montgomery who was in the front seat[67].

Brian Robertson was delighted to have his achievement as an 'ironmonger' so fully recognised. He was allocated a two hour slot in Montgomery's famous 'teach in' at the Del Mahari Hotel in Tripoli, which was attended by senior officers from both the American and British armies[68]. He was made a Companion of the Bath 'as an immediate award and not in the general ruck of periodicals'[69], but he was proudest of all of the praise given to him by Montgomery. On 26 February he told Edith that:

[Monty] has now written me a note which will be in the little museum which you are preserving for me . . . He says 'I did not think it necessary to say, possibly because you are in the family and a very vital part of it'. The rest of the letter is exceedingly kind and complimentary, but no part gives me greater pleasure than the sentence I have just quoted.[70]

Although he became a personal friend of Montgomery, he was careful to handle that eccentric and egotistical man very carefully. After one 'long and interesting talk' with him, he began to tease him 'on becoming a politician, but stopped when [he] saw that it was a tender spot'[71].

His letters were not only full of his own triumphs. In February and March, when the tempo of his work slackened, he was able to give further thought to his children's future. His advice lacked the driving urgency of Wully's some 30 years earlier, and indeed at times it was perhaps even a reaction to it. For instance, while he wanted his son Ronald to sit a scholarship to a public school in South Africa, he was emphatic that he must not be 'crammed'. Nevertheless, he showed his father's old horror of living beyond one's means. He somewhat testily dismissed Edith's fond hope that Ronald might ultimately become an ambassador on the grounds that a career in the diplomatic service was impossible without a private income and that would involve Ronald in 'a grind for money all his life'. Instead he hoped that his son might pick a more lucrative profession like law. Almost 47, Brian Robertson was above all conscious of time slipping away. He deeply regretted missing the best years of his younger daughter's childhood, but the war, as he wrote to Edith:

> . . . will end one day and if I live to see the end it will be a wonderful joy to come home to you and the children and all that home means. I shan't be as young as I was, but may not to be too old to enjoy life once more[72].

He was not allowed to rest upon his laurels in Tripoli for long. In April, and then again at the end of May, he was sent off to Cairo to help with the detailed planning of HUSKY, as the proposed operation for the invasion of Sicily was called. In an atmosphere thick with personal rivalry and bedevilled by the antics of prima donnas, Brian Robertson's essentially rational and self-disciplined approach, which a fellow staff officer, Sir Edgar Williams, was later to characterise as being rather like a 'grown-up looking down on the children'[73], moved Charles Miller, now the Administrative Officer of the 15th Army Group, to appeal to him to:

> . . . get the Eighth Army Staff to cooperate and to drop the infectious autocratic manner of their commander – all right for him (or bad enough) but quite intolerable in his staff in their dealing with other services and superior staffs and allies. Brian quite saw my point and was of course splendid[74].

In reality, of course, there was little that Brian Robertson could do to soften Montgomery's abrasive approach, particularly as he was convinced that Montgomery was a strategist of genius and was actually right!

With the end of the North African campaign, the importance of Tripoli declined. Its role in Operation HUSKY was primarily to receive Eighth Army casualties. In July, Brian Robertson handed over his post as 'King' of Tripolitania to Major General Clowes and moved over to Sicily on 18 July to become GOC of 'Fortbase' in Syracuse. He went there with the reputation of being the man who had enabled the Eighth Army to advance from Alamein to Tripoli. The years 1940–43 were a formative experience in his career. He had become used to overcoming obstacles ruthlessly and yet to surmount these obstacles he had also, on occasion, to compromise and be flexible.

ALEXANDER'S ADMINISTRATIVE OFFICER IN ITALY 1943–45

For two years, Brian Robertson, whom one of the Official Historians of the Italian campaign called that 'prince among administrative officers' was to play a pivotal role, first as Commander of Fortbase in Syracuse and then as Alexander's Chief Administrative Officer (CAO)[1].

Inevitably, as CAO, he did not dominate the headlines of the newspapers at home, as the public knew little of his work, yet without him Alexander's victories would never have been achieved. As in the Western Desert, much of his work consisted in supplying the advancing armies day in, day out, but he was also responsible for every aspect of the discipline and welfare of the British forces and for the exploitation of the Italian economy and labour force in the interests of the Allied war effort. He was thus at times a stern disciplinarian wondering how best to stem the flow of deserters and to stigmatise those soldiers who contracted venereal diseases; at other times he pondered benignly on the lay-out of rest camps and the supply of beer. Always, however, he was the supreme technician who could plan ahead methodically and ensure that the needs of the heterogeneous armies, which Alexander commanded, could be met without fail. His first duty was to the American Fifth and British Eighth Armies. If necessary, he would ruthlessly defend their interests against the parsimony of the War Office or assert the primacy of the demands of the Allied Armies over the needs of the Italian civil economy or the fate of wretched refugees and prisoners of war caught up in a potential war zone.

FROM SICILY TO MONTE CASSINO AND ANZIO, JULY, 1943–MARCH, 1944

It was not until 18 July that Robertson moved over to Sicily to take command of Syracuse, or 'Fortbase', as it was called by its prosaic military code name. He found a city paralysed by Allied bombing with its homeless citizens seeking shelter in the catacombs of the early Christians or great caves like the 'Ear of Dionysius'[2]. His immediate task was to open up

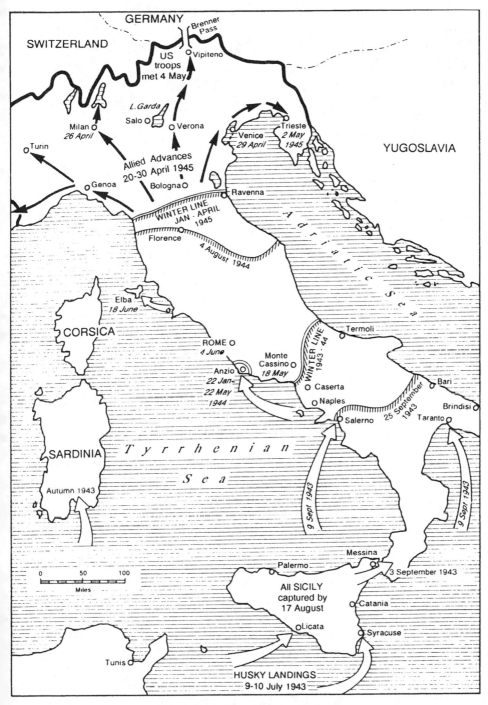

Allied Operations in Italy, 1943–45

the Syracuse docks to ensure that the necessary 'maintenance tonnages' could be unloaded there. He no longer had the experts who had so quickly repaired the North African harbours and had rapidly to have a new team trained to run the port.

He also had to contend with a disturbingly high level of looting and drunkenness amongst the troops. Alexander was sufficiently worried to write directly to Brian Robertson informing him that reports were reaching Britain and America about the bad behaviour of the British soldiers. He concluded his letter by firmly observing: 'I know I can leave it to you to put right, but I must stress that it must be done'. As he had so few military police, there was a limit to what Brian Robertson could do, but he did immediately write to all base and sub-area commanders asking them to ensure whenever a Court Martial was assembled that the President should be informed of the gravity with which these crimes were viewed.

His work was further complicated by the fact that Allied Force Headquarters across the water in Algiers imposed upon him a cumbersome and inefficient maintenance system whereby he had to compile a list of his demands ten weeks in advance, with the inevitable consequence that large surpluses were accumulated in some commodities, while there were acute shortages in others. Allied administration was also positively Byzantine in its complexity. In July, 1943, there were three major headquarters in the Mediterranean whose responsibilities overlapped with each other: the Allied Force Headquarters at Algiers, Headquarters Middle East Land Forces in Cairo and Headquarters 15 Army Group in Sicily. This inevitably led to frequent delays and muddles and made Brian Robertson's work more difficult.

General Miller, who was in overall charge of 15 Army Group's administration, sought to devolve most of the administrative work on Fortbase, only to find that Montgomery insisted on regarding it as an administrative appendage of Eighth Army. Increasingly, Brian was caught between the crossfire of an imperious Montgomery and a resentful and stubborn Miller, while at the same time having his actions scrutinised by the Chief Administrative Officer in Algiers, General Gale. Not surprisingly, there was considerable vagueness amongst the Q staff of the various units in Sicily as to which headquarters was responsible for any particular decision. At the end of August, for instance, the officer commanding the Advanced Ordnance Depot at Fortbase had no idea whether 'his master [was] Eighth Army, Fortbase or Army Group'[3]. In the growing administrative chaos Brian Robertson emerged as the anchorman who ensured that some semblance of efficiency was maintained and that above all the necessary supplies reached the front. When Gale visited Sicily in August, he was impressed by Brian Robertson as ' a man of considerable brain . . . who is really doing the administration behind the Eighth Army'[4]. As plans for the invasion of Italy crystallised, worries about the inadequate administrative back-up multiplied. The invasion evolved out of the occupation of Sicily. Until almost the last moment, 15 Army Group was not sure where its armies should land. Then, when it was at last decided that the Eighth Army should land on the toe of Italy on 3 September, Brian Robertson, whose job it was to maintain it, was not informed of the precise timing of the operation. Not surprisingly, the troops in the first wave of the landings had for a brief period to go on short rations.

Faced with light German opposition, the landings were successful, and in some ways the first month of the Italian campaign was reminiscent of the fighting in North Africa after Alamein. Hopes were raised by the Italian armistice in September, but the Germans soon showed that they would fight the Allies every inch of the way. It was initially a time of rapid advance and lengthening lines of communication, yet the Eighth Army lacked any sound administrative back-up or firm base. Fortbase was put under enormous pressure when Montgomery was ordered on 11 September to link up with the beleaguered Fifth Army which had landed at Salerno two days earlier. This entailed an accelerated advance which was only made possible by switching the axis of supply from the toe to the heel ports. Brian Robertson's success in organising this and dispatching an adequate volume of supplies from Syracuse was regarded by Montgomery's Chief of Staff, de Guingand, as 'one of the major factors in allowing Eighth Army to link up with the Fifth so soon'[5].

By the end of September, the general administrative muddle was beginning to take its toll on military efficiency and slow up Montgomery's advance to the north where he had hoped to reach Rome before the winter. He complained bitterly that:

> The immediate results of a thoroughly bad administrative set-up is that my offensive 'drive' up through Foggia, and right on to the Rome line has got to be limited in scope because of lack of stores, petrol, and so on. When a ship comes in no one knows what is inside the ship until the lid is taken off; thus any planning ahead is impossible. We ought to be allotted certain tonnage, this being loaded to our specification'[6].

His solution was that Brian Robertson should replace Miller and become Alexander's chief administrator in Italy. Gale was in complete agreement and on 12 October Brian Robertson was officially informed that:

> Your title on reorganisation will be Deputy Chief Administrative Officer, AFHQ, Italy, in which capacity you will coordinate US and British administrative supply services in Italy . . . You will also act as General Alexander's administrative adviser on all 'A' and 'Q' matters and obtain from him operational guidance for your administrative planning and co-ordination.[7]

The details of the reorganisation were finalised in a series of conferences chaired by Brian Robertson at Headquarters 15th Army Group on
11 and 12 October. The minutes give an interesting insight into his skills
as a chairman. The Deputy Quartermaster General (DQMG) reported
back to Gale:

> The main conferences were quite excellently handled by General
> Robertson on your behalf. Without any over-emphasis it was made
> quite clear to all who were in charge. In doing this certain matters of
> comparatively minor importance were allowed to pass without a
> clarity of definition, which might have produced controversy. . . .[8]

Although the new organisation was a great improvement, it was still not
quite right. As Brian Robertson himself pointed out ten years later to the
Official War Historian, FLAMBO, as the new headquarters was called,
owed 'nominal allegiance' to General Eisenhower in Algiers, while in
reality 'its real function was to give service to General Alexander'[9]. In
February, 1944, Brian Robertson and his staff were at last fully integrated into Alexander's own headquarters, and he now became the Chief
Administrator of the Allied Armies in Italy (AAI).

At the end of October, 1943, Brian Robertson set up his headquarters
in Naples. His offices were in the city where a building sufficiently large to
house 100 officers and 220 clerks was requisitioned. His mess and living
quarters were in the Villa Lauro, a fantastic castle-like edifice on the
northern shore of the bay of Naples, which had previously belonged to the
shipping magnate Signor Lauro. When appointing his staff he took particular care to ensure that he chose able men who had experienced some
fighting, as he was convinced that he needed officers who would 'be in full
sympathy with . . . the armies'[10]. For his personal staff he chose South
Africans, as he was still a member of the Union Defence Force. Lavinia
Holland-Hibbert, a GSO3 on General Harding's staff, called them 'the
sweet family Robertson' as they were all 'big, well built, fair and South
African'. Brian Robertson's Personal Assistant, Mary or Pixie Vincent,
was 'an attractive streaky haired blonde', who was even allowed to call him
Brian. In later life she was to become a close associate of Trevor
Huddleston and Alan Paton and an ardent anti-apartheid campaigner.
Brian Robertson was able to relax in their company and allowed them to
tease him mildly, yet essentially he always remained 'a grave and distant
figure'. He did, of course, have his quota of cocktail parties and, Holland-
Hibbert noted, enjoyed the company of pretty girls but it was noticeable
that he was far less active on the party circuit than many of the other generals. As CAO of the Allied Armies in Italy, Robertson's work had an
inter-Allied dimension, which had been lacking in the Desert. He had,
above all, to co-ordinate the two separate but parallel administrative

systems – the British and the American. Perhaps because he was a 'South African' rather than a British officer, he got on well with the Americans. After visiting him in November, Gale wrote in his diary:

> . . . there is no doubt about it that he has done a fine job; he has a complete inter-Allied outlook which is needed and is coping very, very successfully with his many problems[11].

Robertson's main priority was to keep the ports open on both the east and west Italian coasts so that the vital supplies of food and ammunition could be quickly unloaded and, whenever necessary, the axis of advance switched. Thus anything that might interrupt their smooth running was a matter of considerable concern for him. He took care to appoint an able American port commandant to Naples and ceaselessly monitored the statistics of the tonnages discharged in the Italian ports. Woe betide any Port Commander who failed to meet his targets. At Brindisi, for instance, after a conference with the Port Committee, Robertson scathingly remarked that ' As usual they countered my request for better tonnages by presenting a long list of demands . . . What they really need is more brains'[12]. He was quick to visit Bari after an air raid on the night of 1–2 December 1943 and was relieved to find its capacity only temporarily reduced, but horrified to note that in one of the ships there were a large number of bombs filled with mustard gas. He complained to Gale that 'If matters had gone slightly differently', the port of Bari would have been knocked out of action for weeks, 'quite apart from the casualties which it would have caused the military and civil personnel . . .'. He urged that if it was really necessary to import such bombs they ought to to be unloaded at one of the smaller ports such as Barletta[13].

By the autumn of 1944, the Eighth Army was bogged down in a sea of mud along the banks of the River Sangro, while in the west the Fifth Army struggled to reach the Garigliano. As the advance slowed down, the campaign became more static and much more of an ammunition rather than a petrol war. Indeed, so intense was the activity of the artillery that on 24 October the Eighth Army was on the verge of running out of 25 pounder ammunition. Brian Robertson had to fly off immediately to Bari to chase up shipments from Sicily. By digging deep into reserves, he was able to guarantee supplies up to mid-November, when the situation was again temporarily eased by the transfer of 20,000 rounds from Fifth Army and the arrival in Naples of a liberty ship carrying 400 tons on 13 November. Nevertheless, the shortage of ammunition was to be a constant worry right up to May 1945.

When the fighting died down in December, supply problems eased. However, over Christmas, Churchill resurrected the latter day 'Dardanelles scheme', Operation SHINGLE, whereby an Allied force would be landed at Anzio. Its purpose was to threaten General Kesselring's lines of communication while the main Fifth Army attacked at Cassino, and so force a German retreat and the fall of Rome. Brian Robertson was, of course, a pivotal figure in working out the logistics of the landing, but when Montgomery was recalled to London at the end of December to start planning OVERLORD (the invasion of France), there was a possibility that he might take him back with him. On 29 December Robertson flew over to Algiers to discuss both SHINGLE and ' the future GHQ Europe set up' with Gale, who was also about to depart to the UK. The whole afternoon and evening of that day were given to discussing the new headquarters in London, and a possible replacement for Brian Robertson in Italy was even lined up, General D. M. Smith from Cairo[14]. In the end he remained in Italy. It is not clear whether this was a result of Alexander's intervention or his own choice. If he had moved to London at that juncture it would certainly have made the planning of SHINGLE more difficult.

The following day, Robertson got down to discussing the details of Operation SHINGLE with the new CAO of AFHQ, General George Clark. They both agreed that the operation would have to be mounted by a joint Anglo-American force as there was no time to set up a new British corps headquarters and above all 'the sharing of risks and hazards together was of importance'. Originally, SHINGLE was to have been launched once the Fifth Army had advanced far enough to make a link up with the Anzio bridgehead feasible. By December it was clear that the Fifth Army was firmly pinned down at Cassino and that any force at Anzio might have to be maintained indefinitely. Thus the more Brian Robertson looked at SHINGLE, the more uneasy he became. He was particularly alarmed by the proposal that troops should be landed with a mere eight days' rations, as the Navy could not guarantee the discharge of further supplies. Five days later, at a conference at Fifth Army Headquarters, he strongly urged that the whole project should be abandoned since it was not 'sound administratively'. He stressed that it was 'dependent on the continuous maintenance over beaches for an indefinite period', which in winter was inevitably a hazardous undertaking. He warned ominously that if the troops landed at Anzio did not quickly break out and join up with the Fifth Army, the whole operation would become a serious 'administrative commitment' which would not only prevent the Allies from eventually landing in southern France (Operation ANVIL), but also reduce the supplies and shipping available for the rest of the Allied forces in Italy[15].

That evening, at dinner in Robertson's mess at the Villa Lauro, conversation was dominated by an intense discussion on tactics and strategy. Almost certainly with Anzio in mind, he argued strongly against dispersing Allied forces too widely, and instead urged, like Wully before him, that they should concentrate on one place, consonant with their resources. He hoped that Montgomery would be able to knock some sense into the higher authorities in London[16]. Nothing, however, could stop SHIN-GLE, and a week later the date of the landing was finalised for 22 January.

Initially, everything went surprisingly well. Anzio harbour was seized and quickly cleared, while fully loaded lorries were driven off the landing craft on to the beaches. On 25 January Robertson visited the bridgehead for the first time and was 'pleasantly surprised with the situation', but by the end of the first week in February it was clear that the Germans were going to stay south of Rome in force and fight every inch of the way. The bridgehead had to be reinforced and the Allies were now committed to maintaining five divisions there for an indefinite period. Inevitably, this entailed the careful husbanding of ammunition and other supplies. Brian Robertson's task was made even more difficult by the inability of the Navy to land more that 2,500 tons a day at the bridgehead. Admiral Cunningham curtly advised AFHQ that 'the time has come to cut our coat according to our cloth'[17]. Yet Alexander's warning that the troops would have to put up with 'an austere standard of living' and 'dispense with accessories such as laundries, canteens, etc.' was proved wrong[18]. In March, General Penney, the Commander of the first Division at Anzio wrote to Brian Robertson:

> For 'well being' generally I and the troops have nothing but praise. Rations are excellent, bathing arrangements are good, mails 'in' are first class and a great deal is due to you. On the more warlike aspect, the ammunition build-up is marvellous.[19]

The leave arrangements were also both efficient and humane. Penney was particularly appreciative of how:

> . . . batches of officers and men are going on leave every few days. Practically 100% speak very highly of arrangements, and the men, particularly of freedom from petty restrictions and of early tea brought to them[20].

In April, Robertson visited Anzio, staying with the American Commander, General Truscott. His ADC vividly remembers them touring the perimeter in an open jeep. He also made a particular point of congratulating Truscott on the efficiency of his administrative staff[21].

One of the most intractable problems involved in the maintenance of British forces in Italy was the shortage of manpower. As CAO, Robertson was inevitably concerned about this. He managed to squeeze nearly another 15,000 reinforcements out of the War Office to add to a rein-forcement pool for the whole Italian theatre of 20,000 but, given the high casualty rate in the Anzio Bridgehead, this was not sufficient. Only 700 reinforcements a week could be sent to Anzio and throughout Italy battalions could no longer be maintained at full strength. The shortage of manpower led to divisions remaining longer in the line and to the cross-posting of troops to unfamiliar units where they did not feel at home. In the spring of 1944 the chances of being posted back to the UK or being given home leave were virtually nil unless a soldier had completed six years' continuous service abroad. Not surprisingly, there were times when morale plummeted and desertion statistics rose. In September 1943, there had even been a mutiny on the beaches at Salerno when several drafts of convalescing Eighth Army men, all of whom had been groomed to see themselves as an élite, instead of rejoining their own regiments and sailing back to Britain to train for Operation OVERLORD, suddenly found themselves transported to Salerno where they were required to join battalions of complete strangers in the Fifth Army.[22] Overall, deserters accounted for only about 0.1 per cent of the million British personnel in the Central Mediterranean Forces, but amongst the infantry divisions, particularly those which had served for a protracted period in the line, desertion did lead to a significant loss of manpower. Like most senior officers of the time, Brian Robertson felt that 'there was no single panacea for the evil of desertion unless it be the re-institution of the death penalty'[23], which the Government resolutely refused to sanction. He did, however, attempt to attack the problem by a mixture of improved welfare measures and, once the Anzio emergency was over, a more sensitive policy of posting men to familiar units. This was to be combined with a much tougher line on desertion. There were to be prompt trials, proper prisons and strict discipline. On the other hand, he did not advocate a purely punitive approach as 'men in prison are a commitment to their country and . . . [are] doing nothing to win the war'. He thus supported suspended sentences where possible, and pointed out that statistics have shown that 'quite a high proportion of such men completely vindicate their character'[24].

Brian Robertson backed up these measures with a propaganda campaign against desertion in the army newspapers and a 'racey pamphlet' on the significance of the Italian campaign by the novelist Eric Linklater. The British press was not so easy to influence. He was particularly worried by reports in the 'tabloids' about the alleged infidelity of soldiers' wives in Britain, which naturally had a negative impact on morale in Italy. Senior British officers in the Anzio bridgehead also drew his attention to 'highly coloured articles in the *Sunday Pictorial* which, by depicting Anzio as 'suicide corner', were frightening reinforcements waiting to be landed. He appealed to AFHQ

. . . to convince those responsible at home that they must not, for the sake of a good story create false impressions, which have an adverse effect on morale.

It was a request which echoes the classic military dilemma of a democratic power in wartime. Anzio had undoubtedly been a 'suicide corner', even though Brian Robertson played this down, but his main case for censorship rested on the argument that:

> Divisional commanders there are having a hard task in reforming units which have had heavy casualties replaced by large drafts of reinforcements. If these reinforcements arrive quaking in their shoes, it does not make their task any easier'[25].

Later in May, after reading a large number of military medical and prison reports as well as many extracts from the field censorship units, Robertson distilled his thoughts on the desertion problem and on how the armies of democratic powers could be motivated to fight, in a long memorandum to Alexander[26]. It is an interesting document which was a mixture of a personal credo, and an intellectual response to an issue to which there was no instant solution. He wrestled with the difficult task of turning men who had matured in a relatively easy-going democratic society, which after 1918 had evinced a deep revulsion to war and 'allowed discipline to be ridiculed' into ruthless fighting machines that could equal their German and Russian counterparts. He felt that the official British war aims in 1944 were too diffuse to inspire the average soldier:

> We say that our cause is freedom. Some say it is democracy. If by freedom we mean freedom for all men to do as they please, freedom for Poles, Czechs, Norwegians, Serbs, Abyssinians and Chinese, then small wonder if the doctrine evokes little fire in the hearts of our soldiers. We can admire and like all these peoples. But the only kind of freedom for which men will gladly lay down their lives is freedom for themselves and for the country to which they belong. Democracy may be a good form of government, but it is not a good battle cry.

His solution then was to urge that 'day and night' officers should emphasise to their soldiers that their freedom was threatened, ' their personal freedom and the freedom of their country and Empire'. He hoped that this would produce a burning hatred for the Germans, which would turn the British soldier into a fearsome fighting machine:

> Hate can be so strong as to make men thrust out fear. It appears to be unethical to preach hate of one's enemies today. I do not pretend to argue the ethics of the matter, but say without fear of contradiction that a good hater is a good fighter. By their correct behaviour towards prisoners and by their own fighting powers the Germans have persuaded many that they are quite good fellows really. The fact remains that they

want to put their feet on our neck and it is not a soft boot. There is a good and sufficient reason for us to hate them collectively and individually.

While not specifically calling for a religious crusade against Nazism, Robertson also stressed that it should be pointed out to the troops that Nazism directly attacked Christianity, in which most of them still professed to believe. Finally, and here he was almost certainly speaking from his own experience, he observed 'that in the face of death there can surely not be a greater comfort and support for a man than his own religion'.

How much Brian Robertson personally believed in this exhortation to hate is hard to determine. In the Western Desert, if his letters home are any guide, he too was inclined to see the Germans as honourable opponents. In retrospect, the message also reads oddly coming from a man who was to became an enlightened Military Governor of the British Zone in Germany and did so much to rehabilitate Western Germany and restore German self-respect. However, forgiveness is a Christian virtue and helping a defeated enemy is a very different process from defeating him in the first place. To turn average men into killers, faith in their cause and hatred of their enemies are essential ingredients.

THE CAMPAIGNS OF THE SUMMER AND AUTUMN OF 1944–45

Once the Anzio bridgehead had been firmly established, Brian Robertson moved up to Caserta where Alexander's main operational headquarters was situated. His offices were in the palace, but his mess was in a rather dilapidated villa nearby owned by an elderly and querulous Contessa, who still remained in residence. Alexander was directed in early February to prepare a plan for the prosecution of the battle north of Rome. On 28 February, the first of a series of planning conferences was held. The gist of Alexander's plan, Operation DIADEM, was for the Fifth and Eighth Armies, which were to be temporarily expanded to 28½ divisions, to attack the German Gustav Line with overwhelming force from Monte Cassino westwards to the coast and then to advance up the Liri valley towards Rome. At the appropriate moment, the divisions in the Anzio bridgehead would break out and cut off the retreating Germans. With the German Army destroyed, the rest of Italy would fall into Alexander's hands. The administrative aspects of the plan were vetted by Brian Robertson. A crucial part of it was to move the Eighth Army westwards to the Liri valley secretly without alerting the Germans to the ultimate object of the manoeuvre.

Throughout March and April, Brian Robertson worked on plans for supplying the armies up to the Pisa–Rimini line. An assessment of the capacity of the ports between Naples and Leghorn was rapidly carried out and on 17 March a provisional maintenance plan involving sea, road and rail was in place. Important, too, were plans for setting up administrative sub-areas in the newly liberated territory and, in the event of a rapid advance, for moving Alexander's headquarters nearer to the front[27].

On 11 May, Brian Robertson lunched with Leese, the new commander of the 8th Army, and at 2300 hours that evening witnessed the enormous barrage which preceded the Eighth Army's attack. On 19 May, Cassino fell and over the next six weeks the Fifth and Eighth Armies raced north-wards, although they failed to trap the retreating Germans. The Eighth Army headed for Florence via Terni and Perugia, while the Fifth Army advanced on Pisa via Lucca and Pistoria. Between 31 May and 30 June, the Eighth Army advanced some 175 miles. Robertson's main task was to ensure that the administrative back-up functioned as smoothly as possible. The war diaries record that during these weeks he was constantly travel-ling around the battlefields and lines of communication, checking casualty stations, the pace of railway construction and monitoring traffic control[28]. Rome fell to the Fifth Army on 4 June and a few days later, Brian Robertson visited the city to confirm plans for its administration which had been prepared some six months earlier. An integrated Anglo-American command was set up which was responsible for law and order, traffic control and the functioning of public utilities as well as the rationing of electrical power. On any matter of 'major policy or difficulty' it was to refer to Brian Robertson's headquarters[29]. Above all, he was anxious to prevent a repetition of the looting and ill discipline that had so marred the liberation of Syracuse and Naples. 'Other ranks', much to the annoyance of General Mark Clark, were initially banned from staying overnight in the capital and their behaviour was anxiously monitored, while only a limited number of officers were allowed to be in Rome at any one time[30]. Lavinia Holland-Hibbert noted that on the evening when she dined at the CAO's mess, the whole conversation was dominated 'for ages about discipline and saluting in Rome'[31].

As the armies advanced northwards, Brian Robertson moved his head-quarters first up to Frascati at the foot of the Alban hills where, after a series of German booby traps had been cleared, he set up his headquar-ters in a mobile caravan. Then, shortly afterwards, he moved up to the shores of Lake Bolsena. When George VI visited this headquarters in July, Robertson received the insignia of a Knight Commander of the Royal Victorian Order from the King (for his services during His Majesty's visits to North Africa and Italy) and was knighted, together with several other senior officers. He very nearly missed the ceremony as his car was delayed by two punctures on the way back from Assisi. After the second puncture he had to hitch a lift in order to arrive in time.

At the end of August, he moved his headquarters up to Siena. His offices were in a hotel in the centre of the city, while in the evenings he retired again to his caravan in the woods outside, where Alexander also had his headquarters. In August, an element of almost Falstaffian comedy was afforded by Churchill's visit. Not only did Brian Robertson have to insist that Churchill took mepacrine or 'those nasty little yellow tablets', as the Prime Minister called them, as protection against malaria, but his staff also had to order several cases of Chianti, which duly ensured 'that the nightly dinners lasted until the early hours of the morning'.

At a conference on 23 June, Alexander unveiled his plans for breaking through the German Apennine line and securing bridgeheads over the Po. Brian Robertson was quick to point out that this would cause considerable administrative difficulties as the further the Allies advanced into the Apennines, the more distant would be their ports of supply. Consequently a rapid advance to secure Venice and Trieste was essential. Initially he feared that the withdrawal of key fighting and administrative units for Operation ANVIL would cause the Allied armies in Italy to be 'administratively hamstrung'[32], but his worst fears did not materialise and he was confident in early July that there were sufficient reserves to carry both armies up to Venice where a fresh base could be developed[33]. By 16 July, Robertson had worked out the administrative plan for the advance, which, as always, involved, amongst many other factors, laying down the lines of communication, pin-pointing areas for petrol dumps and calculating the tonnages that could be moved by rail[34]. His task was made easier when AFHQ moved to Caserta from Algiers and in September took over the administration of the rear areas, leaving HQ AAI only with the responsibility for the war zone.

Alexander had hoped that the Allied armies would reach Bologna by September, but after some early successes, the campaign was halted by fierce German opposition in the Appennines and Bologna did not fall until 21 April 1945. As the second winter of the Italian campaign approached, the Eighth and Fifth Armies were again confronted with the familiar problems of manpower and ammunition shortages and desertion. By August 1944 there was a worldwide scarcity of ammunition and the impact of this on the fighting in Italy was exacerbated by the unprecedentedly heavy expenditure of shells in September. The manpower situation also deteriorated sharply. In November two whole infantry brigades had to be reduced to functioning on a cadre basis. In attempts to maximise Allied fighting strength, Italian troops were used wherever possible in non-combatant roles. Brian Robertson continued to try to stem the flow of deserters by the usual mixture of stick and carrot. John Mackeurtan, his ADC, remembers him visiting one detention camp:

. . . where deserters and other miscreants were held . . . it was typical of General Robertson's outlook that a very sharp directive was sent by him to the officers in charge of the camp to tighten up the rather lax discipline which he had noted, for, as he pointed out, he failed to see why these men who had deserted their comrades should be allowed anything more than the barest comfort.[35]

At the same time, he urged the AAI's Morale Committee to study ways in which 'an informed public opinion' hostile to deserters could somehow be created within the ranks of the army[36]. On the other hand, this was balanced by an unremitting campaign for improving the welfare of the troops. For instance, he pressed hard for an increase in beer supplies, which were 'woefully inadequate'[37]. Although in the spring of 1944 he had regarded home leave as impractical, he was now convinced that it must be made available on an adequate scale as soon as possible. On 5 November, 1944, he flew over to London to discuss a whole range of problems involving leave, ammunition, the expansion of the Polish Corps and, not least, increasing the beer ration in Italy[38]. His ADC remembers how, after breaking the journey at Paris, Brian Robertson's Dakota:

. . . headed for Hendon Airfield just outside London and shortly after setting course for London the co-pilot came back into the body of the plane to ask just where Hendon was! On requesting a map I was shown an atlas with Great Britain some four inches long, so I suggested they found London first and we would then direct the pilot to the northwest side of London. In the event he encountered really foul weather with very low cloud and driving rain . . . and the pilot wisely headed for an airfield on the coast in Sussex at Ford.[39]

Once in London, Robertson first secured a room at his Club. Then for the next four days, in a series of lengthy interviews with the Deputy CIGS he attempted to persuade the War Office to increase the amount of ammunition to be delivered to the Italian theatre. His arguments that a shortage could delay the spring offensive by three months made little impression. He was simply told that if economies were carried out during the winter, there would then *ipso facto* be sufficient ammunition for a spring offensive[40]. He was more successful in working out a home leave scheme. By the time he left London on Friday 10 November, it was agreed that leave convoys taking some 3,000 men at a time would sail every 20 days to the United Kingdom from Italy. Any soldier who had served not less than three years abroad was now eligible for a month's leave. The plan was well received amongst the troops even though they realised that relatively few of them would in reality be able to take advantage of it[41]. It was not until February, 1945, that Brian Robertson himself was able to fly home to Durban for his first spell of home leave since the summer of 1941.

***

In December, 1944, in a radical reorganisation of the command structure in Italy the headquarters of AAI were downgraded to just being the operational headquarters of the 15th Army Group. Alexander was appointed Supreme Allied Commander of AFHQ and together with Harding and Robertson, who remained his CAO, moved back to Caserta. To many this was yet more confirmation that the Italian theatre had now become a backwater. In her diary, the headquarters of AAI and its 'group dynamics' were given a generous obituary by Junior Commander Lavinia Holland-Hibbert:

> It's been a happy and efficient headquarters . . . inspired of course by General Alex and General John [Harding] . . . kept firm by the ability and calm of General Robertson . . .[42]

CIVIL AFFAIRS

Brian Robertson had no direct responsibility for the civilian population. This was exercised nominally by General Alexander through the Allied Military Government of Occupied Territory (AMGOT) and by the Allied Control Commission (ACC). However, the nature of his work ensured that he had to liaise carefully with both these organisations. Anything that might affect adversely the fighting efficiency and welfare of the troops in Italy immediately fell into his brief. Thus he was, for example, particularly concerned in December, 1943, by an alarmist report from the Cardinal Archbishop of Naples which suggested that the large-scale soliciting of troops in Naples by local prostitutes was organised by pro-Axis elements in order to infect them with venereal diseases and to gain military information. He immediately wrote to the relevant officers urging them to help the Italian police and:

> to encourage among the soldiers a definite feeling of hostility towards these pimps . . . An army boot placed with firmness and accuracy in the right place seems to be the most effective and fittest medicine for these gentlemen.[43]

As Chief Administrative Officer, Robertson was the vital link between two very different but inter-dependent worlds: the newly liberated, but impoverished 'King's Italy', which governed itself under the supervision of the Allied Control Commission, and the armies with their own administration, lines of communication, supply systems, rest camps and prisons. The Army was not, however, self-contained. It employed Italian labour on a large scale and exploited, where possible, Italian resources like power stations, railways and engineering plants. Consequently it exercised a decisive influence on the Italian economy. The main instrument for ensuring that the Italian economy was run in the interests of the Allied armies was the Allied Forces Local Resources (Italian) Board. It met officially for the first time on 29 November 1943 under the chairmanship of Brian Robertson. As ever, he was anxious to avoid time wasting and waffle. In his introductory remarks he emphasised strongly that the task of the committee was

> . . . to provide speedy and brief solutions to the questions placed before it and that members must be in possession of the information at least 48 hours before the meeting and were not to bring advisers with them.[44]

Its potential scope can be gauged by the committees on Engineering and Materials, Labour and Wage Controls, Forage, Food Supply, Electrical Power and Prices, which it spawned over the next few months. Theoretically, the Board was supposed to monitor and control only those sections of the Italian economy which concerned the Allied forces. In practice, however, this meant keeping a tight grip on virtually the whole economy. For instance, the Labour and Wages Control Committee was supposed only to co ordinate the wages and labour conditions of those Italians working for the Allies, yet as they were the largest single employer of labour in Italy, the Committee's policy inevitably influenced the whole labour situation in liberated Italy. Similarly, the scope of the Electric Power Committee was enormous. It was responsible for rehabilitating the damaged grid system and for allocating bulk electrical power to both the military authorities and the civilian population.

By the spring of 1944, the impact of military demands on the economy was causing considerable criticism in both the British press and amongst ACC officials. In the *Daily Telegraph* Virginia Cowles painted a bleak picture of rocketing food prices and inadequate bread rations[45], while HF Grady, the American Vice-President of the Economic Section of the Control Commission, was bitterly critical of the Army's cavalier and often wasteful policy of requisitioning factories, the output of which was vital for the rehabilitation of the Italian economy. Grady, who personally disliked Brian Robertson, somewhat spoilt his case by arguing that the Army was 'too preoccupied with winning the war'[46]. Obviously no soldier, least of all Brian Robertson, could deny the overriding nature of this 'preoccupation'. Nevertheless, there was of course a genuine clash of interests between the

Army and the ACC. What the Army really wanted at that stage, although later it too had to learn the economic facts of life, was immediate and effective service regardless of whether the prices and rates it paid for food-stuffs or labour fuelled inflation on a national level. Brian Robertson candidly conceded this at a meeting of the Allied Resources Board on 10 April, 1944, when the question of the rates of payment for Italian workers employed by the armed forces was discussed. He pointed out that:

(a) The Armed Forces require contented willing and industrious workers.
(b) ACC require a stable economic set up in Italy.
These two requirements may conflict. If they do, the armed forces must take priority'[47].

By late summer 1944, economic reality was beginning to impinge on the Army. Firstly, in July the report of the Anti-Inflation Committee of the ACC was published, and then, as the Allied forces advanced further northwards, the extent of the social and economic problems facing the Italian Government was becoming clearer as indeed were the consequences to the Army's efficiency if they were not mitigated in any way. In August, Sir Noel Charles, the British Ambassador in Rome warned that:

The internal situation here is precarious and our lines of communication become longer every day, while there are fewer British troops to keep order in case of necessity. The Communists are aware of this and await their opportunity[48].

Ominously, there were food riots in Lucca, Pisa and Florence in October. In December, Brian Robertson was instructed by Alexander to draft a telegram to the Combined Chiefs of Staff in Washington stressing the threat to internal security if the bread ration was not raised to 300 grammes a day. It was not, however, until February that sufficient grain could be imported to enable the bread ration to be raised.

Although Alexander understandably refused to concede the primacy of civilian over military needs as long as the war lasted in Italy, he did nevertheless agree to the creation of an Industrial Coordination Committee to monitor the problem of military requisitions of factories and workshops. The CAO was initially warned by a member of his staff that this new committee was out to control the local resources in the interests of Italian industry[49], but by January he had overcome his suspicions and was fully in agreement with what Macmillan, the British Resident Minister in the Mediterranean, called the 'New Deal' policy for Italy[50]. Brian Robertson wanted to give the committee extra powers so that it would in effect:

exist as a court of appeal to study and to make recommendations in cases which are referred to it by either the military or civil agencies where military requirements conflict with Italian industry'[51].

By the late winter of 1944–45 it was becoming increasingly difficult to separate military from civil affairs. As CAO, Robertson could, for instance, no longer ignore the threat of inflation to the Allied war effort in Italy. Fearful that

. . . if runaway inflation should occur, it would not only be of serious consequence to the military operations but would have social, political and economic implications of grave consequence[52],

. . . he opposed the recommendation of the Allied Control Commission in February, 1945, that Britain and America should grant credits to the Italian Government in support of the lira. He believed that this would fuel inflation and merely grant short-term financial relief, which would rapidly evaporate, leaving the situation worse than before. This experience of economic problems in Italy served, of course, as a useful apprenticeship for the infinitely more complex problems he was to encounter later as Military Governor of the British Zone in Germany.

THE FINAL OFFENSIVE AND THE CONFRONTATION WITH TITO

After Christmas, planning for the spring offensive began but the chronic shortage of troops had been made more acute by the eruption of the Greek crisis. In December, the British forces in Greece under the command of General Scobie had to be speedily reinforced to prevent a Communist take-over. By the end of the month, there were three British divisions as well an armoured brigade there. Their maintenance through the port of Piraeus, once it was secured, was, of course ultimately the CAO's responsibility. In early January, he flew over to Athens and reorganised the Q side of Scobie's staff, 'purging' a considerable number of officers in the process. He returned again at the beginning of April to hold a further round of what Scobie called 'very useful talks'[53]. Brian Robertson was particularly worried about the welfare of the British troops in Greece, as there was little spare accommodation available, and he was anxious to bring them back to Italy as soon as possible. Nevertheless, two divisions had to remain there until the end of the war[54].

Further troops were drained away from Italy to reinforce Montgomery's 21st Army Group in North-West Europe. Brian Robertson was concerned that the withdrawal of key logistic staff would badly handicap the administrative preparations for the spring offensive in Italy. He pleaded with Miles Graham, who was then Montgomery's CAO:

> . . . we quite realise that we are now the Cinderella of the family. We have two formidable sisters in the shape of yourselves and ALFSEA [Allied Land Forces South-East Asia]. I hope old associations and an appreciation of the conditions out here will make you, for your part, more considerate than the sisters in the fairy story[55].

In the event, he was left with sufficient administrative staff to plan the logistical backup for the final major offensive of the Italian campaign. Once again, railroads and pipelines were pushed forward to within a short distance of the front line and stocks of ammunition were gradually accumulated, thanks to a severe policy of rationing throughout the winter which had forced the artillery to be more economic in its expenditure. The lines of communication for the advance into Venezia Giulia and southern Austria, both of which were dependent on the opening up of Trieste, were confirmed. Plans were drawn up for dealing with the surrender of Kesselring's army and its internment between the Po and Highway 9, the Rimini–Modena road.

The liberation of the northern provinces was bound immeasurably to increase the economic problems facing the Italian Government and the Allied authorities, as their total population was the equivalent of the population of the whole of the rest of Italy. In planning the advance, it was assumed that the Germans would retreat into north-east Italy and that the industrial region of the north-west would be a 'hiatus area' in which the army would have no direct military interest. In this region Brian Robertson's main aim was to give himself 'some personal guidance on the rehabilitation problem' and to ensure that the troops did not interfere unnecessarily with any factory or plant which was not strictly essential for operational requirements[56].

The final offensive opened on 9 April. The Eighth Army attacked across the Senio in the east, while the Fifth Army at last cut Highway 9 and took Bologna. The German retreat rapidly became a rout. On 28 April, German delegates arrived at Caserta to negotiate a surrender, which took effect on 2 May 1945.

There were, of course, celebrations and dances at Caserta, but the German surrender did not lead to an immediate easing of the immense burden on the CAO. Not only were there the immediate logistical problems of interning the German POWs and repairing the transport infrastructure of northern Italy, but there was also the very real danger of a military confrontation with Marshal Tito, the leader of the Communist forces in Yugoslavia. As the Eighth Army, commanded by General McCreery, advanced into Venezia Giulia and southern Austria it was becoming increasingly obvious that Tito was hoping to exploit the hiatus between the German surrender and the effective assumption of British control to create a 'greater Yugoslavia'. On 2 May, the New Zealand Division entered Trieste at the same time as Tito's troops. Several unsuccessful attempts were made to negotiate a *modus vivendi* with him, which would ensure Allied control of the docks and railways in Trieste and the lines of communication to the British Zone in Austria[57]. On 8 May, the crisis escalated significantly when the advanced forces of General Keightley's 5 Corps reported not only that southern Austria was teeming with Tito's partisans but that they were also supported by units of the Yugoslav Army. On 10 May, Alexander, after conferring with his staff and political advisers, Macmillan and the American Alexander Kirk, ordered his staff to draw up a detailed study of the degree of force needed to eject the Yugoslavs from Venezia Giulia and Carinthia. In the meantime, he sought political advice from London and Washington and sent Macmillan up to Eighth Army headquarters to explain the political ramifications of the situation to General McCreery, who was asking permission to use his troops, if necessary, in support of the newly established Allied Military Government. Macmillan then went on to see the two Corps Commanders. Harding of 13 Corps was relatively confident that he could maintain 'the uneasy position' in Venezia Giulia, but Keightley, at Klagenfurt in Carinthia, gave him a much more worrying picture. Not only were the Yugoslav partisans and regular troops actively disputing the powers of the Allied Military Government, but the resources of 5 Corps were being stretched to breaking point by having 'to deal with nearly 400,000 surrendered or surrendering Germans'[58]. Amongst these, together with their families, were some 40,000 Cossack and White Russian troops, who had fought as allies of the Nazis. Also, as Macmillan chronicled in his diary:

> To add to the confusion, thousands of so called Ustachi or Chetniks, mostly with wives and children are fleeing in panic into this area in front of the advancing Yugoslavs . . .[59]

Then, on the evening of 13 May, it suddenly seemed as if the 5 Corps area was about to be swamped by a further 500,000 German and Croat troops, who wished to surrender to British rather than Tito's forces. This vast influx of prisoners of war and refugees, coming at a time when military operations against the Yugoslavs seemed imminent, created a major crisis. Not only did it threaten to block 5 Corps' lines of communication, but guarding and feeding it would absorb the attention of troops who, it seemed, would be needed to fight Tito. Consequently, McCreery sent off a telegram that evening to General Mark Clark, the Commander of 15 Army Group, pressing for immediate steps to be taken to deal with the crisis. He urged that the Cossacks should be returned to the Russians and the responsibility for disarming the Germans and Croats should be either handed over to 12th Army Group, which controlled the American Zone in Austria to the north of the British and was part of Eisenhower's command (SHAEF), or 'a proportion at least of their numbers should be moved into Italy'[60]. As these decisions could only be taken at the highest level, Clark forwarded McCreery's telegram to Caserta where it was in due course considered by Brian Robertson, as the handling of prisoners and refugees was technically an administrative matter within the CAO's brief. He was, of course, aware of the political nature of the problem, but also acutely conscious of the exposed position of 5 Corps in Carinthia. He discussed the contents of McCreery's telegram either with Macmillan directly or his officials and then with Kirk personally, whose telegram to the State Department in Washington is the only account of these deliberations[61]. There was little debate about the Cossacks, as it was agreed Anglo-American policy at that date that they should be repatriated to the USSR, so as to give the Russians no excuse for delaying the return of Allied POWs from Eastern Europe. The fate of the Yugoslavs was a more complex matter. On 7 May, General Mark Clark had instructed General McCreery that he should only accept the surrender of those Croat and German troops who had actually fought against the Eighth Army. Any others would have to be handed over to the Russians or their Allies[62]. Consequently, according to Kirk, Macmillan had recommended the handing over to Tito of 'a large number of dissident Yugoslavs with the exception of Chetniks'. The term 'Chetnik' was however ambiguous. Strictly it applied to the Royalist supporters of General Mihailovitch, yet it was used loosely to describe a considerable number of anti-Tito Yugoslavs, including guerrilla forces raised by the Germans. Thus when Kirk pressed Brian Robertson to define what he meant by it, not surprisingly 'he was very vague on this point'. Kirk then insisted on referring the matter to Washington. At the prospect of the endless delays and mounting chaos in Carinthia which this would cause, Robertson expressed his disappointment and then bluntly added that as he was confronted 'with a grave administrative problem' involving 'hundreds of thousands of German POWs on his hands' and consequently 'could not bother at this time who might or might not be turned over to the Russians and Partisans to be shot.'

That evening, Brian Robertson sent off the following telegram to the Main Eighth Army Headquarters, which then sent a copy on to 5 Corps:

ONE. All Russians should be handed over to Soviet forces at agreed points of contact established by you under local arrangement with Marshal Tolbukhin's HQ. Steps should be taken to ensure that Allied PW held in Russian areas are transferred to us in exchange at same time. TWO. Movement to Italy of all Germans is not acceptable because it would cause serious blockage on our L of C . . . We are approaching 12 Army Group immediately with request that they accept concentration . . . THREE. All surrendered personnel of established Jugoslav nationality who were serving in German forces should be disarmed and handed over to Jugoslav forces[63].

In response to McCreery's SOS, Brian Robertson, with the concurrence of Macmillan and presumably Alexander and his Chief of Staff, General Morgan, had acted rapidly and given him the necessary authorisation to repatriate the many thousands of POWs and refugees who threatened both to reduce to ineffective chaos the Eighth Army's efforts to prepare for military action against Tito and completely to block its lines of communication. He had taken care to frame his instructions sufficiently widely so that no significant loophole remained which might enable tens or perhaps even hundreds of thousands of refugees to remain as a serious obstruction to the British troops in a potential war zone.

Inevitably, this order has given rise to considerable controversy in view of the terrible fate that awaited so many of the returning Cossacks and dissident Yugoslavs[64]. In instructing McCreery to return the 'Russians' in exchange for Allied POWs, Brian Robertson was following the Foreign Office's interpretation of the repatriation clauses of the Yalta Agreement, which was sent to Caserta on 19 February[65], but the order to hand over the Yugoslavs to Tito was not covered by any such agreement. At the end of April, Churchill himself had ruled that all anti-Partisan Yugoslavs should be 'disarmed and placed in refugee camps', but it is arguable that this was only intended to refer to North East Italy[66]. In its reply to Kirk's telegram quoted above, the American State Department criticised Brian Robertson for following a policy of 'administrative expediency' in relation to these Yugoslav units[67]. Yet essentially, at that precise moment on the evening of 14 May, could any other decision have been taken? General Lemnitzer, Alexander's Deputy Chief of Staff, defended the decision in a letter to Kirk in August by stressing that it was 'a matter of military necessity in light of the conditions prevailing at that time in Austria'. This was endorsed by Alexander, who also told Kirk 'that he was obliged to receive surrender of almost one million Germans in mid-May and could not deal with anti-Tito Yugos as he would have liked'[68].

He clearly spelt out the threat that this situation posed to operations in a telegram on 17 May to Eisenhower:

With possibility of hostilities in Austria against Jugoslavia, it is essential to free my L of C immediately from this embarrassment. Operational efficiency of my troops is gravely prejudiced, both by necessity for controlling these multitudes and also by general congestion of the area. It is further essential that military supplies should be built up to support possible operations. It is impossible to do this and feed vast numbers . . . simultaneously[69].

By the time Alexander had sent this telegram, the pressure on 5 Corps in Carinthia had lessened. The 300,000 Germans were prevented from entering the British zone by Yugoslav troops and the 200,000 Croats after crossing into the British area at Bleiburg were then persuaded to surrender to Tito's forces. Yet the situation was still tense and confrontation with Tito seemed imminent. On 16 May, Alexander ordered 15 Army Group to draw up a detailed operational plan for ejecting Yugoslav troops and partisans from Carinthia and Venezia Giulia. AFHQ therefore pursued at times a variety of contradictory policies aimed at clearing the decks. The Robertson order remained in force, but simultaneously the alternatives to forcible repatriation of the Chetniks and Cossacks were also followed up. On 17 May three separate messages were despatched which all contradicted Robertson's signal of 14 May: Alexander asked Eisenhower to accept the transfer of surrendered German forces, including the Cossacks from Carinthia, the Deputy Adjutant General sent out an order, probably intended to refer only to Venezia Giulia, to 15 Army Group instructing them to evacuate 'Chetniks and dissident Jugoslavs infiltrating into areas occupied by Allied troops' to British occupied territory south of the River Po, and Brian Robertson himself, under the signature of Alexander, urgently requested the Chiefs of Staff to clarify what should be done with the Cossack, Chetnik and German Croat troops[70].

On 19 May, Tito at last withdrew his forces from Carinthia although Yugoslav troops remained in Venezia Giulia until June. Two days later, the Eighth Army asked for fresh guidance from AFHQ on the repatriation of the Yugoslav dissidents, which was in the meantime continuing. In a memorandum, written for Brian Robertson by the G-5 section of AFHQ, which dealt with displaced persons, it was suggested that 'all classes and types of dissident and anti-Tito Jugoslavs . . . should not be forced to return to Jugoslavia . . .', but this was modified by a handwritten amendment which added the words 'against their will'[71]. On 26–27 May, two staff officers from AFHQ, one of whom was from the CAO's department, attended an Eighth Army conference on the whole problem of repatriation. It was agreed that the Cossacks and Soviet Nationals would be handed over by whatever means were necessary. As far as the Yugoslavs went, a compromise was decided upon to the effect that they could be repatriated provided that force was not used. What constituted force was not clearly defined and it was left to the local commanders to use their discretion. Many of the dissident Yugoslavs were, as the *Cowgill Report* shows, in fact persuaded into returning to Yugoslavia peacefully by first being led to believe that they were being sent to Italy. However, after complaints from the Red Cross and the Allied Military Government, McCreery, to the relief of his own men, at last called a halt to this policy of 'deception' and the forcible repatriation of the Cossacks on 13 June. It is only fair to add that in May 1945 British commanders initially believed the assurances given them by Tito's officers that surrendered personnel would be given humane treatment and that war criminals would face orderly trials[72].

On 20 June, the Combined Chiefs of Staff answered Brian Robertson's telegram of 17 May and confirmed that the 'Chetniks and the German Croat troops' should be held by the British until a political decision had been taken, while approving the repatriation of the Cossacks. The return of defeated troops, sometimes with their women and children, to brutal Communist victors is, of course, hard to justify from a post-Cold War perspective, but in May 1945, Russia was still an ally and many of those men who were repatriated had in fact fought for the Germans – even the Royalists or Chetniks had at times cooperated with them against Tito, whose partisans had been supported by the Allies. It is also important to remember the context in which repatriation took place. In western Austria alone there were two and a half million refugees and displaced persons at a time when food stocks were virtually exhausted, while the shortage of accommodation and food made AFHQ equally reluctant to accept any more refugees into Italy. This was evident at the Bolzano Conference in June, which was chaired by Brian Robertson, where the future of the Displaced Persons and POWs within the SHAEF-AFHQ areas was discussed. Both AFHQ and Allied Control Commission officials were adamant that they would only accept Yugoslavs from the SHAEF area if their 'actual shipment to Jugoslavia was in sight'[73].

June and July, which were Brian Robertson's last two months in Italy, continued to be dominated by the logistical problems of arranging for the return of British troops to the United Kingdom, the administration of prisoners of war and displaced persons camps and the gradual return of Germans and Austrians to their homeland. His tours of inspection sometimes had their lighter moments. For instance when visiting 5 Corps in southern Austria in early July he found that the local commander had conscientiously tried to enforce the non-fraternisation regulations:

> . . . by segregating the beaches into two separate areas, one for troops, one for the locals, with barbed wire running right into the lake. Many of the Austrian girls, however, made a point of sunbathing and swimming stark naked in full view of the troops, which practically created a mutiny, and the local commander was quick to see the futility of non-fratting and at once advised General R. of the situation.

Surprisingly perhaps, for so stern a disciplinarian, Robertson recognised the reality of the situation and sanctioned 'fratting', as his ADC observed, 'to the delight of all concerned'[74].

Then, later in the month, as he was beginning to think about returning to his old job at Dunlop, he was suddenly requested by telegram from Sir James Grigg, the War Minister, to replace General Weeks, who, because of illness, was retiring as Montgomery's Chief of Staff in the British Zone in Germany. Robertson was to fly to London the following day, meet Weeks and then go with him immediately to Germany. His sudden departure took Caserta by surprise and was genuinely regretted by his senior colleagues. General Lemnitzer, the Deputy Chief of Staff, for instance, wrote:

> I cannot tell you how sorry I was to have you leave. Our long association through the Mediterranean campaign has been and always will be, one of the highest points in my army service. It has indeed been a privilege and a pleasure to have served so long with so fine a soldier as you[75].

Brian Robertson's appointment to the challenging post of Chief of Staff or Deputy Military Governor in Germany, as it was later called, was to change the course of his life completely. It was also, as Lord Ashfield, the Chairman of the London Transport Passenger Board and an old friend of Wully, observed, gratifying evidence that he had established for himself 'a splendid reputation as an administrator of the very highest order'[76].

THE POWER BEHIND THE THRONE: DEPUTY MILITARY GOVERNOR TO MONTGOMERY AND SHOLTO DOUGLAS, 1945–47

Brian Robertson's five years in Germany, from August, 1945, to June, 1950, were undoubtedly his 'finest hour'. First, as Deputy Military Governor to Montgomery and Marshal of the RAF Sir Sholto Douglas until November 1947, then as Military Governor in his own right and finally as British High Commissioner, he played a crucial role in German affairs, becoming a figure of international importance. He was just 49 when he arrived in Germany at the end of July 1945. In October he was restored to the Active List of the British Army in the temporary rank of Lieutenant General, made substantive in May 1946. The *Observer* described him as 'a tall slender man . . . with the colouring of a typical Scot – thinning sandy hair and penetrating blue eyes under bushy brows'[1]. He was at the height of his administrative and intellectual powers and, in the words of Lord Longford, then Lord Pakenham, who as Chancellor of the Duchy of Lancaster from April, 1947, to June, 1948, was the minister responsible for the British Zone, was 'quite clearly an alpha man capable of making a hundred complex decisions a day'[2]. Ernest Bevin, the Foreign Secretary, rapidly found his advice and grasp of detail indispensable, and, initially to the pique of some of the professional Foreign Office officials, relied heavily upon his expertise when German issues were discussed at the meetings of the Council of Foreign Ministers. He appreciated that Brian Robertson had the first-class staff officer's ability to sum up complex problems in clear logical prose[3]. Edward Playfair, a Treasury official who was seconded to the Control Commission, remembered some 45 years later how:

> He always had a clipboard in hand, and a clever habit of writing on it as he went along during a meeting and ended up by saying, as it might be, 'Well Secretary of State, I wonder if we might sum up our conclusions on the following lines, which I have just jotted down'. Then he read out something consistent with what had been said during the meeting but infinitely clearer; so that was adopted at once[4].

Like a Chief of Staff in battle, who must never forget his commander's overall objectives, he judged each fresh issue in the complex web of problems that constituted the German question after 1945 firmly within the context of the degree to which it would enable the British government to further its main aim of achieving a viable peace settlement in Europe. It was this rigorous and logical process he had in mind when he used to argue that the 'principle of war is applicable to the politics of peace'[5].

As in Italy and North Africa, he struck all who met him for the first time as rather an austere and severe character. Some, particularly the junior members of the Control Commission who observed him from afar, were 'petrified of him'[5]. At times, his silences and apparently cold demeanour seemed positively disconcerting. His manner was precise and stiff and he reminded Lord Longford of 'a very academic kind of Oxford don'[7]. Above all he hated the verbose and self-important, who wasted that most precious of all commodities, time. General Sir John Cowley, who was then Deputy Head of the Economic Division of the Control Commission, recalled years later how:

> His outstanding habit was to say nothing. Many times I have been alone with him in his office when an excited officer came in and told him about some important problem (or so he thought) and Brian kept quiet. Eventually the excited officer over did his problem. The only method of working with Brian was to say as little as possible and then to keep quiet[8].

Initial encounters with Brian Robertson could thus be something of an ordeal. Harry Collins, the Deputy Director General in charge of coal production in the British Zone, was, for instance, mortified when on his first interview with Robertson, he was not even asked to sit down. He came out of his office complaining bitterly, 'Who does he think I am – one of his damned privates or what?'. Collins' anger eventually subsided when his departmental chief advised him to attribute his brusque handling to Brian Robertson's shyness[9]. This was an opinion shared by many of those who came to know him well. Sybel Cowley, the wife of Sir John, perceptively observed that 'he appeared to be arrogant, but was in reality very modest; he was shy'[10].

He had, as one journalist wrote, 'something of the reputation of a man-eating tiger'[11], yet his staff rapidly came to realise that his bark was worse than his bite. Once an official had won his confidence, Brian Robertson was always ready to listen to him and in light of what he said revise his own ideas. Above all, he won the respect and eventually the genuine affection of his senior staff through his superlative administrative skills and the leadership he gave during the many economic, political and diplomatic crises that buffeted the Control Commission from 1945–49.

During the Berlin blockade in particular, Brian Robertson was appreciated as 'a rock in a swirling sea'[12] by both his own officials in Germany and the British Government at home – despite some policy disagreements. The spirit that animated and inspired him can be found in one of Horace's most famous odes, which he often enjoined his officials, much to their alarm, to read[13]:

> The man who is just and sticks to his purpose, neither the tumultuous pressure of his citizens' bidding him to do what is wrong, nor the face of an insistent tyrant stops him from his solid determination . . . nor the right hand of thunderous Jupiter; if the world shall fall shattered, the ruins will strike him unafraid.

PICKING UP THE THREADS, JULY–DECEMBER, 1945

When Brian Robertson flew over to Germany at the end of July, 1945, to take over from General Weeks, as Montgomery's Chief of Staff, he could hardly have been less prepared for this complex and demanding post. As he himself readily conceded:

> I didn't speak a word of German; I'd never been in the country before. I had been in South Africa for half a dozen years or more. I knew nothing about the situation *at all, nothing,* nor had I taken any part in the great preparatory work that had been carried forward in London[14].

When he arrived in Germany, he was presented with a copy of Brigadier Morgan's book *Assize of Arms*, which, as it gave a detailed account of Germany's clandestine rearmament in the Twenties, was regarded by the War Office as being almost on a par with the Bible[15], and also of the official handbook. This contained a series of directives which were so loosely phrased that they were of little value to military government officials. Rather more definite guidelines were provided by the Protocol of Berlin, which was issued at the conclusion of the Potsdam Conference on 2 August: the Allies were to restore local democratic self-government ultimately up to state (or *Land*) level, encourage the formation of democratic parties and treat Germany as an economic whole under a central German administration. They were also to disarm and to demilitarise Germany and 'to convince the German people that they have suffered a total military defeat and that they cannot escape responsibility for what they have brought upon themselves . . .'. Specifically for the British Zone, the immediate economic and social consequences of this protocol were a commitment to dispatch as reparations to Russia some

Germany Under Allied Occupation

15 per cent of the Zone's surplus industrial and capital equipment as well as having to accept a large number of east German refugees from the areas of the former *Reich* which were to be ceded to Poland[16].

Brian Robertson came rapidly to realise in the late summer of 1945 that disarmament, re-education and punishment were not the immediate problems facing the occupying powers. A much more pressing matter was to win the coming 'battle against the winter'. Twenty years later, he told a distinguished audience at the Royal Institute for International Affairs that:

> . . . the first discovery which I made very quickly was that the men on the spot had their minds on other things. Very soon I could see that the assumptions on which our policy had been based were false, and that the objectives chosen were quite irrelevant. The real menace for the future of Europe and to world peace was not Germany but Russia. The immediate objective was not to batter Germany down – she was sprawling in the dust already – but to build her up and do so wisely. We had to save Germany physically from starvation, squalor and penury, spiritually from despair and Communism[17].

To British officials in Germany, Brian Robertson communicated this message in a simple but direct way in their 'house magazine', *The British Zone Review*. He compared Germany to an errant child, who urgently needs educating:

> There are some who advocate the frequent application of the stick. There are others who think that it can all be done by kindness. The majority of parents, however, do not belong to either of these extreme schools of thought, nor do I believe that we should govern our actions either by vindictive harshness or by sentimentality. Of the importance of this task there is no doubt. Just as in the case of children, what happens has a lasting effect on them for the rest of their lives, so it may well be in the case of the German nation, which in a sense is being reborn in the present stage of its history. What happens during the early years after its rebirth may have an effect upon its character for centuries to come[18].

In August 1945, the British Zone was full of stark contrasts. The countryside bathed in late summer sunshine presented a picture of peace and beauty and the small towns and villages off the main roads were for the most part undamaged. The cities and larger towns were, however, in ruins. Dortmund, for instance, was almost totally destroyed except for its outer fringes. The transport system had broken down. Out of some 8,000 miles of railway track only 650 were able to take any traffic, while many of the roads were blocked by destroyed bridges and bombs had burst the banks of the canals. Across the Zone 50 per cent of the housing stock was either destroyed or badly damaged. Coal production in the Ruhr, which in the early years of the war had reached around 400,000 tonnes per day, had declined to a mere 30,000 tonnes[19].

As Montgomery's Chief of Staff, Brian Robertson acted as his deputy both on the Control Council in Berlin and in co-ordinating the work of the British military government in the Zone[20]. The Control Council was theoretically the supreme governing body in Germany, where the American, British, French and Russian Commanders-in-Chief met to discuss matters affecting Germany as a whole. Brian Robertson prepared Montgomery's briefs for the Control Council and sometimes deputised for him. He attended the Coordinating Council and the Meeting of the Combined Deputy Military Governors where the issues discussed by the Commanders-in-Chief were analysed in greater detail.

In dealing with his Allied colleagues on the interminable and fractious committees in Berlin, his reputation as an outstanding inter-Allied bureaucrat was tested to the full. He worked patiently to establish a close working partnership with the mercurial American Deputy Military Governor General Lucius Clay, a powerful and flamboyant figure. Quite soon both men and their families became friends. He found American policy short-sighted and incalculable, largely because it was so influenced by the press:

> They go from one extreme to another in their zone and are very unpop-ular in consequence. They are impatient and not very adroit in negotiation . . . Their main contribution to Quadripartite government is to produce a series of unpractical [sic] laws which have little bearing on the main problems[21].

His French colleague General Koenig could usually be relied upon to support Robertson, particularly when British policy was under attack from Clay or his Russian counterpart, Deputy-Marshal Sokolovsky. However, the French wished to set up a separate Rhineland state and detach the Ruhr from Germany by putting it under international control and were bitterly hostile to the re-creation of a united Germany. They thus vetoed any policy which might be seen to anticipate this. British officials, whilst recommending a 50-year Allied occupation of the Ruhr and Rhineland, were opposed to their ultimate separation from Germany, although Montgomery advocated the annexation of the latter territory by France, Belgium and Holland. In December, Brian Robertson feared that French rather than Russian obstructionism over the future of Germany would lead to 'a serious explosion between the four powers represented on the Council'[22].

Nevertheless, he had few illusions about Russian policy and was convinced in October 1945 that she aimed 'to extend her influence over the whole of Germany'. He also realised that if her 'iron curtain policy' continued to paralyse the Four Power administration, important decisions on currency, taxes and loans would have to be taken on a zonal rather than a national basis, the outcome of which would inevitably be partition. He was genuinely anxious to save the quadripartite machine because he believed that 'it would be a tremendous step forward in preparing for improved national relationships' and he feared that its failure would have serious repercussions on international cooperation elsewhere[23].

In those early days of the Control Council, the Russians were exacting and difficult colleagues who kept a suspicious watch on Allied zonal policies. When, for instance, it emerged that the British were using, as pioneers, some 250,000 German prisoners of war, organised into formations or *Dienstgruppen* which were administered by their own headquarters staff, General Zhukov, the Russian Commander-in-Chief immediately accused Montgomery of breaking the Potsdam Agreement and demanded that an inter-Allied commission of inspection should be sent into the British Zone. Montgomery played for time and discussed his approach with Brian Robertson, who astutely advocated acceptance coupled with the demand that the commission should also visit the three other zones. Zhukov backed down and the problem was eventually referred to the Coordinating Committee. Privately, Brian Robertson felt that General Templer, who headed Montgomery's Military Government Directorate, had been 'very injudicious' in his formation of the *Dienstgruppen* and he insisted on their dissolution[24].

Brian Robertson grew to like and respect Sokolovsky, his Soviet opposite number. By December, after agreement had been reached on the procedure for valuing reparations and the rate of transfer of German refugees from Poland and Czechoslovakia to the British Zone, he felt much more sanguine about the prospects for future quadripartite cooperation. Indeed, he was positively optimistic, as his notes for a Corps Commanders' conference in December revealed:

. . . Their attitude towards ourselves has undergone complete change in recent weeks. This is due to the discovery that we intend to honour our obligations on Reparations.

General conception of Russians is that they are insincere and incapable of decisions without reference to Moscow. This is not our experience, but they are very realistic, they hate the Germans and they still distrust us considerably . . . [25].

Initially, the administration of the Zone had been in the hands of the Army, but in September the Military Government was subordinated to the British Element of the Control Commission and General Templer now became Brian Robertson's deputy. Gradually, over the course of the winter of 1945–46, the soldiers were replaced by civilians as far as possible. The British element of the Control Commission initially consisted of 12 separate divisions each concerned with a particular aspect of the occupation. The directors of the divisions were a formidable team. For instance the Finance Division was headed by Paul Chambers who, in 1960, became the Chairman of ICI, and the Economics Division by Percy Mills, who was appointed Minister of Power in the Macmillan Cabinet of 1957. The Political Adviser to the Commander-in-Chief was William Strang, who was later promoted to be Permanent Under-Secretary of State at the Foreign Office.

The decisions taken at Potsdam eventually to recreate a central German administration and to treat Germany as a whole ensured that one of the first actions Brian Robertson had to take was to move to Berlin all the British officials dealing with higher policy, long-range planning and the supervision of the future German central administrative agencies. This was no easy task in that bomb-shattered city of 1945. Most of the offices, living quarters and messes had to be located in the semi-ruined outer districts of the British sector. For his living quarters, Brian Robertson's staff managed to find him a large and undamaged mansion in Hohmannstrasse on the edge of the Grünewald, which had been owned by Henschel, the industrialist, while his offices were located in premises on the Kurfürstendam. It was in the Höhmannstrasse mansion that Brian Robertson had to entertain a never ending stream of VIPs passing through Berlin as well as laying on drinks, dinners and cocktail parties for the senior Allied and British personnel on the Control Commission. Eisenhower came to play bridge and, much to the evident disapproval of Brian Robertson's elderly German butler, Sokolovsky was an occasional visitor. In his turn, Robertson was exposed to the hazards of Russian hospitality where huge amounts of alcohol were drunk. He used to survive the evening unscathed by carefully responding to each toast by sipping only a small amount of vodka. This feasting amidst a sea of German misery must have made Brian Robertson uncomfortable, particularly as each morning the first thing that he would see as he looked out of his windows in the Höhmannstrasse was an emaciated procession of elderly Berliners dragging small sleighs en route for the Grünewald in a desperate attempt to find fuel. However, good food and wines were an essential lubricant for international understanding amongst the victors in the winter of 1945–46. Indeed, Brian Robertson had to despatch his Dakota to bring in delicacies from Denmark as they could not be found in either the Zone or Britain. To obtain fresh meat, he would occasionally allow some of his staff to go rabbit shooting along the disused and overgrown tramlines running into Berlin[26].

The administrative Centre of the Zone remained in Lübbecke, which was conveniently near to the headquarters of the British Army of the Rhine. In the Zone, Brian Robertson had a second residence, *Schloss* Benkhausen, which initially he had to share with Generals Templer and Lethbridge. Several times a week, he had to leapfrog between Berlin and Lübbecke. Usually he flew by Dakota to Bückeburg, near Braunschweig, and was then picked up by a light aircraft, an Auster or 'whizzer', and taken on to Lübbecke. Sometimes he would snatch the chance to take some exercise and his ADC would meet him off the 'whizzer' with a horse, on which he would then canter briskly down to his office[27]. At other times, he travelled down in splendour from Berlin in what had originally been Goebel's special coach, which was a luxury hotel on rails with its own sitting room, bathrooms and bedrooms.

Ultimately, the fate of the British Zone was dependent on inter-Allied cooperation in Germany. If that worked, the British Zone would gradually be reintegrated into a united Germany, but if Four Power agreement broke down, the options facing the British Government were uncertain. Should there be, as Brian Robertson put it, 'one Germany or two or four'[28]? Until this question was answered in 1948, it was difficult to draw up long-term plans for the future of either the British Zone or Germany as a whole.

In administering the Zone, Brian Robertson had constantly to be aware of the political consequences of any action he might authorise. In Britain, the Churches, the political parties, Parliament and the media closely and critically monitored the work of the Control Commission, while former German SPD politicians often had contacts with individual Labour or Independent Labour Party members and MPs to whom they could bring their complaints about heavy handed treatment in the Zone[29]. In August, 1945, the journalist Ritchie Calder described the British Military Government as 'a benevolent autarky' lacking any long term purpose. This was echoed even more forcefully in Hamburg at the end of October when a meeting of senior German local government officials complained to Strang that the British were trying to superimpose upon German structures 'an unsuitable foreign system based upon British colonial practice'[30]. Such criticism had considerable impact on John Hynd, the Minister for occupied Germany, and his staff at Norfolk House, the headquarters of the Control Commission in London. Pressure was put on Montgomery and Robertson to accelerate the civilianisation of the military government in the Zone, initiate local government reform and allow the formation of political parties. Templer and the Corps Commanders, in the midst of the 'battle of winter', considered such developments to be premature. Brian Robertson handled them tactfully but firmly. Over the civilianisation issue he reassured them that generally far from 'treading on the accelerator all the time . . . my idea is to apply the brake', but he was nevertheless adamant that 'it was quite useless to attempt to build a brick wall in front of any movement in this direction'[31]. He employed similar arguments over the proposal to allow the formation of democratic political parties in the British Zone. He also warned the Corps Commanders that as the formation of the political parties was being encouraged in the other zones, particularly the Russian, there was real danger that when the inter-zonal barriers were lowered, the Germans in the British Zone might well be overwhelmed by a flood of Communist-inspired propaganda if they had no political organisation of their own.

In December, the Four Power Internal Affairs and Communications Directorate began tentative discussions on the date when the various parish, district and provincial elections in the occupied territories should be held. As far as electoral procedure went, Brian Robertson reported that the British Element not surprisingly favoured small single-member constituencies rather than proportional representation[32]. Ambitiously, the Directorate then set up a working party to consider the future governmental structure of Germany. This prompted Brian Robertson to give 'a good deal of thought' to the problem. He argued that the most viable scheme was for a loose federation, based on the four zones of occupation with possibly an extra state composed of the Ruhr and Rhineland, since this would be the most acceptable basis to the Russians and the French for a reunited Germany. It also had the advantage of accommodating 'a degree of diversity in the type of regime for each unit, as is already, of course, an accomplished fact'[33]. The British Element did, however, ultimately envisage that:

> . . . with the departure of the occupying troops it is not unlikely that, despite the different ways of life that have grown up in the Zones, the unifying force of German nationality will be strong enough to break down the Zonal barriers. The Zones may disappear and the regions be left as the constituent federal states of Germany, with no level between them and the central administration. But this need not concern us at the present, and its results may in any case be as harmless as they would be natural if reorganisation of the various regions of Germany has been carried out in such a way as to stimulate and foster regional patriotism[34].

Events over the coming year were, however, to make even this scheme for a loose federation of German states seem academic.

'1946 IS GOING TO BE A VERY DIFFICULT TIME'
Montgomery

Throughout 1946, the administration of the British Zone was a Sisyphean task. Food and coal shortages steadily sapped the strength of the

population while growing disagreements with the Russians over reparations and inter-zonal trade prevented the Zonal economy from making
even the limited recovery necessary to ease the financial burden on the
British Exchequer. Brian Robertson's problems were further compounded
by the almost permanent flux in which the British Element of the Control
Commission found itself. In the course of 1946 it lost a third of its personnel, delegated much of its power at local level to the Germans and
changed from being a military to a predominantly civil organisation.

With Montgomery's backing, Robertson worked hard, but ultimately
with only mixed success, to weld the British element of the Control
Commission into an efficient administrative apparatus. His first priority
was to regroup the 14 Divisions of the Control Commission into an
Economic and a Governmental Sub-Commission under Sir Percy Mills
and General Erskine respectively. He thus spared himself endless paperwork and detail by dealing directly with two rather than 14 subordinates.
He skilfully overcame both the opposition from the Divisional Chiefs,
who naturally feared for their own authority, and also from their parent
ministries in London by appealing over their heads to Norfolk House
and the Treasury. In a positively Machiavellian way, he sugared 'the pill
very slightly without in any way altering its potency' by calling the heads
of the two sub-commissions 'Presidents' instead of 'Chiefs'[35], which was
supposed to convey the idea that they would chair conferences rather
than interfere directly in divisional affairs. He aimed to complement these
administrative reforms by concentrating the Zonal offices of the Control
Commission in Hamburg. This decision was logical but not politic. It
stirred up a hornet's nest of opposition in both Britain and the Zone as it
meant moving some 13,000 Germans in a devastated city where most of
the inhabitants lived in appalling conditions. Stubbornly, he persisted
with his plans which were derisibly nicknamed the 'Poona'[36]. However, by
1948, the further contraction of the Control Commission and the decision
to set up a West German government made the 'Poona' redundant and it
was never completed.

Robertson's tenacity was shown to rather better effect at the vital level
of industrial negotiations. These dragged on in Berlin from late December
1945 to March 1946. The negotiations were crucial for the future of
Germany because they were to determine the level of Germany's industrial production. British policy was to make Germany self-supporting so
that the Zone would cease to be a drain on the British economy, while at
the same time ensuring that Germany would have no surplus capacity for
rearmament. Hence the British initially proposed that German steel production should be reduced to the level of about 10.5 million tons annually.
However, the Americans suggested 7.8 million, the French 7 million and
the Russians 4.6 million. Brian Robertson threw himself into what at
times became a bitter fight to retain this capacity for steel production, as

he believed passionately that a viable economy was an important preliminary to the restoration of German self-respect and the creation of a stable German democratic state.

On 10 January, it appeared that a compromise was in sight. Both Sokolovsky and Robertson agreed in the Coordinating Committee, where the details of the Plan were worked out, that the actual production of steel should be limited to 5.8 million tons, while a maximum steel making capacity of 7.5 million tons should still be retained. Normally Brian Robertson would have been delighted that inter-Allied unity had been preserved and a compromise brokered, but when it emerged that Clay and Sokolovsky not unreasonably interpreted this agreement to mean that the production of all the steel-dependent industries would be also pinned down to 5.8 million tons, he surprised them by vehemently insisting that the 7.5 million figure was to serve as the basis for the rest of the economy[37]. In this he was backed by Bevin and at the next meeting of the Coordinating Committee he made 'a strong and candid exposition' which made Clay 'physically quiver with rage'[38]. Montgomery was inclined to concede the argument to the Russians and Americans and he advised Brian Robertson that it was 'not worth having a first class row over the matter'[39]. Robertson disagreed and fought on for a few more days until it was clear that Clay was more interested in negotiating a compromise with the Soviet Union than in conceding points to the British. Grudgingly, he agreed to cooperate in preparing a level of industry plan based on the 5.8 million steel production figure, although he still refused to commit himself to it absolutely[40].

It was unusual to see Brian Robertson cast in the role of an intransigent negotiating partner. Usually he was accused of being too ready to make concessions or else congratulated on being 'inter-allied' in outlook, but, pondering the lessons of Versailles, he felt passionately that if the Allies set too low a level for the permitted development of German industry they would alienate the Germans once again and in due course unleash a third world war. The best guide to his motivation during these protracted negotiations is a curious fable, or 'dream' as he called it, which he dictated to his Assistant one morning during a brief lull in his work[41]. In its own way it is also an interesting and subtle comment on the policies of the Four Powers towards Germany in early 1946:

Four animals were met together in the jungle to discuss the fate of the dragon. They had fought long and hard against the dragon and all had suffered. Now the dragon lay at their feet, transfixed to the ground by four spears.

'He's a bad dragon', said the lion. 'We must see he does not do this again. I favour clipping his claws and his wings. Then there is that apparatus inside him for producing fire and brimstone. We should apply treatment to that. I think we might succeed in giving him the sweet breath of democracy.'

'Cockadoodledoo!' said the cock, which made the others stare at him sharply. 'I am in favour of leaving those four spears through his rear leg and I am prepared to sit on mine for all time . . .'

'Did you say rear leg or Ruhr leg?', said the lion . . .

The eagle spoke up sharply. 'The attitude taken up by the lion and the cock is intolerable. Their proposals have all been discussed before and we do not agree with them. I consider it imperative that we should accept the bear's plan immediately and that anybody who does not do so should be held responsible before the eyes of the jungle world.'

'But the bear has not spoken yet', said the lion.

'I did not say that he had spoken but I inferred that he would do so and I agree with him. I do not doubt anybody else's sincerity. Nobody should doubt mine.'

. . . Then spoke the bear. 'This is a terribly bad dragon', said he and I cannot agree to leaving him any of the means for repeating his badness. Clip his claws. Nonsense, pull them out. Clip his wings. Certainly not – amputate them. And his eyes, too – they must come out. . . .

. . . Then suddenly the dragon caused a sensation by making a remark. Everybody had forgotten him.

'You have not mentioned my teeth, gentlemen', he said. 'Maybe you are busy sowing them already in the field of the years.'

The lion's tail came down with a bang and he moved off scowling with rage, but whether he was more angry with the dragon or with the other animals or with himself is not clear.

By March, after further haggling, compromises were reached right across the board on the future level of German industry. Brian Robertson was unable to secure an upward revision of the figure of 5.8 million tons for the permitted production of steel, but with the full backing of Bevin, he fought a successful rearguard action to have included a key clause insisting that this figure must be subject to review if any of the fundamental assumptions on which it was based should change. The British were convinced that the plan would soon be seen as impracticable and would inevitably have to be modified.

When Robertson announced the details at a press conference on 28 March, he had the difficult task of defending a plan which he was convinced was seriously flawed. He did not hide his belief that the level of steel production would have to be increased and he emphasised particularly that the plan was only valid as long as Germany remained an economic whole. He could offer little comfort to the Germans, but he did stress their amazing powers of recovery:

Anybody who fought against them during the war knows but too well
that this is so. If the skill and organising power of the German people are
developed not to war but to overcoming their economic difficulties, we
believe that sufficient productive resources have been left to them to
enable them to obtain a tolerable living in line with the European average. I say that we believe this, but I cannot say categorically that it will
be so. There is no margin of safety to counteract any unforeseen political or economic developments which may occur within or without the
frontiers of Germany to disturb the rehabilitation of the country[42].

Even as Brian Robertson spoke, the British Zone was facing an acute
food crisis, which certainly threatened to disturb this 'rehabilitation'.
Before the War some 50 per cent of north-west Germany's food supplies
came from outside the area. By 1946, not only had its population
increased by two million, as a result of the influx of refugees, but Germany
had also lost 25 per cent of her agricultural land to the Poles in the east.
In November, 1945, an inter-Allied committee of nutritional experts had
recommended a personal ration of 1,550 calories per day, and to reach
this target imports into the Zone were accelerated from December, 1945,
onwards. Then, at the end of February, 'very bad news'[43] arrived: as a
result of global shortages, wheat imports into the three western zones were
to be drastically cut. Food rations had therefore to be reduced to a mere
1,015 calories a day and even this standard was dependent on the steady
maintenance of further wheat shipments.

Robertson had a major, although not unexpected, crisis on his hands.
He had already set up a separate division within the Control Commission
to deal with food and agriculture. This had launched a propaganda campaign to persuade the German farmers to produce as much as possible
and also greatly increased the number of inspections and checks on the
farms to prevent hoarding and food passing into the hands of the black
marketeers. Ultimately, however, he knew that the crisis could only be
solved by a political decision taken at the highest level in London to
import more food into the British Zone, even if this meant cutting
Britain's own ration scales. He thus went out of his way to make sure that
the public in Britain, and indeed the whole international community,
were fully informed of the gravity of the crisis. He requested permission to
hold a press conference on 7 March where, for once, nothing that he said
was 'off the record'. He described succinctly what the consequences
would be of a breakdown in food supplies for the cities. With an eye on
British public opinion, which was still anti-German, he was careful to
avoid any appeals to sentiment. Instead, he gave an unemotional staff
officer's explanation of why it was important to feed the Germans
adequately:

The problem for Germany should be viewed from a practical and not a sentimental point of view. The Germans have brought this situation on themselves, and indeed on the world. We consider that they should be adequately fed, not because we are sorry for them, but as a matter of policy. It is no part of British policy to starve Germany, nor is it Allied policy. To do so would be to defeat one of the principal objectives of our occupation, namely that the German people should be given the opportunity to prepare for the eventual reconstruction of their life on a democratic basis[44].

Privately, however, he was much more outspoken. He was very critical of both the Minister of Food, Sir Ben Smith, and the Chancellor of the Exchequer, Hugh Dalton, for their apparent parsimony and political cowardice in not cutting the British food ration. In a discussion with Hynd he threatened to send over to Britain 'pictures of starving children and dying women'[45]. He had no doubt in his own mind that a cut in the British ration scale would provide the necessary food for Germany. To prove his point, the Information Room at the Zonal headquarters at Lübbecke contained contrasting models depicting the normal amount of food eaten by the average person in Britain and Germany – the latter on the basis of 1,000 calories. By April, the ration cuts were already beginning to make the population in the cities look greyer and more pinched and at the beginning of May there was only sufficient grain in Germany to last until the end of the month. Brian Robertson returned to the attack and sent Hynd a hard-hitting memorandum which one civil servant in Norfolk House called a 'first rate document'[46]. It graphically outlined what would happen if present trends continued:

> . . . the economic life of the British Zone will stop almost simultaneously. Coal production will stop. The trains will stop. The lights will go out . . .

And then he added a chilling observation calculated to cause panic amongst democratic politicians sensitive to the swings of domestic and world opinion:

> The sporadic looting and unrest which is occurring now would increase. It is not, however, likely that the situation would get out of hand, provided that our own soldiers will be prepared to shoot down starving rioters.

This memorandum, combined with a further telegram from the new Commander-in-Chief, Sir Sholto Douglas, stressing the dangers of an administrative breakdown in the British Zone, finally pushed the Cabinet into action. Herbert Morrison, the Lord President, was sent to Washington where he negotiated the dispatch to the British Zone of 675,000 tons of grain for the period up to September 1946 in return for a cut of 200,000 tons to the UK. Disaster was thus narrowly averted but the imported grain merely enabled the authorities to increase the daily ration by about 400 calories a day. Even this meagre standard could not be maintained in the bitter winter of 1946–47.

The food crisis came to a head at a time when the Control Commission was in a state of transition. The new Regional Commissioners were in the process of being appointed in London to take over from the Corps Commanders. Brian Robertson feared that this transition might lead to a decline in the quality of his staff. He told the Corps Commanders:

> We are losing some of our best soldiers like Templer. In the near future we shall lose some of our key civilians like Mills. I have an uneasy feeling that the importance of the task out here is not realised at home[47].

He was also concerned about the mounting German criticism of the British administration, which, largely because of the food shortages, was no longer seen as fair and efficient. Above all, he feared that this would lead to a rejection in the Zone of democracy and Western values. To the Germans, he adopted the policy of telling the plain, unvarnished truth about the gravity of the crisis, yet at the same time he tried to give them hope, even if this meant that he had to hide his own worst fears for the future. Thus he told the German Zonal Advisory Council on 6 March:

> I offer you no hope of an easy life but I tell you that it is our intention that the bleakness of the present austerity shall be progressively mitigated until a position is reached in which the German people by hard work and sober living may secure for themselves a decent and reasonable existence[48].

He conceded that the current economic situation made political reform more difficult, but he was adamant that it would nevertheless proceed and outlined the British policy of democratising from the bottom upwards.

The food crisis was compounded by an equally grave crisis in coal production. This was partly the result of food shortages sapping the strength of the miners, but also of an indiscriminate de-nazification process which had removed from the pits many of their managers and safety personnel. After an explosion at the Monopol Grimberg pit in the Ruhr on 20 February with the loss of 402 lives, Brian Robertson personally suspended the denazification policy. He also urged the government, in the interests of the economy of the British Zone, to reduce the French allocation of Ruhr coal. He wrote almost in despair to Arthur Street, the Permanent

Secretary at Norfolk House, two days before the announcement of the Level of Industry Plan:

> The Germans are beginning to feel that in the Russian Zone their people have hope and that a measure of recovery is being made possible. In our Zone, in spite of protestations, we provide very little grounds for hope. We must find employment and we must get their basic industries going. Next winter we must find them some coal for their homes[49].

The cost of averting famine in the Zone inevitably intensified the financial pressure on the British Exchequer and made a revival of inter-zonal trade and the treatment of Germany as an economic whole increasingly urgent. Only within this context could the crippling expenses of the British Zone be shifted from the British taxpayer to the Germans.

Yet just when it became so pressing to implement this policy, Quadripartite cooperation began to unravel. In March 1946, Winston Churchill, now Leader of the Opposition in Britain, had already drawn the World's attention to the Iron Curtain that had fallen across Europe from Stettin to Trieste. In that same month, the Western Powers were forced to watch impotently while the SPD and Communist Parties in the Russian Zone and the Eastern Sector of Berlin were forcibly amalgamated. Bitterly, Brian Robertson observed that the fight was unequal because the Russians did not scruple to use force whereas 'we must go about our job with kid gloves on'[50]. Reluctantly, he was coming round to the conclusion that he had been 'taken in' by his liking for General Sokolovsky's 'ability and wisdom'[51]. A more serious blow to Allied unity came when, in April, the Russians rejected a paper tabled by Brian Robertson at the Coordinating Committee calling for the pooling of indigenous resources and the use of the profits from exports to pay for such vital imports as food. When the Russians prevaricated, Clay announced the suspension of the delivery of all reparations from the American to the Russian Zones and then at the next Coordinating Meeting Brian Robertson announced that he was requesting permission from London to follow suit.

Like military offensives, the policies advocated by the Great Powers at the regular meetings of the Council of Foreign Ministers required meticulous planning. Not surprisingly then, it was to Brian Robertson rather than to Hynd that Ernest Bevin turned for advice and information on Zonal and Quadripartite affairs. The Conference of Foreign Ministers, which was held in Paris in the summer of 1946, was a watershed in the history of post-war Germany. Its consequences were succinctly expressed by Robertson:

> The results were negative in the sense that no agreement was reached, but they were positive in the sense that lack of agreement defines the position more clearly[52].

Two important developments occurred. First, in response to a point blank refusal by the Russians to treat Germany as an economic whole, Bevin declared that the British would have to reorganise their Zone so that it ceased to be a financial liability. In practice this could only mean levying duties on all goods leaving the Zone and allocating less Ruhr coal to the French. Byrnes, the American Secretary of State, then proposed a scheme, to which Bevin responded immediately and positively, for the economic fusion of the American Zone with any other Zone willing to cooperate.

On 26 July Brian Robertson was authorised to begin negotiations with Clay. Plans were rapidly agreed upon for setting up a Bipartite Board to work out plans for harmonising ration scales and the standard of living in the two zones and for creating a joint bizonal administration for food, agriculture, trade, industry and transport. To underline that this was merely an economic and not a political agreement, aimed at setting up a West German state, there was to be no elected assembly or council and the head offices of the newly created agencies were to be spread around the two zones. At the Zonal Advisory Council on 14 August, Brian Robertson readily conceded that the proposed fusion was only a second best to economic unity for the whole of Germany. In an effort to assuage the fears of his audience about the implications of this for the future political unity of Germany, he emphasised that the British and Americans had no intention of partitioning the country, although privately many leading Germans in the western zones already thought that this was inevitable. He then spelt out clearly the advantages which he hoped the fusion would bring: interzonal trade, economic cooperation and a common and more generous ration scale[53].

In the late summer and early autumn of 1946, the atmosphere of crisis and pessimism which had for so long hovered over the British zone briefly seemed to lift. The fusion agreement with the American Zone was an ultimate safety net and the food situation had even improved to the point where reserves could begin to be accumulated. The local *Kreis* elections had taken place leaving the SPD overall the strongest party in the Zone and plans were well advanced for replacing the former Prussian territory within the British Zone with new and more compact *Länder*. The key state of North Rhine-Westphalia had already been set up and the decision taken to vest the assets of the Ruhr industries in the Commander-in-Chief with the ultimate intention of putting them under some form of international control.

On 11 August, Brian Robertson's family arrived in Berlin and for the first time for over six years he was able to enjoy a domestic life. *Schloss* Benkhausen gradually ceased to be a general's mess and became a real family home where he could relax, play bridge and entertain his colleagues and numerous important visitors in a happy and informal family environment. Lord Pakenham, who usually found him a daunting and severe figure, felt that he mellowed within his family circle and appeared 'in a most attractive light with Lady Robertson ragging him, and for that matter everyone else, to the general enjoyment'. The *Schloss* and the Grünewald house were truly oases amidst the ruins of Germany in 1946. With the limpid clarity of a small child, his six-year-old daughter, Fiona, once asked him, 'why do only the British live in whole houses?[54]

It was, however, to be several more years before the Germans could even begin to think about living in undamaged houses. After the dramatic events at the Paris Conference there was a feeling on the Co-ordinating Committee in Berlin that nothing of substance could be decided until the next meeting of the Council of Foreign Ministers in New York in November, when it was hoped that some way out of the deadlock over the future of Germany might be found. This, as Brian Robertson drily observed, was 'possibly a rather optimistic assumption'[55]. In both the Foreign Office in London and in the British Element of the Control Commission in Berlin, there was a flurry of preparation for the Conference. Strang and Brian Robertson were summoned over to London to discuss the wording of a general directive to be sent to Sholto Douglas. In its final form, it spelt out the long-term aims of the British Government in Germany, which essentially amounted to creating a peaceful, demilitarised and democratic federal republic[56]. Within the British Zone, this aim was to be advanced by the creation of more *Länder* on the model of the state of North Rhine-Westphalia and by the devolution to their administrations of as much political responsibility as was compatible with the existence of a united Germany. Bevin also needed detailed advice on the future of the Ruhr, the boundaries of Germany, reparations and the Level of Industry Plan. Above all he requested their opinion on whether Britain should:

> . . . seek the immediate establishment of a single Germany or should we maintain the independence of the combined Anglo-American Zone until it has achieved greater political and economic stability?

Patrick Dean, the head of the Foreign Office's German Department, was sent out to Berlin to assist the Control Commission with drawing up its responses to these questions. He was warned specifically to be on his guard against any arguments on efficiency which Brian Robertson and Strang might advance in Berlin. Oliver Harvey, one of the deputy Under-Secretaries reminded him that 'We do not want an efficient Germany but one with strong local vested interests'[57].

Brian Robertson was interested not so much in an efficient Germany as in a peaceful Germany. He lucidly spelt out his thinking on the German problem in a talk in August to British officials in both Lübbecke and

Berlin[58]. He explained to them how in 'military parlance a distinction is drawn between the object which a commander seeks to gain and the objectives which he aims to secure as the means for obtaining his object'.

The overall object or prize was 'lasting peace in Europe'. To seize this, three objectives had to be attained: the demilitarisation of Germany, the establishment of a democratic Germany and a negotiated settlement with 'our great allies, America and Russia'. He warned his staff against being too sentimental about the Germans:

> Let there be no mistake about it. The Germans are a warrior race. They have a strong streak of cruelty running through them.
>   Given an opportunity, they will very quickly get up to their old tricks again.

The demilitarisation measures would therefore have to be thorough although not vindictive.

Robertson was strongly opposed to the division of Germany for reasons which he was frequently to reiterate up to July 1948:

> Germany is the focus of Europe. A break with Russia on the German question would be highly dangerous to the cause of peace. I think that we should do everything short of compromising our essential principles to avoid such a break. There is some evidence at least that the Russians have a sense of responsibility about Germany and a conception of the peril to themselves as well as to others which disagreement over Germany would produce. It is easy to become impatient with Russian obstruction and their rather Asiatic methods of negotiation. If, however, I am right in thinking that fundamentally they want to reach agreement on Germany, then our patience with them should be great and our perseverance unrelenting.

A near bankrupt Britain did not, however, have the time to be 'patient and persevering' in its quest for a settlement with Russia. In London, the priority was increasingly to create a viable economy in Western Germany rather than to achieve a united Germany at any price. Not surprisingly then, Brian Robertson's proposal made during the Paris Conference for avoiding a break with the Russians by allowing them to defer payment for exports from the Western Zones met with little support from the Foreign Office. Consequently, in his response to Bevin's key question about German unification, Sholto Douglas, advised by both Brian Robertson and Strang, sought to reconcile the pressing need to alleviate the financial burden of the Zone on Britain with the eventual aim of achieving German unification. He argued strongly for German unity, but made its realisation virtually impossible by proposing that no reparations to Russia from the

British and American Zones should be made for at least seven years until their economy had recovered. In effect, he advocated unity on terms which the Russians were bound to reject[59].

As part of the British delegation, Brian Robertson sailed for New York in November for the next Council of Ministers meeting. He shared a cabin with Strang, who, much to his irritation, kept him awake at night by noisily eating chocolate. The British delegation was booked into the Hotel Roosevelt. His Administrative Assistant recalls that one evening when Brian Robertson returned from a lengthy Conference session, he found that his key would not work. When he tried to elicit help from his neighbour, who was not a member of the British Delegation, he was somewhat surprised to find that she was stark naked!

Although all the crucial quadripartite decisions on Germany were deferred until the next meeting in Moscow in the New Year, important bilateral discussions took place between Britain and America over the Bizone, which made German unity in the near future even less likely. The Americans firmly refused to pay more than 50 per cent of the costs of the Bizone, but nevertheless the British did gain an important concession from them. At a meeting between Byrnes and Bevin, also attended by Clay and Robertson, on 3 December, it was agreed that the Level of Industry Plan as far as it affected the Bizone was no longer valid and that the two Military Governors should make a joint study and produce recommendations for a new plan. They were also to discuss proposals for financial reform including the issue of a separate currency for Bizonia – as the Anglo–US zones were called – in the likely event of the failure of the Moscow Conference. When Clay brought up the question of political fusion it was ruled out as being premature, yet the possibility of a separate currency for Bizonia, as Brian Robertson observed, was in itself an issue with 'very important political consequences'[60]. The momentum towards the division of Germany was gathering speed.

On his way back to Berlin, Brian Robertson stopped off in London to discuss the results of the Conference at the Foreign Office where he stressed the crucial importance 'in all German questions' of reaching initial agreement with Clay, who had direct access to Byrnes[61]. He also saw Montgomery, now CIGS, at the War Office. In May 1946, Montgomery had virtually promised him the post of Quarter Master General with effect from June 1947 on the assumption that he would by then have 'had enough of Germany', but it was abundantly clear that Brian Robertson had made himself indispensable not only to the Commander-in-Chief but also to Hynd and Bevin. Thus, as he put it, '[Montgomery] was flattering enough to say that in his own opinion it might be unwise that I should be taken from Germany yet', and he agreed to remain in Germany but only on condition that responsibility for the Control Office at Norfolk House was placed 'squarely and directly on the Foreign

Secretary'[62]. This did indeed happen in April, 1947, when Hynd was replaced by Lord Pakenham, who was made directly answerable to Bevin for German affairs. Over the coming bitterly cold winter months, when the average daily food ration fell again to about 1,000 calories, coal output plummeted and bitter jokes were circulating amongst the Germans to the effect that starvation was the norm under British rule, Brian Robertson may perhaps occasionally have regretted that he had thrown away the chance of a safe and comfortable job in Whitehall. On the other hand, that he stayed was clearly to the long-term gain of at least those Germans lucky enough to find themselves in the western zones.

THE MOSCOW CONFERENCE AND THE DEVELOPMENT OF BIZONIA

In the Arctic weather of January 1947, it was easy to be pessimistic about the state of Germany with its acute food and coal shortages. *The Economist*, for instance, painted a bleak picture of a 'situation even more unmanageable than it was at the time of Potsdam' and observed critically that then 'the victors only had Hitler's errors to repair. Now they have added their own'[63]. Brian Robertson certainly did not dispute that analysis. He made no secret of his belief that the Level of Industry Plan of March 1946 was a major error entered into because 'at that time to reach agreement seemed important almost at any price'[64] and that the inevitably unpopular process of demilitarisation or demolition of surplus industrial capacity was proceeding far too slowly. Later he also conceded that initially British officials acted like colonial administrators and 'were too slow to build up again the German administrative machinery except at a very local level'. But he was surely right that the root cause of the paralysis in Germany in the winter of 1946–47 lay in the fact that quadripartite government in Germany had become a 'farce'[65].

During this turbulent year, when the occupying powers stood on the threshold of great decisions about the future of Germany, Brian Robertson clung tenaciously to his belief that the Control Commission had a mission to create a democratic and peaceful Germany. At its lower levels, the Commission was 'an amateur bureaucracy struggling with colossal problems in a foreign country and largely through interpreters'[66]. Its members were exposed to great temptations in a land where one hundred cigarettes represented a fortune on the black market. Control Commission officials lived, as Victor Gollancz so tellingly observed in his book *In Darkest Germany*, cocooned in islands of relative luxury with a ration of 200 cigarettes and 'a fair amount of chocolate every week'[67]. Inevitably there were a series of embarrassing black market scandals which Parliament and the press picked up[68]. Perceptively, the *Financial Times* referred to the Control Commission as 'that mixture of missionary and beachcomber'[69]. By tightening up regulations and working through the Regional Commissioners, Robertson had some success in removing 'black sheep' and 'beachcombers', but his main technique was to attempt to inculcate in his staff a sense of pride in their work and a mission to build democracy in Germany. He had a positively Victorian belief in the sense of mission. Neatly turning the tables on the vociferous critics at home, who accused the Control Commission of creating a new British Raj in Germany, he told his staff:

> We here are Empire builders, not in the sense repeated to us maliciously by some of our critics. The Empire whose boundaries we struggle to extend is the Empire of true democracy, of peace and decency . . . We have had our difficulties and we have had our disappointments. Allied disagreements, food shortage, shortage of many things, and perhaps worst of all the very complexities of our problem, the complication of doing anything, the number of factors that have to be brought into account and the number of people who have to be consulted before anything can be done. These are the obstacles and exasperations in our way . . . They are just mountains to be scaled and rivers to be crossed, and it is our plain duty to get on with the job and to stick to it unremittingly . . .[70]

In early 1947, Brian Robertson had a veritable Alpine range of mountains to scale. Not only had he to oversee the devolution of more power to the Germans and cope with the pressing economic and social problems of the Zone, but to organise the preparation of detailed reports for the Foreign Office and the Control Council for the coming conference in Moscow – the final Control Council report covering all four zones weighed six pounds! Bevin also informed him that he was expected 'for much if not all the time' at the Moscow Conference.

★★★

The initial plan for Bizonal Fusion came into force on 1 January 1947. It was obvious from the beginning that its organisation was inadequate and, if, as was most likely, the Moscow conference failed to produce an agreed formula for German unity, it would have to be considerably tightened up. Thus, as early as 2 January, Clay and Robertson began detailed and secret talks about how to improve the administrative structure of the Bizone. Since they were in effect discussing giving to Bizonia some of the attributes of an independent state, they had to be careful, particularly before the Moscow Conference, not to provoke Russia into taking retaliatory measures. Together with an Economic Council of 52 delegates, which were to be nominated by the German *Länder*, they agreed that at the appropriate time there should be set up a second chamber or 'house', as Brian Robertson called it, and an executive committee, a court of appeal on constitutional questions affecting Bizonal economic legislation and a central bank. Brian Robertson was uneasy that Clay was obviously using the American constitution as his model. He disliked the proposal that the Chairman of the Executive Committee should be appointed by the second house or 'senate' for a fixed term, but in view of the 'transitory character of the organisation', he let Clay have his way. When, as he was convinced they would eventually have to, they came to drafting a more permanent constitution, he was determined to take up this issue again. Reflecting his British background, Robertson felt that any constitution, in which the 'cabinet' could not be removed from office if it lost the confidence of 'parliament', would be unworkable by the Germans and produce even more serious deadlocks than it did in the United States. Significantly, they also agreed quietly 'in due course' to drop the term 'economic' from the Council's title[71]. These discussions, although only between the two military governors and about economic rather than political powers, were an interesting exploration of constitutional issues that the West Germans themselves were to start discussing the following year.

On 25 February, the expected Soviet attack on the Bizone was launched in the Control Council. Brian Robertson neatly deflected the not wholly unjustifed accusations that it was a political agreement by offering to make it quadrizonal. He and Clay also embarrassed Sokolovsky by sarcastically asking whether his diatribe should be published in the German press. Indeed, Clay even offered to publish it himself. These remarks were made the more pointed because, nearly three weeks earlier, Brian Robertson had protested strongly over the verbatim publication of a particularly bitter Russian attack on Britain and America in the Co-ordinating Committee in the German press in the Soviet Zone. Sokolovsky 'who had all along betrayed acute embarrassment' then 'dissolved into helpless laughter saying he could give no answer'. In Strang's words, this then 'closed one of the most comic scenes the Council had witnessed'[72].

The first session of the Moscow Conference was convened for 10 March. Flying to Moscow proved surprisingly difficult. On Saturday 8 March, Brian Robertson arose at 4.30 in the morning only to find that the weather was so bad that the Dakota could not take off. He spent the rest of the day in his office, apart from a break to look at his horses, and did not return home until 11.30 in the evening. The following day, he and his ADC again got up at 4.30 and motored out to Gatow. This time the plane actually took off, but then developed engine trouble and had rapidly to return to Gatow. On Monday, this exhausting routine was once more repeated, and again the plane had to turn back because it received no clearance from Moscow to land. Only on Tuesday, despite a gale and packed ice, did Robertson's Dakota finally manage to arrive in Moscow, one hour late[73].

Bevin went to Moscow quite prepared to break with the Russians over Germany. His officials had drawn up a radical plan which became known as the 'new Potsdam' or 'Bevin Plan'. This laid down conditions for the revision of the Potsdam agreement, which they knew Russia would not be able to accept. Not only would Russia have to return some of the reparations, which she had already illegally taken from her own zone to help balance Anglo-American deficits, but also contribute to the bills of the Western powers and receive no steel or coal deliveries until Germany was self-sufficient.

The first week of the Conference was taken up with the report of the Allied Control Commission on the state of Germany. In the second week, the foreign ministers moved on to making a series of speeches laying down their basic principles. When Oliver Harvey fell ill, Brian Robertson temporarily took his place as Bevin's adviser, sitting on his left hand side in the conference room. The Council of Ministers met in the Hall of the Aviation Industry in the late afternoon for a three or four hour session. Then, after a brief dinner, the British delegation worked deep into the night preparing papers for the following day. One of Brian Robertson's tasks was to help draft a section of the speech on reparations which Bevin gave on 17 March. Once again, in a hurried draft scribbled in pencil, he rehearsed his arguments against the existing Level of Industry Plan and the need for a moderate and realist reparation programme to be achieved by a set date. Remembering Molotov's successful bid to woo the Germans with his speech at the Paris Conference, he also advised Bevin to 'end up with some sob [stuff] of the sort which would appeal to the Germans'[74].

By 21 March, this 'phase of general statements' was coming to an end and two days later Brian Robertson was appointed to a special coordinating committee set up to report on the drafts for the future political organisation of Germany which were contained in the mass of papers which made up the Control Council's Report. He threaded his way expertly through the familiar areas of disagreement and deadlock. Even on the days when he was not chairman, he was able succinctly to sum up his colleagues' views and move the meeting on from one contentious issue to another. On 29 March, the coordinating committee then went on to look at the key issues of German economic unity and reparations[75].

Robertson remained in Moscow for another three weeks. In that time, very little was agreed upon with the Russians, except that they did concede that the level of steel production should be raised to somewhere between 10 and 12 million tons. Otherwise, decisions were once again deferred until the next Conference of Foreign Ministers met in London in November. Later, Brian Robertson himself summarised the results of the Conference for his staff:

. . . the debates were on the whole very friendly. The discussions were quite good, but the results were zero; and they shook each other by the hand and said, 'Well, Good-bye, old boy! It has been very nice and we must start talking again at a later date'[76].

Like everybody else, Robertson was convinced that the time for inconclusive debate had passed and that at the London Conference:

. . . there will be a decision to run Germany as a whole . . . or there will be no agreement and that will in itself be a decision for the partition of Germany.[77]

He flew into Berlin on the afternoon of Saturday 19 April. As his ADC noticed 'all the slackness goes directly the General returns – the house is full of generals, air marshals and C's-in-C within half an hour'[78]. In the evening, the President of the Economic Sub-Commission, Sir Cecil Weir, and several of his key officials came to dinner to discuss the future of Bizonia after the failure of the Moscow Conference to achieve any settlement of the German question. Bevin, with Brian Robertson's and Weir's support, was pressing hard to have the various departments of Bizonia concentrated in Frankfurt and made much more efficient. Although Bevin and Byrne's successor, Marshall, had agreed in Moscow on this, Brian Robertson found detailed discussions with Clay so difficult that they virtually broke down and on 28 April the fusion agreement seemed, as he put it, for a time to be 'in suspended animation'[79]. Clay was highly suspicious of British plans for what he called 'a detailed regimentation of the German economy'[80], while the British felt that he wanted to move too quickly towards political fusion and a *laissez-faire* economy. In the end an acceptable compromise was proposed by Bevin: British plans for a controlled economy would be tactfully played down, while a Bizonal German Advisory Council would be set up, which if the London Conference failed to produce an agreement on Germany would be given 'legislative and executive functions'[81]. It was also agreed that Frankfurt should become the capital of the Bizone and that its various agencies and boards were to be concentrated there. On 13 May, Robertson, Strang and Weir flew over to London to report to Bevin on the details of the agreement[82].

Throughout the summer and autumn of 1947, Brian Robertson commuted regularly to London to see Bevin or to confer with Foreign Office officials about the workings of Bizonia and the political implications of Britain's inability to finance 50 per cent of its cost in dollars, and to prepare for the next Conference of Foreign Ministers. On one of these occasions, in a taxi going down Whitehall, he explained to his ADC the tactics he used to employ at the numerous committees and conferences he had attended. This made such an impact on the ADC that he remembered them 44 years later:

> I counted the number of people who are going to be at the meeting today. There are 36 and I am going to be the most junior and that gives me a great advantage. I can speak last. I will try to speak at exactly half-past one. Their tongues will be hanging out for their gins and tonics. There is both a time when you want to speak last and a time when you want to speak first at such meetings, but at this meeting everybody will have made up their mind before the meeting what they want. If it's a balanced thing, then the ideas of the last person who speaks sticks in their minds and that's when you speak last. . . .[83]

He then went on to explain that speaking first was effective when people had not had time to think about an issue. Once they had made observations on a particular question, it was difficult to persuade them to change their minds. Thus a persuasive and well balanced opening statement could often influence the whole subsequent meeting.

As the pace of change quickened in Germany, so the burden on Brian Robertson increased. At times his office was besieged by those seeking advice or decisions. On 13 June, for instance, another of his ADCs noted that:

> Even when he leaves 20 minutes late one person talks in the passage, another on the stairs, a third outside the car and a fourth on the way to Gatow.[84]

Although, in the long term, the Bizone represented the best prospects the West Germans had for escaping from poverty, hunger and political impotence, this was by no means clear in the summer of 1947. After five visits to the Zone, Lord Pakenham informed Bevin that:

> Germany is in a shocking position. It is a complete illusion to suppose that things are getting steadily better . . .[85]

This was strongly endorsed by Cecil Weir who argued that the existing organisation of the Bizone was an unsatisfactory compromise which tied the hands of both the Germans and the British and Americans. He pointed out to the Deputy Military Governor:

> The German economy is running down in an alarming way largely because there is at present no clear sighted and authoritative direction of the economy. Military Government has deliberately handed over a large part of its responsibility to the Germans without putting the Germans up till now in a position to exercise authority effectively.[86]

In essence, Brian Robertson agreed, but counselled patience as radical changes would almost certainly be made after the London Conference.

During that hot summer of 1947, as the Control Commission staff sweltered at their desks by day and played tennis or polo and socialised in the cool of the evening, change was very much in the air. Not only was a break with Russia after the next meeting of the Conference of Foreign Ministers in November regarded as almost inevitable, but the serious and possibly even terminal weakness of the British Empire was painfully displayed to the world when the Chancellor of the Exchequer, at the end of June, revealed that most of the American loan authorised in the autumn of 1945 had been spent and that Britain was virtually bankrupt. The consequences of this for the British in Germany were quite simply that America would have to shoulder more of the costs of running the Bizone with the unavoidable corollary that Washington would demand a greater say in crucial policy matters. In a seminal memorandum, aptly entitled 'He who pays the piper calls the tune'[87] Brian Robertson set out to forecast 'the shape which these demands are likely to assume and to propose a method for satisfying them without sacrificing too much'. He based his arguments on the assumption that France would join the Bizone, that political fusion would be accomplished by the end of the year and that it would be impracticable to renegotiate the whole fusion agreement to take account of the changes in the balance of power among the Western Allies. Although he was scathing about the American denazification policy, he felt that the key differences between the British and Americans lay in the disagreement about the efficiency of socialism versus private enterprise and, what was really an extension of this debate, 'centralism versus *laissez-faire*'. Robertson was confident that what he saw as the worst excesses of the American free market policy could be controlled. His experience of administering the British Zone had turned him into ' a military socialist', as one of the officials in the Political Division, Austen Albu, called him[88]. He argued for instance that:

> Ownership is a word which is temporarily devoid of any real significance in Germany. Everything of consequence is, or should be controlled by the Government – that is to say by Military Government or by German administration which has been set up by it. During this period of scarcity which will inevitably continue for several years this situation will prevail. Assumption by the Government of the functions of ownership is not so much a political issue as an inescapable fact. What will matter in regard to this issue is not that which is done but that which is said.

These assumptions were, however, to be strongly and successfully challenged by the free market economy of Adenauer and Erhard within two years.

Robertson's solution for ceding to America a decisive say in German policy, whilst safeguarding British influence, was to advocate the setting up of a permanent committee in Washington staffed by representatives of the British, French and American foreign ministers. This body would formulate policy and issue instructions on matters of principle. Within Western Germany, or 'Trizonia', Britain would assist the revival of the German economy by supplying commodities from the sterling area.

> In this way we should avoid getting ourselves into the position of paid help. In Germany we should be equal partners in a joint enterprise. In Washington our influence on policy would necessarily be tempered due to the fact that we should not be equal subscribers to the support of the joint enterprise.

A permanent committee in Washington along the lines advocated by Brian Robertson never materialised, but inevitably the balance of power within West Germany tilted decisively towards the Americans. In December, as the price for relieving the British of their share of dollar payments for subsidising Bizonia, the Americans assumed a controlling voice in the joint Import-Export and Foreign Exchange Agencies. Brian Robertson, however, remained adamant that Britain was still a great power with a unique mission in Germany. As he was to tell his officials in a confident and relaxed survey of the situation in July:

> Our difficulties are temporary. Our greatness is enduring, at least it is enduring as long as we have the spunk in us which is the essential ingredient of greatness[89].

Sadly, in the light of history, this optimism can be seen to be unjustified. Nevertheless, as long as *he* remained in Germany, British influence would still be an important factor. Through his close links with Clay, his administrative and negotiating skill and towering intellectual ability, Robertson was able to defy, for a time at least, this shift in the balance of power.

In the middle of August, after having finalised the arrangements for setting up and staffing the Bizonal offices in Frankfurt, Brian Robertson decided at very short notice to take a family holiday near Klagenfurt in southern Austria. It could, as his ADC confided in his diary[90], easily have been a disaster. There was no running water in the house, the catering department at Benkhausen forgot to send any wine or whisky and the tennis court was overgrown with grass. Nevertheless, such was the beauty of the scenery and the perfection of the weather, that 'the General' was able to take all these tribulations 'very calmly' and just relax in the sun.

When he returned to the Zone at the end of August, the revised Plan of

Industry for Bizonia, which had been agreed upon by American and British officials in July, was at last ready to be implemented. All the relevant officials in the Control Commission were instructed to explain to the Germans why Britain and America had somewhat belatedly revised the Potsdam agreement. On 15–16 September, Brian Robertson himself made an almost vice-regal procession through the Ruhr where, apart from a brief detour to visit a prison camp for Nazi war criminals, he met industrialists, trade unionists and German politicians to discuss the Level of Industry Plan in detail and to listen to their complaints. He went out of his way to emphasise that the Plan was 'firm fair and reasonable', even though not perfect. In tone, his discussions with the local industrialists and businessmen were reminiscent of the way he used to address similar gatherings in South Africa. He took an informed interest in their problems. When, for example, he was asked whether permission could be given to increase the production of artificial rubber or 'buna' he could give expert advice and point out that the price of raw rubber was currently very low, while the 'buna' process was uneconomic as it required coal[91].

These speeches were delivered in English and translated by his interpreter, Lieutenant Lederer, but ever since August 1945 he had been taking German lessons twice a week, paying particular attention to stress and tonal accent. Increasingly, when public relations demanded it, he was able to read out a short prepared speech in German[92].

An important consequence of the new level of Industry plan was a drastic cut in the number of plants potentially capable of producing war material which were scheduled to be dismantled. In the two zones the total was reduced from 1,626 to 682, but even this number was increasingly difficult to justify as it risked alienating the Germans at a time when it was Anglo-American policy to make Bizonia economically self-supporting and ultimately politically self-governing. The building up of Western Germany on the one hand, while simultaneously dismantling key industries, seemed to many Germans to be a Jekyll and Hyde policy. Nevertheless, the British Government was still uneasy about Germany's military potential. In July, Brian Robertson justified the dismantling to his staff with an interesting parallel from the 1920s when the British no longer thought of Germany as a threat but were concentrating their minds on Russia. He was firm that 'those things which are really dangerous for future peace' will have to be removed[93].

Yet by the end of September he feared that neither the German politicians nor people would willingly accept the dismantling plan. Thus its implementation had to be planned like a military operation. Every step was to be taken to minimise German opposition. The Regional Commissioners were to do all they could to find the Germans alternative work *before* their factories were closed down but, on Brian Robertson's instructions, detailed contingency plans for dealing with opposition were also drawn up. He was aware of the political dangers of an open confrontation between German workers and British troops and the Regional Commissioners were told to exercise 'a mixture of restraint, patience and firmness' and for as long as possible to let the German authorities themselves deal with any incidents[94].

Careful planning, which was anxiously monitored by the Foreign Office, also went into the initial announcement of the dismantling. On Thursday16 October, there was a press conference, a radio broadcast in German to the Zone by Brian Robertson and a film programme to be shown in the cinemas by *Welt im Film*. Great efforts were made to sugar the bitter dismantling pill by stressing the positive aspects of the new Level of Industry Plan. On Saturday, Brian Robertson then went down to the Ruhr and explained the programme to the German ministers of North Rhine-Westphalia, the politicians and the trade union leaders. In essence, his message was that the programme was inevitable but that he wanted it implemented by consent rather than coercion. He told the trade union leaders that 'we want to do things in a humane way that will inflict the least possible disturbance on the economy of the country'[95]. He tried too to explode the notion that any German cooperating with the British to implement the plan were collaborators. He firmly told the ministers of North Rhine-Westphalia:

> Now if we were sitting here as an occupying power sucking the best out
> of the country and using our occupation entirely for our own purposes,
> it would be a good word to use, but as our objectives are exactly the
> opposite of that, it is a very stupid word to use[96].

The Germans accepted the programme unenthusiastically but with considerable stoicism, which Brian Robertson was quick to appreciate. Indeed he went out of his way to congratulate Hans Böckler, the Secretary of German Trade Union Federation, for speaking with 'outstanding dignity'.

That evening, he flew back back to Benkhausen to host the usual dinner party for senior Control Commission personnel. On Sunday afternoon, he was able to go out hare shooting in the late autumn sunshine but in the evening he had to return to Berlin in his private train.

It was his last relaxing weekend at Benkhausen because on 1 November he took over the post of Commander-in-Chief from Sholto Douglas and was also made a full general, a promotion which had been approved by Attlee himself in June. This entailed moving to the C-in-C's official residence at Schloss Ostenwalde and, of course, even more entertaining either there or in Berlin. From 13 to 16 November, for instance, the Chancellor of the Duchy of Lancaster was in Berlin and there was a non-stop series of dinner and tea parties to which both Germans and Control Commission personnel were invited. On Sunday 16th there were 'hundreds of people' to lunch and later four different sets of tea had to be served in four different rooms so that Lord Pakenham could meet as many Germans and members of the Control Commission as possible.

As Military Governor and Commander-in-Chief, Robertson now had overall command of all British Forces in Germany. Inevitably, almost all his time was taken up with Control Commission and Zonal business. The day-to-day running of the British Army of the Rhine was the responsibility of General Sir Richard McCreery, the GOC-in-C, but occasionally Brian Robertson was able to manage meetings with him and the Corps and Divisional Commanders. In March 1948 he was able to conduct a three day tour of inspection of the Rhine Army, at that time full of half-trained young national servicemen. There could be no shadow of doubt about the Army's unreadiness for operations.

On 17 November, the Robertsons left for London to attend the wedding of Princess Elizabeth and Prince Phillip, and five days later the London Conference of Foreign Ministers began. Although Brian Robertson had produced a memorandum for Strang on the future governmental structure of a united Germany, he was very sceptical as to whether the Russians would ever agree to it. 'Partition', he felt, 'seems to be in the air'. His own advice was that the Western powers should give up the pretence of quadripartite control and instead aim to reach a *modus vivendi* with Russia on certain matters like disarmament, and such matters as the allocation of reparations, posts and telegraph for which standing consultative committees could be set up[97]. Even this cautious and pragmatic approach was too optimistic. The Conference merely served to show how deeply divided the Western powers and Russia had become. The Russians recited a long litany of complaints in which they accused Britain and America of violating the Potsdam Agreement by setting up Bizonia and denying them their share of reparations, while Bevin and Marshall rejected Soviet proposals for the formation of a German government on the grounds that they would merely lead to the creation of an unrepresentative Communist puppet regime. The Conference broke down on 17 December amidst bitter recriminations.

The day after the collapse of the talks, Bevin and Marshall invited the two Military Governors to discuss future developments in Germany[98]. Both urged the introduction of a new currency into Western Germany, including the French Zone, if a quadripartite agreement could not be secured, but Clay was somewhat more optimistic than his British colleague about the prospects for an agreement with the Russians. Both also wanted to set up what Clay called 'a live working organisation' in the Bizone by 'adding slowly but surely' to the political responsibilities of its economic council. Brian Robertson indeed felt that a Bizonal Government should be in place by the summer of 1948. This was, of course, a major step towards partition, but Bevin insisted that Anglo-

American plans should still make provision for the eventual free election of an all-German government 'so that any irredentist German movement would be based on the West rather than the East'. Brian Robertson then went on to raise the whole question of French participation and suggested with Clay's agreement that trizonal talks should begin unofficially in Berlin. He hoped that the French could 'be educated and worked round'. Finally the two Generals were then instructed by Bevin and Marshall to have the details of these recommendations ready by early January. Ominously, Clay also raised the question of a potential threat from the Russians to the Western Allied position in Berlin, but he reassured Marshall that there were sufficient reserves 'on which to live in Berlin for some time'. These conversations showed how formidable the combined political influence of the two Military Governors had become. Marshall willingly conceded that anything on which they were both agreed 'would probably be accepted by the US Government'. Brian Robertson's policy of patiently maintaining his special relationship with Clay was paying dividends in that it enabled Britain to maintain her influence over events in Germany at a crucial stage, despite her economic decline.

Although the breakdown of the London Conference was undoubtedly a serious international event, it was of course in many ways a liberation for the Western powers in Germany. On his return to Berlin, Brian Robertson stressed at the press conference that 'the German people in the two Zones can feel that the new phase now beginning is likely to be a phase of progress and recovery'[99]. He followed this up by striking a new, albeit seasonal note in his Christmas Broadcast on the British Forces Radio two days later:

> The German people love Christmas day, and so do we. In many places at this season German children and British children will be standing round the same Christmas tree. May we hope that when these children grow up, they will remember that Christmas tree and so be an influence for peace between the nations to which they belong[100].

On the evening of Christmas Eve, he travelled down with a party of 17 to Ostenwalde where he was able momentarily to forget Bizonia, the Russians and the vulnerability of the West's position in Berlin in a relaxing atmosphere of carol singing, eating, drinking and cracker pulling with his family and colleagues who had become friends.

MILITARY GOVERNOR AND HIGH COMMISSIONER, 1948–50

In January 1948, the British Zone was still suffering from chronic food and coal shortages. It was governed by a swollen bureaucracy of both German and British bureaucrats, whom Arthur Bryant scathingly described as constituting 'a third and negative sex', which bred only paper[1], while its economy was dominated by the black market, the main medium of exchange of which was still the cigarette. The impending food crisis was averted by extra imports and a massive effort by the British authorities through Operation STRESS to make the Germans aware of its causes, the steps that the Control Commission was taking to alleviate it and how best they could help themselves. The Germans were inundated by leaflets, articles in the press and talks on the radio, including a school-masterly broadcast by Brian Robertson, aimed particularly at the black marketeers and the inefficient German bureaucrats[2].

Operation STRESS was, of course, only a palliative measure. It did not solve the deep malaise which faced the Germans in the British and American Zones in early 1948. Only the introduction of a new currency and the granting of a real measure of political independence could begin to do that. At the meeting of the two Secretaries of State with Clay and Brian Robertson in the immediate aftermath of the collapse of the London Conference on 18 December 1947, an embryonic programme for the political and economic revival of West Germany had at last emerged. By early January, it had been elaborated more fully and Bevin had been able to secure the Cabinet's backing for it. This cabinet paper[3] was a vital document which was to determine the British Government's German policy over the coming year. Its underlying principle was to stop at all costs the development of a Communist-controlled Germany. It aimed to create:

> a stable, peaceful and democratic Germany, if possible by agreement between the four controlling Powers. If, however, such agreement cannot be secured, then those controlling Powers who are prepared to cooperate must proceed so far as necessary with such practical measures as cannot be delayed any longer.

In practical terms, this meant that over the coming year the Bizonal organisation at Frankfurt would first be given more responsibility then, later in the year, there would be elections for 'German bodies exercising most of the functions of a Government and a Parliament'. Simultaneously, efforts would be made to associate the French with these developments, thereby in effect creating a trizone, and to carry out currency reform on a Four Power basis. If, however, agreement with Russia could not be secured, then a new currency would have to be introduced on a bizonal, or preferably trizonal, basis.

The first step in this programme was relatively easy to accomplish. In early February, the constitution of the Bizone was strengthened by the introduction of measures which the two Military Governors had prepared over the preceding year: the Economic Council was given power to raise taxation, a second house was set up representing the *Länder*, as were a high court and a central bank. However, the next steps were inevitably both more complex and controversial and were discussed in detail by the Foreign Secretaries of Britain, France and America and, later, Belgium and Holland, at a conference in London which began on 23 February.

Meanwhile, Brian Robertson had carefully analysed the flow of Cabinet and Foreign Office memoranda that had passed through his office. In what one Foreign Office official called 'an extremely useful and clear statement' he employed his usual staff officer tactics of unambiguously setting out the short-term objectives which needed to be secured before the overall aim of blocking the spread of Communism and creating a democratic Western Germany could be reached[4]. Thus, although he feared that it would be 'an administrative embarrassment of the first order', he strongly endorsed attempts to fuse the French Zone with Bizonia because it was obviously a 'political necessity' if an independent West Germany was to be created as a barrier to Communism. To overcome French objections to the renaissance of West Germany he advised that:

> . . . we should raise the discussion to another plane. We should point out that it is our intention to build up in Western Germany a system which is politically sound enough to withstand Communism and to take its place besides the other Western European democracies. We also intend to construct a system which is economically sound and which will enable the Germans to play their proper part in the reconstruction of Western Europe and their own country.

He enthusiastically embraced Bevin's plans for the Western European Union, which had been set up by the Brussels Treaty, signed on 17 March, 1948, and put forward a proposal which was ultimately adopted by the Western Allies for drawing in the Benelux powers for regular consultations on developments in Germany. He was quite convinced that any discussions about an all-German constitution would be 'a waste of time' and was already beginning to reorganise the British element of the Control Commission on the assumption that a government for Western Germany would be set up in Frankfurt, yet he was equally sure that Germany would eventually have to be reunited if war was to be averted. It was this desire to avert the ultimate threat of war that sometimes seemed to introduce an element of apparent inconsistency into his actions during the coming year. To the alarm of the Foreign Office, at times he went out of his way to advocate agreement with Russia. Despite his previous scepticism in December about achieving a currency agreement with the Russians, he hoped that the American plans for quadripartite currency reform, which were submitted to the Control Council at the end of January, would be acceptable to the Russians, and he had to be dropped a strong hint by the Foreign Office that a breakdown in the negotiations would be preferable to the acceptance of an unworkable scheme[5]. Brian Robertson was no appeaser in the negative sense of the word as it was used after 1938, but if he saw the chance of a genuine agreement that would defuse a potentially dangerous situation he did not hesitate to recommend it.

THE DEVELOPING CRISIS

As the process of setting up a West German state gathered momentum, the uncertainties surrounding the future of Berlin came sharply into focus. The Russians were already beginning to wage a war of nerves there by discriminating against non-Communist politicians and interfering with inter-zonal traffic. By threatening the vulnerable Western sectors with a blockade, they hoped to deter the Democracies from pressing on with their plans for setting up a quasi-independent German state. To help allay the fears of the West Berliners that the Allies were about to desert them, Brian Robertson authorised several low key measures such as setting up an Anglo-German club and arranging long-term cultural programmes, all of which had to be met by a miserly £10,000 grant[6]. A Foreign Office Committee chaired by Strang and attended by Brian Robertson, which met a few days before the Three Power conference in London began, was anxious that the Democracies should avoid an ostentatious show of determination in the early stages of the crisis only then to 'give way when the screw is turned a bit tighter'. This, it argued, would 'damn us in the eyes of the Germans'. Accordingly it was extremely cautious in its recommendations and did not rule out an eventual orderly evacuation 'if and when it becomes clear that the Russians intend to take drastic steps to force us out'[7].

By the time Bevin had the opportunity to read the Committee's report, the nature of the Soviet threat had been brought sharply into focus by the

Communist coup in Czechoslovakia which had occurred on 27 February. This both strengthened Bevin's resolve to keep a British presence in Berlin and also introduced a greater element of urgency into the process of setting up a West German state. When the first phase of the Three Power talks was adjourned in London on 6 March, Brian Robertson was instructed to proceed quickly with a study of how the French Zone and Bizonia could be harmonised and to set up working parties on the political and economic organisation of the future West German state. In anticipation of the signature of the Brussels Treaty, he was also asked to make arrangements for the closer association of the Benelux countries with the occupying powers[8]. The Treaty, by which Britain, France and the three Benelux states agreed to give mutual support against any aggressor, was theoretically aimed against Germany. In reality, given the growing tension over Berlin, the real enemy was much more likely to be the Soviet Union. The conclusion of this new Western European alliance, which had created a need for all its members to be kept briefed on matters pertaining to Germany, inevitably increased Brian Robertson's workload at the very time when the Berlin crisis was coming to a head.

In Western Germany, the Communist coup in Czechoslovakia had made the Allied task easier. It went a long way towards annulling the effectiveness of Soviet propaganda which, with considerable success, had been arguing that the Russians were the real champions of German unity, while the Western Allies were about to split the country. This argument had persuaded many potentially able German civil servants and politicians not to cooperate with either the *Länder* or Frankfurt administrations. In the battle for the 'soul of Germany', Brian Robertson was now able to exploit the fear inspired by the Czech coup to win over the West Germans. In an address to the *Landtag* of North Rhine-Westphalia on 7 April, which was later described as the most outspoken speech in Germany since the end of the war, he did not hesitate to urge his audience to:

> Come forward, determined to make the best of that larger part of your country which is on the right side of the Iron Curtain. The rest will come in time. We offer you our good will and cooperation. Don't be frightened by the mischief-makers who scream 'collaborators'. The time has come to realise that the interests of all Europeans are converging. Our needs and your needs cannot be dealt with separately for we all form part of Europe. . . . Make up your minds to stand together against these gentlemen who with democracy on their lips and a truncheon behind their backs would filch your German freedom from you[9].

Throughout the spring and early summer, relations with the Russians continued to deteriorate. Sokolovsky withdrew from the Control Council on 20 March and quadripartite discussions on financial reform ended without any results in April. Simultaneously the Russians tightened their grip on Berlin. At the end of March, complex regulations were introduced at a mere 24 hour' notice stipulating that all military freight trains destined for the Western zones would have to be specifically authorised by the Soviet military authorities, while Russian officials would check all personal belongings and documents. Clay immediately sought permission from Washington to order his guards to shoot any Russians who attempted to board American military trains, but Brian Robertson's attitude was more subtle. He suggested to Bevin that the Western Allies should be prepared to threaten retaliation on a global scale by denying Soviet shipping and aircraft access to harbours or landing strips within their control[10]. Closer examination, however, revealed that the vital lines of Soviet communications ran well clear of areas of Anglo-American influence. Clay was also beginning to talk in a bellicose way of forcing an armed convoy through the Russian check posts, but Robertson rightly pointed out that road traffic was still being allowed through provided that it was properly documented, and that 'a few tanks across the road at a defile' would be sufficient to stop any convoy 'quite apart from the fact that the Russians might get the best of the shooting match'[11]. Brian Robertson's inclinations at this stage were still to work out an undramatic *modus vivendi* that would 'get our trains running without too much loss of face'[12]. He suggested to Clay, for instance, that they should allow unarmed Russian inspectors to board the trains while still in the British Zone, but Clay was adamant that any appeasement of the Russians would merely lead to further demands, an attitude which Brian Robertson found 'most pessimistic and bellicose'[13].

On the afternoon of 5 April, a serious incident occurred which caused even Brian Robertson's iron self-control momentarily to crack. His children remember that this was one of the few occasions when they saw their father really angry and upset[14]. A Soviet Yak fighter, which had been performing aerobatics, suddenly dived underneath a BEA passenger Vickers Viking as it was coming in to land at Gatow. It then climbed sharply, ripping the Viking's starboard wing off. The Soviet pilot and the crew and passengers of the Viking were killed. Robertson and Clay immediately ordered fighter protection for all British and American passenger and transport planes. Brian Robertson then personally delivered a letter of protest to General Sokolovsky, who was 'ill at ease and on the defensive',[15] but did state that the incident was an accident rather than a deliberate attempt to interfere with the plane. This persuaded him to withdraw the fighter escorts but he had hoped that Sokolovsky as a friend would at least make an unofficial apology. Instead, Sokolovsky defended the Russian pilot's right to be in the air corridor and even argued that the Viking had rammed the Yak. He proposed a joint Soviet–British enquiry, which Brian Robertson rejected on the grounds that a four power investigation would be more effective.

In the midst of this 'electrical atmosphere of suspicion and mistrust'[16] Montgomery arrived on Tuesday 6 April without any fighter escort to talk to the four Commanders-in-Chief about the growing crisis in Berlin. He lunched with General Koenig and then in the evening Brian Robertson threw a dinner party for him to meet Sokolovsky and General Dratvin. According to one junior participant:

> Dinner is very light hearted . . . Monty rags Soko, Soko laughs back. No political talks and all goes excellently. Then Monty talks alone to Soko; at 10.15 they get up and are gone before you can say knife. The Russians are reserved but polite and take care to think before they speak'.[17]

On 7 April, Sokolovsky firmly rejected a Four Power enquiry, and blamed the Viking pilot for the accident. In reply, Kit Steel, the Military Governor's new Political Adviser, drafted a strongly worded note which not only rebutted Sokolovsky's accusations but announced that a tripartite enquiry would be set up. This draft was sent for approval to London where it was toned down by the Foreign Office and Brian Robertson was told to accept Sokolovsky's proposal for an Anglo-Soviet enquiry in a 'firm, calm and dignified' manner[18]. Bevin remained unmoved by Brian Robertson's subsequent protests because he feared that British public opinion would misunderstand the reasons for not taking up the Soviet offer of an enquiry[19]. The revised note was thus so mild in tone that Clay regarded it scornfully as 'an appeasement reply'[20]. The investigation opened on 12 April but the Russians refused to allow any witnesses to be called who were not of Soviet or British nationality. Consequently, on the following day the British withdrew and set up their own court of enquiry. In due course this confirmed that while the collision was an accident, it was caused 'by the action of the Soviet fighter aircraft which was in disregard of the accepted rules of flying . . .'. Many contemporaries believed that Brian Robertson's initial prompt decision to order fighter escorts for transport and passenger planes and contemptuous withdrawal from the joint court of enquiry so impressed the Soviet Military Administration that later, even during the height of the Berlin blockade, it never dared seriously to threaten Allied aircraft in the corridor again.

On 20 April, the Three Power talks resumed and for the next six weeks Brian Robertson commuted frequently between Germany and London. He flew into Northolt aerodrome on Sunday 18 April and remained in London until the end of the month for a series of conferences and meetings. One Thursday morning he had to drive up to Hampstead to see Lord Pakenham who was recovering from a broken Achilles tendon. While he was discussing the intricacies of the German problem, his ADC was left to amuse what seemed to be ' hundreds of children all over the house'. This same indefatigable ADC was also able to buy new polo sticks and blotters for 'the General' and miraculously obtain tickets for him for the popular musical, *Annie Get Your Gun*.

While the future of West Germany and indeed of Western Europe was being decided at the conference meeting in the Old India Office, there were ominous signs that the 'battle for Berlin' was about to begin. The consensus of opinion amongst British officials was that the Russians were not ready to risk war, but instead would try, as Brian Robertson put it, 'to undermine the position of the Western Allies and of the anti-Communist Germans by a series of gradual steps'[21]. Clay on the other hand was convinced that the Russians were ready to risk war, which he thought was inevitable 'within the next year or 18 months'. On 28 April, at lunch in London, he confronted Strang and Brian Robertson with an apocalyptic scenario in which 'we shall have to face the alternatives of war or an ignominious retreat from Berlin'. Clay believed that the Americans would sooner face war than such humiliation, although Douglas, the American Ambassador, was not quite so certain[22]. Brian Robertson's policy was altogether more subtle and cautious. Montgomery described him in April as walking:

> calm and collected through this highly charged atmosphere trying to keep the ship of state on an even keel and above all trying to keep General Clay and the Americans from crashing headlong into an open conflict; through being unreasonable, unwilling to talk things over[23].

In late April Robertson's inclination was still to negotiate a compromise with the Russians, although he recognised that the chances of securing this were now slim. His caution was largely dictated by the weakness of the Allied position in Berlin. While it was possible to supply the British garrison indefinitely by air unless the Russians actually used force, a land blockade would sever the economic arteries of West Berlin and expose the civilian population to considerable hardship. Brian Robertson feared that they would turn in desperation against the American, British and French administrations in the Western sectors. At this stage it was simply not deemed possible to supply the whole population of West Berlin by air. After his visit to Berlin, Montgomery succinctly summed up the problem:

> For instance the bulk of the source of electric power for the city is in the Russian sector; they could cut the supply lines to the British sector; this would stop factories, lead to mass unemployment, and cause unrest among the civil population; the Germans might well begin to ask us to go[24].

Small wonder then that Brian Robertson privately raised the question whether it would be worth keeping the troops in Berlin 'after we have lost the effective control of our administration'[25]. In a series of meetings held in London just before the Three Power conference resumed, Brian Robertson continued to advocate a cautious waiting policy. On 23 April, he told the German Department of the Foreign Office for instance:

> . . . that he expected the position to get considerably worse owing to increased Soviet pressure. He thought that the line we should take should be to decide to stay in Berlin in spite of any inconveniences, however serious. We should not, however, make any statement to the effect either that we should stay in Berlin at any cost; or if the Russians used force in order to evict us or if they made our position impossible we should go to war. In his view we should simply say nothing and stay put[26].

Both Strang and Robertson were of course aware that a humiliation in Berlin would be 'bad for prestige and for our standing with the Germans' and would also undermine Allied efforts to build up a West German state. Thus the longer defeat could be staved off, the greater would be 'the political and economic progress achieved in the Western Zones'[27].

This eminently sensible but unheroic line drew criticism, of course from Clay, but also from Lord Pakenham, who put his finger neatly on the element of ambiguity in their advice. Pakenham argued uncompromisingly that Britain should stand firm over Berlin. She had a special moral obligation:

> . . . to the three million citizens of Berlin (two million in the Western Sectors) whom we have taught to look to us on the grounds that we are the courageous and honourable champions of democracy. The same moral arguments which justify our occupation of the Germans' country compel us . . . to accept a special responsibility for defending them from external aggression and persecution.

He also disputed the argument that the loss of Allied prestige would be less the longer evacuation was postponed on the grounds that

> . . . the longer we do lead the people of Berlin to believe, as I presume we should, during the intervening period, that if they stand for democracy, we should stand by them, the greater our loss of moral prestige now and in the years to come[28].

Pakenham's memorandum was a powerful document. He was inspired by the disasters of the pre-war appeasement policy and impatient of compromise over an issue which he saw essentially as a moral one. His tone certainly appealed to Bevin, who announced in the Commons on 4 May that 'we are in Berlin as of right and it is our intention to stay there'[29].

Brian Robertson appreciated that if the Western Powers were to remain in Berlin, their 'great weapon' would be the support of German public opinion[30]. By early May, all the signs were that America, Britain and France had the backing of the West Berlin population, but this very support also bound the West more firmly to Berlin, because as Brownjohn, the Deputy Military Governor, observed, 'whole sections of the population of all classes have now committed themselves on our side and are known by name'[31]. A scuttle would deliver them to the tender mercies of the Russians and the East German Socialist Unity Party.

Brian Robertson feared that the conclusion of the London Conference and the announcement of the currency reform for the Western Zones would trigger a full Soviet blockade of Western Berlin. Towards the end of the Conference, he gave some thought as to how the decision to set up a West German government should best be presented to the Russians. He wanted to keep the door open, even if only ajar, for future negotiations. He argued that by:

> careful presentation we may not only deter the Soviet from taking some of the more violent counter-measures but we may even prepare the way for that ultimate settlement with the Soviet which is essential for world peace. Even if such a settlement cannot be reached for some years, it is still desirable to prepare the way for it[32].

In essence he urged that the Soviet Union should be informed about the London Agreements before the official communiqué and be invited to join the other three powers in establishing a united Germany with a single currency. To pave the way for Soviet adhesion, talks could be held either at the Council of Foreign Ministers or in the Control Council as to how the Agreements could be adapted to include the Soviet Zone. To sidestep Soviet delaying tactics he did however stress that the Agreement in its essentials could not be modified and would not be suspended pending negotiations. At the very least he hoped that this would make it more difficult for Stalin to justify before his own people the pursuit of a policy that might lead to a third world war. This advice was not heeded by Bevin who had the official communiqué of the Conference handed over to the Soviet Ambassador in London on 7 June only very shortly before it was released to the press[33].

The next few weeks were a period of intense activity, worry and strain as the three major strands of the German problem converged. Work on implementing the London Agreements was to begin as soon as possible, while plans for introducing the new currency into the Western Zones were also finalised. Both these decisions, as had long been predicted, provoked the Russians into drastically tightening their blockade on West Berlin.

The London Agreements laid down that the Minister-Presidents of the *Länder* should convene a constituent assembly not later than 1 September, which would then draw up a federal constitution. The Military Governors in their turn were to draft an occupation statute which would define the residual powers of the occupiers. Largely to placate the fears of France and the Benelux countries, a Tripartite Military Security Board was to be set up and an international Ruhr authority would allocate the coal and steel production of the Ruhr throughout Western Europe. The agreement was worded in such a way as to make possible the eventual participation of the East German *Länder*, but the strength of Soviet hostility to it made clear that this was a very distant prospect indeed. The initial reaction to the London Agreements in West Germany was for the most part negative as they were seen as a *diktat* and a camouflage for an extended occupation. To counter this, Brian Robertson invited the four Minister-Presidents in the British zone to dine with him on 14 June in his new residence in Bad Homburg, near Frankfurt, where he discussed the Agreements with them for 4½ hours. His main argument was that 'some common basis for the reorganisation of the West European system was essential' and that the price Germany had to pay for this was not excessive. They were clearly flattered by the way he discussed confidentially the details of the Agreements with them and he managed to assuage their worst fears[34].

The drafting of the constitution was to be a slow and protracted business. Of more immediate urgency was the introduction of the new currency. Since April, a tripartite technical committee had been working on the details of currency reform and on 3 June the Military Governors of the three Western Zones agreed in principle to introduce the new *Deutsche Mark* (DM) on Sunday 20 June, but the French delay in ratifying the London Agreements and then the belated discovery that not enough bank notes had been printed to give each German a 60 DM *per capita* allowance conspired to complicate the planning of the operation and necessitated a series of protracted discussions. On 16 June, Brian Robertson was asked to go to Clay's house in Berlin at 9.30 in the evening to help him finalise plans with Noiret, the French Deputy Military Governor. The talks, however, lasted so long that he had mercy on his young interpreter and sent her home to sleep. When they adjourned at 3am, the participants were so exhausted that they still had no idea what the French position was[35]. It was only on the following day, when the French Assembly ratified the London Agreements, that they were at last able to agree to divide the *per capita* allowance into two instalments of 40 and 20 DM. On Sunday 20 June, the new currency was introduced into the Western Zones without any incident.

Meanwhile, relations with the Russians deteriorated and their blockade of Berlin was progressively tightened. On 16 June the Russians walked out of the Kommandatura, the Allied Military Government of Berlin. By the weekend of 19–20 June, only some four out of an average of 18 trains a day were able to cross the Russian Zone to West Berlin, all German inter-zonal passenger trains had been suspended and the *Autobahn* bridge over the Elbe at Hohenwarte was closed. Brian Robertson and Clay delayed making a formal protest until the following week because they realised that the Russians could argue that they were taking legitimate, but presumably only short-term, measures to protect the currency circulating in the Soviet Zone. That weekend, then, was something of a lull for Brian Robertson. On Saturday evening he had to entertain that inveterate critic of the Control Commission, the MP Dick Stokes, who true to form proceeded to attack both him and the administration of the British Zone. However, despite the strain of the last few weeks, Brian was sufficiently relaxed to enjoy 'parrying and attacking back'[36].

The next week saw a further escalation in the crisis. Four Power nego-tiations for a uniform Berlin currency broke down and both sides proceeded to introduce rival currencies into the city. Although fraught with danger, as it could result in the economic absorption of West Berlin into the Soviet Zone, the Western Powers had been ready to accept the circulation of the Soviet Mark in West Berlin as the sole currency provided that it was firmly put under quadripartite control. The Western *Deutsche Mark*, indelibly stamped with a 'B', was introduced into West Berlin on 23 June. The Russians retaliated by introducing their own currency and claiming it to be the only legal tender for the whole city. So as not to rule out a future political settlement for the city, the Western Allies allowed both currencies to circulate together in West Berlin and to be acceptable as payment for fuel bills, taxes and rents. On 24 June, the Russians cut the last rail and road links to the West and halted the supply of electricity from East Berlin to the Western sectors. The crisis had reached a new and more dangerous stage.

THE BERLIN BLOCKADE AND THE AIRLIFT

The Berlin crisis was the turning point of the Cold War. If the Russians had forced the Western Allies out of Berlin, their plans for consolidating Western Europe would almost certainly have failed. While the great pol-icy decisions were made in London, Paris and Washington, Clay and Robertson – and to a lesser extent General Koenig – became the pivotal figures who had to cope with the daily and sometimes hourly task of cri-sis management. During the Schleswig-Holstein crisis in 1864, Bismarck once compared himself to a hunter crossing a marsh who never advanced 'a foot until certain that the ground to be trod is firm and safe'[37]. In Berlin, Brian Robertson's technique was not so different. To achieve the object of preserving a British presence in that city he had to probe the possibilities of talks with Sokolovsky, restrain Clay in his wilder moments from sending armed convoys up the motorway and monitor as a dispassionate statistician the weekly tonnage achieved by the airlift. As the Military Governor with responsibility for the small British garrison there and for the security of the tens of thousands of Germans in the British Zone who had openly identified themselves with the Western Allies, and whose fate in the event of a Russian takeover would be the firing squad or the *Gulag*, he had also to keep the ultimate escape routes open to West Germany in case of war or the failure of the airlift.

Over the next ten days, Brian Robertson, following instructions from Bevin[38], went through the motions of complaining both in writing and verbally to Sokolovsky. With an eye on world opinion he hung the blame for causing unnecessary suffering to the West Berlin population fairly and squarely around the neck of the Soviet authorities[39]. In Sokolovsky's reply, Robertson detected a glimmer of hope that the Russians would not persist in starving out the German population in the Western sectors of the city, but he saw no chance of re-establishing quadripartite administration. Indeed, he feared that the Russians might well proceed to integrate their sector into the Soviet Zone and set up barricades cutting it off from the rest of the city[40].

The idea of supplying by air, not just the Allied garrisons in West Berlin but also the civil population, was first suggested to Brian Robertson in his own drawing room by Air Commodore Waite, who had presided over the Viking enquiry. Both men then went to see Clay, who preferred the alternative of forcing a convoy up the motorway, but agreed to the airlift as a temporary measure, that would buy time and be more acceptable to the doves in Washington[41]. On the American side, the airlift began on 25 June and three days later had 70 aircraft on continuous service. The British were slightly slower to get going. On Sunday 27 June, Brian Robertson's house in Berlin was 'like Victoria Station with people pouring in and out'. He took Brownjohn, who had returned from London, to brief Clay on Bevin's determination to stay put in Berlin and also to broach the possibility of using Dutch and Belgian airmen. In the afternoon he flew down to Buckeburg to finalise instructions to the RAF. The Wunstorf base near Hanover was to be the main British airfield for supplying Berlin.

Brian Robertson felt that a workable *modus vivendi* with the Russians could only be negotiated from a position of strength. This could best be achieved by pressing on with the launch of the London plans for Western Germany and by building up the airlift to 'really sensational proportions'[42]. A start on the first part of the programme was made on 1 July when the London proposals were unveiled to the rather sceptical Minister-Presidents of the West German *Länder*, but of more immediate importance was the development of the airlift.

Primarily on Bevin's initiative, Clay, Brian Robertson and Noiret went on 3 July to Sokolovsky's headquarters near Potsdam. Bevin wanted them to find out more about Soviet intentions in the city. It emerged, however, from the subsequent discussion that Sokolovsky had been given no authority to negotiate and that the whole blockade was essentially an attempt by Moscow to prevent the implementation of the decisions taken in London. Responding to Brian Robertson's accusations about his callous treatment of the West Berlin population, Sokolovsky pointedly stated that 'he was much more concerned about 20 million Germans in the Soviet Zone whose economy had been disrupted by the measures taken by the Western Allies as regards currency reform and the decisions of the London Conference'. He continued to belabour this point throughout the meeting and there was obviously nothing that could be done in Berlin by the Military Governors to break the deadlock[43].

It was clear that only at governmental level could this now occur. On 6 July, the Western Allies sent a joint note to Moscow reaffirming their legal rights in Berlin, but stating that once the blockade was lifted they would be ready to negotiate on the future administration of the city. During the next few weeks, the world hovered on the brink of nuclear war. On 17 July, 60 American B-29s, which were capable of carrying atomic bombs, flew to Britain, while the Chiefs of Staff in London began to draw up mobilisation plans for war. In Germany, where all British forces were to be withdrawn to the Rhine as soon as hostilities broke out, Brian Robertson was particularly worried by the poor quality of the Rhine Army. He told Bevin that it did not constitute, 'properly speaking, a trained army and to put it in the field if a crisis arose would present very great difficulties indeed'[44].

Against this alarming background, it is not surprising that Brian Robertson returned to his original proposal for trying to square the circle by reopening discussions on the German question with the Soviets whilst simultaneously pressing on with the London Agreements. Before he flew to London on the evening of Sunday 11 July to challenge the mandarins of the Foreign Office, he was able to take a brief break from importunate telegrams and the statistics of the airlift. He flew down with his family to a Highland Ball at Lohausen, and then on the Sunday afternoon played polo, which he enjoyed so much that his ADC had considerable difficulty in dragging him away to catch his plane for London.

The next day, he handed over a lengthy memorandum[45], which urged the Foreign Office to make a radical U-turn in its German policy. He acknowledged that the struggle in Berlin was:

a test case between the Soviet and the Western Powers, in which prestige on both sides is engaged to the hilt. For Great Britain and the United States to retreat from Berlin would involve the abandonment to

Soviet persecution of tens of thousands of Germans who have with great courage committed themselves irrevocably to an anti-Communist policy and would have an incalculable effect on our plans for Western Germany.

On the other hand, he argued that the Allied position in Berlin was not tenable in the long term. The airlift had certainly bought the Western Allies time, but its organisation on a large scale in winter was 'not practicable'. Similarly, he maintained that the introduction of the *Deutsche Mark* as the sole currency in West Berlin was also not 'practical' as Berlin had a heavy deficit in its trade with the Western Zones and would thus prove 'a constant drain' on their currency reserves. There would therefore eventually have to be a political settlement unless the Western Allies were contemplating war. He believed that the great wave of anti-Soviet feeling sweeping Germany could be skilfully exploited to set up a united Germany which would be genuinely independent of Soviet influence. Discussion with the Russians, however, could only begin once Moscow had conceded a restoration of quadripartite control in Berlin and communications with the West were fully restored. He strongly emphasised that 'to enter upon discussions while the Soviets have the whip-hand of us in Berlin and can at will relax or increase pressure on us, would place us at a hopeless disadvantage'. He was also adamant that as a safeguard against Soviet machinations aimed at delaying the setting up of a West German state:

> The early implementation of the London decisions is essential, not only to the reconstruction of Western Germany, but also to the success of the European Recovery Programme. We must refuse to defer execution of our plans for Western Germany pending discussions or so to modify them until an agreement on Germany as a whole has been reached.

On the assumption that genuine negotiations could be opened with the Russians, Brian Robertson proposed that the Western Allies should insist on the setting up first of all of a German administration in Berlin with the four Powers only exercising very general powers of veto through a reconstituted *Kommandatura*. He conceded that

> The Soviets would be very reluctant to accept this; on the other hand it would not be easy for them to reject it on account of its obvious appeal to the Germans. A Soviet rejection would give us a strong plank for propaganda.

He then moved on to reopen the whole question of German unity and it was here that his advice ran contrary to the accepted wisdom at the Foreign Office:

> Some new approach appears inevitable or at least some device by which faces all round are saved. The most promising solution of this kind seems to lie in an adaption of the Soviet proposal already made in their propaganda for a general evacuation. It would be impossible for the Western Allies to concede total evacuation because once British and US troops left Germany, the Soviets would have their country at their mercy. There is no reason, however, why the armed forces of the Allies should not withdraw into given frontier areas, leaving Berlin and the main part of Germany to a single central government after which a peace treaty should be made on the analogy of the position immediately after Versailles. It would be essential that freedom of movement throughout the country should be guaranteed.

He thought that while a German Government would be inevitably sensitive to Russian pressure, 'a coup on the model of Czechoslovakia' would be most unlikely because of the strength of anti-Soviet opinion in Germany. Also it could be countered by Western troops in the Rhineland and 'possibly the Ruhr'.

The Foreign Office, while seeing some limited value in Brian Robertson's proposals for Berlin self-government, rejected his central thesis that Germany could be reunited on an anti-Soviet basis. The consensus of opinion was that the 'Robertson Plan' would enable Russia to demand a place on the proposed International Authority for the Ruhr. She would then be able to unpick the whole economic settlement so laboriously created over the last year. This was succinctly summed up by the Assistant Under-Secretary, Roger Makins, who called it a recipe for 'an economic "Munich" of major proportions' and added that 'the plain fact is that we have gone too far with the Western European policy'[46].

It was a decade since Munich and British politicians were determined to apply its lessons to Berlin. Significantly, when Anthony Eden, who was then opposition spokesman for foreign affairs, boarded Brian Robertson's plane on the way back to Berlin on 14 July, he brought with him a copy of Wheeler Bennett's book, *Munich: A Prologue to Tragedy*. In this climate it took considerable moral courage even to explore the possibilities of a negotiated settlement. Brian Robertson was not advocating a betrayal of those West Berliners who had stood up against Communism. He believed firmly that the Western Allies should do all within their power to strengthen their position, but ultimately he was convinced, as indeed were most soldiers, that the airlift and troop reinforcements could only buy time for a successful political initiative to be launched. In the jittery mood of July 1948, he provided reassuring, unflappable leadership in Berlin. Eden was clearly impressed by his 'firmness and calm common sense with which he confronts his multitudinous daily problems' and told Bevin that he was 'doing a wonderful job'[47].

On 14 July, the temperature was further raised by the Russian reply to the notes of the Western Allies. It refused to accept any preliminary conditions to be attached to the opening of negotiations and insisted that the Berlin problem could not be divorced from the German question as a whole. To Robertson, the tone suggested that the Russians did not want to fight, but would be ready to do so if challenged. As usual, Clay reacted by threatening to send a heavily armed convoy up the *Autobahn*, a suggestion which Robertson found both dangerous and unrealistic:

> It is based on the hypothesis that war will not result. Personally I think that it will probably start a war though I admit it might not do so. In any case, the convoy would probably not get through and even if it did, one convoy would not make much impression on the needs of Berlin[48].

Koenig, on the other hand, wanted to delay for a year the outbreak of war, which he regarded as inevitable, by evacuating West Berlin. Brian Robertson's own position was somewhere in the middle. He argued that the Western Allies must make an equally firm impression on the Russians by strengthening their military position, but should be ready to seize the moment to negotiate. To Strang he again rehearsed the alternatives:

> *FIRST.* To agree to negotiate on the whole German question subject to conditions regarding the lifting of the blockade.
> *SECOND.* To sit tight and do nothing. This will not be very agreeable and is quite likely to end in war.
> *THIRD.* To go to war now which alternative is difficult to contemplate.

He realised that the first option was complicated by Clay's attitude, but he did not think opinion in America was 'equally pugilistic'. Nor was he deterred by the fact that the Russians had rejected in advance the very conditions which in Western eyes were an essential preliminary for opening negotiations. He advised against any more notes which merely served to sharpen differences and instead proposed that 'the next contact should be oral and that its object should be to arrange discussions as to how discussion could be started'[49].

Brian Robertson continued to press his arguments for negotiations on Bevin and the Foreign Office. On 20 July, he told Strang that while he felt that the Western Powers could now no longer afford to evacuate Berlin, staying on indefinitely without a negotiated settlement would result in war[50]. On 27 July, he flew over again to London where he reported to Bevin on the situation in Western Germany and Berlin before attending a meeting of the Cabinet Committee on Germany. Bevin took the occasion to thank him for his memorandum of 12 July, but rejected its main arguments, although they did 'involve issues which required careful study'[51].

The following day, he had the chance to expound his ideas more fully at a meeting with the officials of the German Section of the Foreign Office, but he was unable to overcome their scepticism. When Strang suggested that the Americans did not want an agreement with the Russians, he was particularly scathing about American ability to formulate long-term policies and spoke of them much as, according to Harold Macmillan, the Ancient Greeks must have done of the Romans:

> . . . the Americans were generally wrong on the big issues. He thought it was best for us to make up our minds now, and then to attempt to persuade them to accept our plans. The USA did not want a war and their bellicose talk was unreal. Unlike the UK they had no machine for working out long term plans. It was therefore up to us to take the initiative[52].

Little of Brian Robertson's memorandum found its way into Bevin's own summary of aims which he drew up on 28 July for the Prime Minister. Bevin argued bluntly that the West could not afford to reach a settlement with the Russians by making concessions in West Germany or the Ruhr, but he did share Brian Robertson's views on one important point at least. Although he believed that the Western Allies should stay put in Berlin even at the risk of war, he thought that they should still maintain contacts with the Soviet Government in the hope that negotiations might eventually become possible.

Brian Robertson did not however change his mind. When, some two weeks later, he was asked for a report on the situation in Berlin, he painted, with the full backing of his top officials, a gloomy picture of a faltering airlift and growing economic dissatisfaction in the Western sectors[53]. He annoyed Bevin by arguing that 'the obvious conclusion . . . is that if we can find a half-way house, it would be better to accept it than admit to a breakdown'. In the meantime he argued that it was 'a matter of mutual interest' to secure a *modus vivendi* in Berlin which would keep the position 'in equilibrium' pending a long-term settlement. He was told that his telegram had been given a 'very limited distribution inside the FO at present' and he had hastily to reassure Bevin that while he felt it right to give his opinion frankly, there was no question that he would not carry out the Government's policy loyally.

Largely as a result of American pressure, the ambassadors of the three Western Powers did engage in exploratory discussions with Stalin and Molotov during August, while firmly insisting that the London Agreements could not be modified. At first an understanding seemed possible. Stalin agreed to raise the blockade provided that the *Deutsche Mark* currency was withdrawn from the Western sectors, and he appeared to accept the Western demand that the Soviet Bank of Issue should be firmly under Four Power control. At the end of the month, the detailed talks for implementing this were transferred to the Military Governors in Berlin.

Throughout the Moscow discussions, Brian Robertson was consulted closely on technical matters. Bevin particularly wanted a contingency plan drawn up for making the *Deutsche Mark* the sole currency in the Western sectors in case the talks should break down[54]. Even though the atmosphere in Moscow was at times conciliatory, in Berlin itself the situation continued to deteriorate to such an extent that the Foreign Office began to wonder whether the Russians had decided 'to embark on the policy of undermining the position of the Western Powers in the city by direct action'[55]. On 27 August, a meeting of the Berlin City Assembly was broken up by large hostile demonstrations assisted openly by Soviet sector police and even Soviet officers. This level of aggression inevitably cast its shadow over the coming talks with Sokolovsky. As Brian Robertson observed:

> Whatever safeguards we may secure about the quadripartite control of currency will be valueless to us if the Soviet refuse to recognise any city administration other than that of their stooges who have seized power by force in the Magistrat building[56].

Despite these incidents, the talks opened in Berlin on 30 August. When Bevin sent his detailed instructions, he went out of his way to repair the rift that had temporarily opened up between himself and Brian Robertson in the middle of the month. Bevin now seemed genuinely to believe that agreement with the Russians was possible. He told Brian Robertson that he had 'always had in mind' his advice on stabilising the situation by holding talks in Berlin and now 'the directive enables this to be done'. Brian Robertson was thus instructed to avoid difficulties over small points and if a breakdown was to occur, it should be over a real matter of principle[57].

The talks lasted up to 7 September, much to the irritation of Clay, who felt that they were useless. Brian Robertson as a master negotiator had little difficulty in sidestepping minor difficulties. At one stage the negotiations were threatened by Soviet air manoeuvres near the Corridor. Clay wanted immediate high-level protests made to Moscow, while Brian Robertson preferred to accept Sokolovsky's assurances that no Soviet plane would exercise within the Corridor. He observed that although he and his colleagues had learnt to distrust the Russians, they should be careful not to 'attribute sinister motives to them on every occasion'[58]. However, by 7 September even Brian Robertson's negotiating skills had failed to secure agreement on a foolproof system for guaranteeing Four Power control over a Soviet *Mark* currency if it were to circulate as the only currency throughout the city. The Russians also suddenly claimed the right to place restrictions on the flight of commercial aircraft into Berlin and to control Berlin's trade with the rest of Germany. The matter was referred back to Moscow, but Molotov's reply was so unsatisfactory that it seemed clear to the Western Allies that the Russians wished to prolong the negotiations in a never ending round of 'discussions of abstruse technical detail'.

The failure of the Berlin discussions led to a reappraisal of the West's policy and ultimately to the decision to take the issue to the Security Council of the United Nations. To this end, Brian Robertson attended a series of meetings in Paris. The mood of Bevin and his officials was both sombre and cautious and they were more prepared to listen to the logic behind Robertson's blunt warnings on the precarious position of the Western Allies in Berlin. Even Bevin conceded that a planning staff needed to be set up to deal with all eventualities, ultimately including a withdrawal from Berlin. However, he preferred to pin his hopes on the success of the airlift which the Americans were convinced could provide at least 7,000 tons of supplies a day. Yet again, Brian Robertson's sceptical mind cast doubt on the figures, which he feared were more the product of propaganda than sober calculation. He was later to tell the Foreign Office:

> The facts are that on US Air Force day, 18 Sept, when a very special effort was made, 825 US and British aircraft were received in Berlin and delivered 5,593 metric tons gross equivalent to 6,150 short tons. The latter figure is presumably the justification for 'approximately 7,000 tons'. I would emphasise that this special effort was only made possible by taking extraordinary measures which resulted in a falling off in figures for subsequent days[59].

Although he conceded that the Americans had 'achieved miracles of this kind in the past', he was still convinced that the airlift would provide no 'permanent answer to the blockade'. Nevertheless, with the failure of the Berlin negotiations and the approach of winter it was the only means the Allies had of supplying West Berlin and of maintaining, even if only temporarily, their position there. Brian Robertson brought all his legendary skills as a former CAO to bear on analysing tonnage statistics, which he rarely found sufficient, ironing out organisational problems and, in early October, helping to set up an integrated Anglo-American command structure[60]. The RAF was very much the junior partner of the American Air Force and Brian Robertson was anxious that it should be seen, if only to safeguard British influence in Berlin, to be making a major contribution. He had considerable difficulties in extracting precise figures for daily deliveries from the Americans. It was not until 15 December that Clay and General Cannon proposed that a figure of 5,620 'short tons' should be taken as the target for average daily deliveries, 1,370 of which would be the British contribution.

By late Autumn, the circulation of both the Soviet and the *Deutsche Mark* in the Western sectors was causing considerable problems and anomalies. Some wage earners were paid in the former currency, others in the latter, and the situation was further complicated because the unofficial value of the *Deutsche Mark* was four times that of the Soviet *Mark*. To head off the growing criticism being directed against the Military Governors by the West Berliners, Brian Robertson came round to recommending that the *Deutsche Mark* should become the sole currency in the Western part of the city[61], but as the United Nations had set up a committee of neutral Powers to find a solution to the currency problem, Bevin temporarily withheld permission for this move.

By December, morale in the Western sectors of Berlin was higher than it had been since the beginning of the blockade. On 5 December, West Berlin went ahead with elections for a new city assembly which produced an overwhelmingly anti-Communist vote. This greatly simplified the task of the Western occupying powers because it led to the setting up of a strong anti-Communist administration under Ernst Reuter that was immune to Soviet interference. Brian Robertson's satisfaction with these developments was tempered with the awareness that:

> . . . they have emphasised our grave responsibility towards the people of this city for finding a solution of the Berlin problem without throwing any fresh light on the way towards that solution[62].

However, he began to become more confident in the capacity of the airlift to sustain Berlin. During the first three weeks of January 1949, thanks to the exceptionally mild winter, the average daily tonnage easily reached the target of 5,260 tons. He also accepted the American estimates that by July 7,000 tons a day could be delivered provided that sufficient heavy American planes could be operated and maintained from airfields in the British Zone. Nevertheless, he did not see the airlift as 'an indefinite solution'. Although it would have to be kept going until a settlement could be reached, he was acutely conscious of 'its prodigious cost' and the danger that it 'might produce a critical situation at any moment'[63]. Also the very success of the Americans brought problems for the British whose organisation was more improvised and partly dependent on chartered aircraft. Robertson was particularly concerned that if the RAF failed to keep up its current rate of deliveries, the Americans might begin to demand a greater say in what happened in Berlin. Thus whenever there seemed to be even the remotest prospect of successful negotiations, he urged that the opportunity should be fully explored and the talks at least kept going until the West German government was set up. At the end of December, despite fierce opposition from the Treasury, he welcomed the report of the United Nations' Neutral Committee of Experts which recommended that the Soviet Mark should be the sole currency in the city. He recognised clearly that this would mean the gradual absorption of the whole Berlin economy in to the Soviet Zone, but it would allow the Western Allies to stay in the city and to protect their sectors. He felt that it was the best deal 'we could hope to get' and was convinced that any agreement with the Russians on Berlin would have to involve 'exchanging the West Mark at a parity with the East Mark'[64]. However, protracted negotiations between the Western Allies, the Russians and the Neutral Committee of Experts, on the technical details of the proposal broke down in February and in the end there was no option but to make the *Deutsche Mark* the sole currency in the Western sectors.

By the spring, the Western Allies were ready to maintain the blockade for as long as was necessary. Unexpectedly, in April, secret talks between Malik, the Soviet representative to the United Nations, and Philip Jessup, the American Ambassador-at-Large, achieved a breakthrough. Only in the later stages of these negotiations were the Military Governors consulted. Then Brian Robertson was emphatic that any revival of Soviet proposals first made in September 1948 for issuing Soviet licences for air traffic in the Corridors must be firmly rejected. On 12 May, the blockade was lifted and a meeting of the Council of Ministers was planned in Paris for later in the month. He realised, like everybody else, that there was little possibility of Four Power agreement on a German constitution. The most that could be achieved, he felt, was some sort of '*modus vivendi*' with the Soviet Government involving such measures as fixing an exchange rate, trade agreements and freedom of movement between the two Germanies, which would have to be worked out by the representatives of the occupying powers in Berlin. He was sure that the growth of a prosperous and secure West Germany would ultimately exert increasing pressure on the Soviet position in Berlin and the Soviet Zone. As was foreseen, the Conference rapidly became deadlocked over the German problem, but the Four Powers confirmed the New York agreement on lifting the blockade and agreed to future quadripartite talks 'normalising as far as possible the life of the City'[65].

The position of the Western Powers in Germany, and in Berlin in particular, was enormously strengthened by the signing of the North Atlantic Treaty on 4 April. Although no effective command structure was set up until 1950, together with the Brussels Treaty, the Organisation for European Economic Cooperation and the Council of Europe, NATO provided a workable framework for Western economic and military cooperation and was the wider context within which Brian Robertson was to operate until he left Germany in June 1950.

In September, the airlift, having built up a stockpile of five months of food and raw materials, was suspended. Berlin, however, remained a potential flashpoint. The Soviet Military Authority continued fitfully to interfere with traffic bound for West Berlin. In October, 1949, West Berlin was confronted with a fresh threat when the East German Government was set up. As Brian Robertson was quick to spot, by allowing the new state to create mass organisations, such as the Free German Youth and its own police force, the *Volkspolizei*, to whom was given the responsibility for controlling West Berlin's communications across East German territory, the Russians had cleverly camouflaged their position in Germany. They were now able to keep themselves 'ostensibly in the background' and provoke 'incidents of lesser or greater importance, possibly eventually a *coup de force* without involving an incident with the Allies'[66].

The success of the airlift, the determination of the Western Allies to set up a West German government and the quick consolidation of the East German state intensified the division of Germany. There was now no question of pulling out of Berlin or negotiating the setting up of a demilitarised Germany with the former occupying powers withdrawing into the border zones. West Berlin had become an outpost of Western democracy, which needed to be reinforced rather than abandoned. Essentially, Brian Robertson accepted this and in March, 1950, he was arguing for measures, which could be included in the Marshall Aid Programme, for channelling industrial orders to factories in West Berlin regardless of the cost[67].

MIDWIFE TO THE FEDERAL REPUBLIC, JULY, 1948–AUGUST, 1949

Fundamentally, Brian Robertson's attitude to a West German state was ambivalent. In the absence of any agreement with the Russians about a unified Germany, it had to be created, if only to prevent a Communist Germany, but its very existence would exacerbate relations with the Soviet Union and, so he believed, ultimately lead to war. At best he saw it as a temporary expedient which would initially strengthen the West at a time of confrontation with Russia, but eventually it would have to act as a magnate to attract the eastern *Länder* into union with it. To him it was never a substitute for a united democratic Germany. Nevertheless, as the Berlin crisis intensified in the late summer and Autumn of 1948, the decks had to be cleared for a possible war and the enormously important strategic prize of West Germany secured. Setting up the Federal Republic then was a vitally necessary operation, like fortifying a strong point in a battle.

The first stage in this complicated process began when the three Military Governors met the Minister-Presidents of the 11 West German *Länder* on 1 July[68]. They handed over to them two documents authorising them to convene a constituent assembly by 1 September, to draft a federal

democratic constitution and to recommend modifications where neces-
sary to the *Land* boundaries. The third document informed them that the
Military Governors were going to draw up an occupation statute regulat-
ing the future relationship between the German government and the
Western occupying powers. The process did not run entirely smoothly.
First of all, General Koenig, in a last ditch attempt, tried unsuccessfully
to question various aspects of the London Agreements. Then the
Germans themselves gave 'a very lukewarm reception' to the proposals.
The Minister-Presidents were wary of the Russians and of potential accu-
sations of collaboration from the Right. Adenauer, too, had been
orchestrating opposition to the proposed International Authority for the
Ruhr. To counter this, Brian Robertson asked his Regional
Commissioners to speak candidly to the Minister-Presidents in the British
Zone and explain to them the political reality of the situation. Over the
Ruhr, for instance, the British and Americans had no option but to make
concessions to the French if they were to win their acceptance of a West
German state. The Regional Commissioners were 'above all to try and
impress' on their Minister-Presidents that both 'restrictive and discursive
criticism' and attempts radically to revise the constitutional guidelines
would be self-defeating and play into the hand of the French who would
then insist on reopening the London Agreements[69].

Over the next two months, against the background of the Berlin blockade, Brian Robertson thought carefully about the problems of reconciling
Western Europe to a revived albeit truncated Germany. As a realist, he
became increasingly irritated with what he regarded as outdated or irrel-
evant attitudes in Britain and even on his staff. A scholarly but rather
pessimistic paper on the future of democracy in Germany written towards
the end of July by Robert Birley, the Zonal Educational Adviser,
prompted him into clarifying his own attitudes towards the new
Germany[70]. He was disturbed by the way Birley treated 'nationalism as a
vice and the antithesis of democracy' when the Germans in the future
would surely need some nationalism which 'differs little from patriotism'
to defend their own independence. In essence, he argued that a balance
was needed between an extreme form of democracy which would leave
Germany 'a ready prey to any powerful evil influence whether from within
or without' and an authoritarian police state:

> This means that, when we and our Allies are no longer in Germany to
> safeguard her independence, she must be given the means to safeguard
> it herself. That is the thought from which we should not shrink.

He urged that the Western Allies should exploit Germany's hatred of
Russia and Communism to anchor her firmly in the West. In fact, he used
the language of the European Union of Federalists when he went on to

stress that her 'nationalism, her efficiency and her strength' should be 'dissolved' into the Western Union. The corollary of this, of course, was that if Western European civilisation was to utilise German strength to defend itself from Communism, it must treat the Germans 'as fellow Europeans'[71], and, as he wrote two months later, stop treating Germany 'as the big sinner of Europe'[72]. German feelings and interests should instead be treated more sympathetically right across the board. Thus not only should the Dutch be persuaded to give up their claims to those 'snippets' of German territory on the coast, but the British Government should go out of its way to refer more sympathetically to the Germans in Parliament and the United Nations. He also thought that legal proceedings against Field Marshals Rundstedt, Brauchitsch and Manstein for war crimes should be dropped because they would reopen old wounds and turn those elderly men into martyrs. He defended himself from any potential accusations that he had gone 'soft' on the Germans by arguing that his approach was:

> . . . a strictly practical one. As you know I believe that we are committed to war with the Russians eventually. We cannot be choosers in such a conflict when it comes to allies. The Germans, the best fighters in Europe apart from ourselves, are basically anti-Russian and anti-Communist in consequence. They are indeed, I should say, more reliable from this point of view than any other Continental country . . . We have to choose whether to have them in the Western Club or not and if they are received with some friendliness and encouragement by the members, they may learn to respect the rules and to support the club. If we do not have them in very soon, we shall lose them to the old national and anarchic forces which have caused so much disaster in the past[73].

The next nine months were to witness the completion of three parallel sets of constitutional negotiations: the Germans drew up the Basic Law, or the constitution of the future Federal Republic, while the Military Governors drafted the Occupation Statute and began discussions on the tripartite fusion of their three zones. As a result of French opposition, the final arrangements for zonal fusion had to be concluded at intergovernmental level. For British Control Commission officials in Germany it was a twilight period in which increasingly they could only advise and act as an 'honest brokers' while they awaited the advent of the new German government.

The Military Governor was sharply criticised by Bevin for tolerating a brief general strike on 12 November 1948. Although it was directed against the German authorities, Bevin argued that it set a dangerous precedent for action against the Occupying Powers. Brian Robertson was so stung by this criticism that he offered his resignation. In his own defence, he argued that at every level consultation with the trade unions had taken place, culminating in talks between their leaders, Clay and himself. The meetings had failed and the only option confronting him was to declare the strike illegal, but since that would not have stopped it, he would then have had to order the arrest of the key trade unionists. Ironically, he then proceeded, albeit indirectly via Strang, to lecture Bevin, a former trade union leader, on the rights of the workers in Germany reminding him that 'the right to strike is a principle which we have admitted since we first came into this country'[74]. When Strang went down to see Bevin in Eastbourne, Bevin immediately went out of his way to stress that he had implicit confidence in Robertson. It emerged that he was more annoyed with himself for not preventing Ludwig Erhard, the director of the Economic Council of the Bizone and the future 'father' of the West German economic miracle, from dismantling the controls over the economy. He was convinced that this produced unrest by driving up prices[75].

The speed with which Erhard had moved towards a more *laissez-faire* system had taken both Bevin and Robertson by surprise, but it was difficult to reverse as it enjoyed the support of Clay. Initially, Robertson thought that he might gradually bring Clay round to his 'military socialist' point of view, but he soon abandoned that hope. In a comprehensive survey of the Bizone economy, which was sent to London on 1 January, 1949, he conceded that it was now too late to reintroduce controls which were anyway discredited by being associated with the Nazi regime and the immediate post-war period. Instead, he pinned his hopes on higher taxation, increased production and foreign investment in Germany cumulatively acting to hold down prices[76].

By the late spring of 1949, the travails heralding the birth of the Basic Law, the Occupation Statute and the High Commission, which was to replace Allied Military Government in Western Germany, were nearly over. On 16 February, a draft of the Basic Law was passed by the Main Committee of the German Parliamentary Council and then given to the Military Governors for their scrutiny. On 2 March, they reached agreement on a list of points involving the financial and legislative powers of the Federal Government, the powers of the police, the creation of a non-political civil service and the position of Berlin within the Federation where they thought that the draft was inconsistent with the original instructions given to the Council. Nevertheless, Brian Robertson was aware that there were limits as to how far the Military Governors could force their advice on the Parliamentary Council. He reminded the Foreign Office that if a real clash occurred between the Allies and the Germans, the Allies would have to choose between giving way and dropping their plans for a West German state[77]. Throughout these negotiations, his philosophy was generally to leave issues to the Germans where at all possible. He went out of his way to reassure Adenauer that the policies of a future German government would neither be crippled by the veto of any one Power nor would the occupying powers promulgate a 'spate of legislation' to hobble a future German government in the last weeks of the military government[78]. He was particularly irritated when François-Poncet, who was appointed French High Commissioner in May, went to Bonn while the Germans were still discussing the Basic Law there. He argued that that they needed a liaison officer, not a 'big gun' who might overawe them[79].

He was quite philosophical about the inevitable disagreements that would arise over the Basic Law because he was convinced that nobody, least of all the French, could really run the risk of a damaging stalemate which might kill the West German constitution at birth. In Washington, his optimism was proved to be correct when Bevin skilfully brokered a compromise on the Basic Law. However, selling this to the Germans was going to be more difficult as the revision by the Military Governors of some aspects of the Basic Law had inevitably reopened divisions between the Christian Democrats (CDU) and the SPD. The members of the Parliamentary Council were anxious to compromise, but Brian Robertson was worried that Schumacher, who was due to address an SPD meeting on 20 April, would make an inflammatory speech that would make agreement more difficult. He spoke privately to two of the SPD members of the Parliamentary Council and gave them 'pretty clear hints as to the contents of the messages from the Foreign Secretaries and urged them to work on them as their own proposals and not as coming from me'. He wanted Clay to announce the Washington compromise to 'take the wind out of Schumacher's sails', but Clay first of all insisted on delaying until 25 April and then, in an extraordinary act of insubordination, proposed to withhold the details of it altogether from the Germans. It took a personal appeal from Bevin to Washington to bring Clay into line. The amendments to the Basic Law were then accepted by the Parliamentary Council and the whole document was approved by the Military Governors on 12 May and shortly after by all the *Länder* except Bavaria. Brian Robertson had taken care to squash any suggestions of a popular referendum, which he feared would only reopen the whole question of a West German state and possibly provide Russia with an opportunity to influence the voting[80].

This trinity of agreements was completed when the Foreign Ministers in Washington also approved the Occupation Statute and signed the 'Agreement on basic Principles for Trizonal Fusion'. The election campaign began in July and voting took place on 14 August, eventually resulting in a coalition government headed by Adenauer.

HIGH COMMISSIONER, SEPTEMBER, 1949–JUNE, 1950

While the West Germans were preparing for their first free election since July 1932, the Military Government was planning its metamorphosis into the High Commission. Both Clay and Koenig resigned and were replaced by civilians, John McCloy and François-Poncet, the French Ambassador to Germany, 1931–38. Thus only Brian Robertson remained of the former Western triumvirate, with his enhanced authority and encyclopaedic knowledge of developments in Germany since August 1945. Seconded to the Foreign Office, he now held what was, in effect, a civil appointment and was no longer Commander-in-Chief. Nevertheless, he was still empowered to request the GOC-in-C of the Rhine Army to take any necessary measures for the maintenance of law and order in the event of a crisis. He was ordered in July, 1949, specifically to keep in 'close touch with McCloy and if possible to establish relations which go beyond the normal, rather spasmodic contact between High Commissioners'[81]. By establishing 'a special relationship' with McCloy, the Foreign Office hoped that Britain, through Robertson, would continue to be able to exert considerable influence on developments in Germany.

Some three months earlier, Brian Robertson had successfully fended off a virtual take-over by the Americans of the British Zone. He had warned the Foreign Office to block American attempts to set up tripartite control at *Länder* level, which he saw as an insidious plan to strengthen their position in the British Zone:

> At the present time it is a British sphere of influence and that is precisely what the Americans want to break down. Our regional commissioners are highly respected. Our *Kreis* officers have made a name for themselves as a fine body of men; British ideas are gaining ground. It is against all this that the American proposal is directed.[82]

Fortunately for British influence, a relatively innocuous system of attaching 'observers' to the Regional Commissioners was acceptable to the Americans. They did, however, insist on a weighted vote in their favour in matters which would involve the expenditure of dollars.

The two months before the elections was an immensely busy time for the High Commissioners elect. Not only did a considerable amount of Military Government legislation have to be harmonised, codified or repealed before the entry into force of the Occupation Statute, but the decision of the Parliamentary Council to make Bonn the provisional capital of West Germany ensured that they had to move their offices to that small university town. This involved ejecting the irate C-in-C of the Belgian Army and his Staff, which took several weeks and a top level meeting between Bevin and Spaak, the Belgian Prime

Minister, before they finally agreed to move out in August.

Inevitably, Brian Robertson gave considerable thought to his new role as High Commissioner and to the future of Anglo-German relations. Officially, he was charged with exercising, together with his two colleagues, the residual powers of the occupation. These enabled the High Commission to monitor and to intervene where necessary in such controversial areas as demilitarisation, reparations, the functioning of the Ruhr controls and foreign affairs. The High Commissioners were also ultimately responsible for the protection of the Allied forces and the maintenance of law and order in the event of the failure of the German Federal authorities to do so. In general, the High Commission was to act like a benign colonial power in the process of divesting the last traces of its authority to a subject people. It would listen, advise and occasionally reprimand, but hope not to have to veto.

Brian Robertson never ceased to remind his government that the real object of creating the Federal Republic was to win Germany for the West. He was haunted by the fear that if the Federal Republic failed, a new right-wing Nationalist government might come into being which, as in the early 1920s, would be tempted to look to Moscow in the hope of securing national reunification and ultimately becoming 'the dominant partner in a Soviet–German alliance'. It was therefore vital to prevent the Republic and its politicians from being seen as mere puppets of the occupying powers by doing everything possible to build up the prestige of the new regime. This meant, above all, that interference in German affairs would have be restricted to the minimum and when problems did emerge they would have to be handled 'with all the wisdom at our command'. He told Bevin to expect the Germans 'to do and to say many things that will irritate us. That is in the nature of the Germans and we must make allowance for the fact'[83].

A month later, in August, after the German elections had taken place and in the shadow of another sterling crisis, Brian Robertson, in a second memorandum for Bevin ruthlessly dissected the inconsistencies and errors in Britain's German policy, which had attracted not only bitter criticism from the Germans, but also from the Americans and both parties in the House of Commons. The essence of his argument was that Britain was pursuing a contradictory policy in Germany. The continuation of industrial dismantling risked alienating the Germans and undermining the central tenet of British policy which aimed at integrating spiritually, economically and politically first West Germany and then later the rest of Germany firmly into Western Europe. He stated quite simply that:

> . . . the political and psychological objections to a continuation of dismantling [war plants] . . . are so strong and operate so adversely against the fulfilment of our main policy as to outweigh the rather doubtful advantage to security obtained by removing them.

Thus he argued strongly for setting a deadline in the near future after which 'we should say, "nothing further will come down".' In return, the Western Allies would expect the full cooperation of the West Germans in the reconstruction and defence of Western Europe. On this latter point, Robertson was quite specific:

> The Western Powers are incapable of holding the Russians either on the Rhine or anywhere else in Continental Europe. A German army fighting on the side of the West is the only solution to that problem: there is no other. We should not regard this as a fearful if inevitable possibility. On the contrary we should be quite clear that it is an essential objective to our own security.[84]

The three High Commissioners designate met for the first time on Friday 2 September. The mood of the meeting was amiable and there were none of the sharp exchanges which had been regular occurrences when Clay and Koenig were there. McCloy's diffidence was more than balanced by the formidable experience and expertise brought by François-Poncet to the proceedings. The *Bundestag* convened in Bonn on 7 September and Adenauer was elected Chancellor on the 15th and then, over the following week, formed his cabinet. During this period of delicate political manoeuvring, Brian Robertson dreaded that the dismantling issue would blow up and harden reactions on both sides so that concessions by the Western occupying powers would be made impossible. There had already been a riot at the *Ruhr Chemie* Plant at Oberhausen, but that had been easily dealt with. The man whose reaction he most feared was Schumacher, who might 'at any moment come out with something quite as bad as that for which we put Reimann [a strident neo-Nazi nationalist] in prison'. To avoid this he asked his officials to stage an accidental meeting with Schumacher while he was visiting Hanover so that he could say something 'to encourage him towards some temperance of language during the coming weeks'[85].

The Occupation Statute was handed over to Adenauer on 21 September. In his weekly report, Brian Robertson made no mention of the now legendary incident of Adenauer pointedly stepping onto the carpet where the High Commissioners were standing. He was, however, impressed by Adenauer's speech stressing Germany's determination to earn the confidence and respect of its neighbours. The relations between the High Commission and Adenauer were frequently stormy, but in the final analysis both sides realised that they could not afford the luxury of a rupture. Consistently, Brian Robertson strove to mediate and conciliate. The turbulent atmosphere of these first few weeks is well described in one of his telegrams to London at the end of October in which he reported on a confrontation between the High Commissioners and Adenauer on the vexed question of dismantling:

Brian Robertson as a schoolboy with his father.

Term Report			Examination Report				
Subjects	Place	Remarks	Subjects	Marks	Max	Place	Remarks
English			Eng. History	140.	195.	2$\frac{nd}{n}$	Fair
History			Geography	268	310	1$\frac{st}{n}$	Very Good
Geography	1$\frac{st}{n}$	Good.	Grammar	91	120	2$\frac{nd}{}$	Fair
Grammar	etc		Spelling &	71	100	2$\frac{nd}{}$	Fair
			Dictation	91	100		Good
Writing Exer-	2$\frac{nd}{n}$	Fair	French	69	90	1$\frac{st}{n}$	Good
cises & Dictation			Arithmetic	70	105.	1$\frac{st}{n}$	Fair
Arithmetic	1$\frac{st}{}$	Good	Tables	37	70	2$\frac{nd}{}$	Fair.
Music	1$\frac{st}{}$	Good	Botany &	70	90	1$\frac{st}{n}$	Good
French	1$\frac{st}{}$	Very Good.	Common Things				
Latin		Good.	Music	61	70.	1$\frac{st}{}$	Good.
Total	1$\frac{st}{}$						
			Total.	968	1250	2$\frac{nd}{n}$	Good.
Conduct	2$\frac{nd}{n}$	Good.					

Top Brian Robertson's school report from Tanllwyfan,
August 1905.

Bottom Brian Robertson on the Wazirstan Circular Road
at 14,000ft.

**Brian Robertson in 1935, shortly before he went
to South Africa.**

Top Brian Robertson with Edith and their son Ronald
at No. 299 South Ridge Road, Durban, 1939.

Bottom Brian Robertson being presented by Montgomery
to King George VI at Tripoli, June 1943.

**Brian Robertson (bottom right) inspecting
the new soldiers' club, Royal Palace, Naples, 1944.**

Top Brian Robertson (left, wearing his hebron coat)
with the American Generals Gruenther and
Lemnitzer at Eighth Army Tac. HQ in April 1944
when Leese outlined his plans for the final
attack on Monte Cassino. *(Official War Office Photograph)*

Bottom Schloss Benkhausen.

Top **The Rolls Royce Phantom III and the Humber Pullmans
waiting for the morning journey from
Schloss Ostenwalde to Lübbecke.**

Bottom **Brian Robertson and Sholto Douglas
(second and third from right)
with other members of the Allied Control Council
and Co-ordinating Committee, 1946–47.**

Top Brian Robertson and Clay (second and third from right)
at Villa Hügel, Essen, October 1948.

Bottom Brian Robertson arriving in the Canal Zone on
24 July 1950.
(Crown Copyright/MoD)

'War Office? Sorry, old boy, can't possibly take any more. There's a drive on against redundancy, y' know'

Top A cartoon from the Egyptian paper *Akhbar El Yom*,
5 December 1953, referring to the recent victory
of the pro-Egyptian parties in the Sudan.
The caption below the cartoon runs:

*(The London Press said that the war dance was the reason
for the British defeat in the Sudan)*

Churchill: 'From now on, I want neither diplomacy
nor talks . . . I want you to dance like this man.'

Brian Robertson is top left, Eden top right and
Churchill bottom right. *(Akhbar El Yom)*

Bottom The cartoonist of the *News Chronicle* (19 January 1955)
depicts Brian Robertson's 'military style organisation' at the BTC.

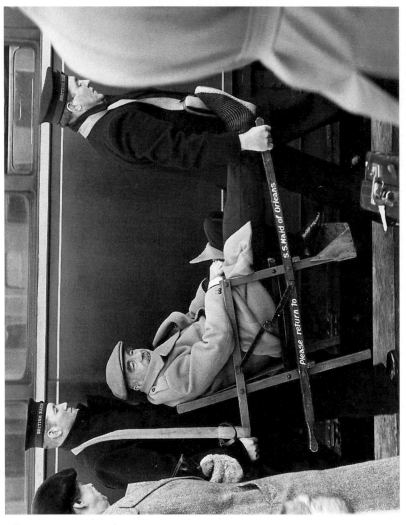

Brian Robertson returning home after breaking his leg in a skiing accident in January 1959. (*Daily Express, 8 January 1959*)

. . . Nothing was settled and no point conceded by either side, and the discussion produced so much plain speaking from Adenauer, François-Poncet and McCloy that at the end of it all they were reduced to exchanging assurances of their belief in each other's integrity and good will. I kept out of the mud slinging and confined myself to replying on dismantling[86].

The crucial issue of dismantling was discussed at the Paris Conference by the three Western Powers on 9 November, 1949. In a cogently argued memorandum, Brian Robertson convinced Schumann, the French Foreign Minister, that the Germans had neither the finance nor the raw materials to produce large quantities of steel and he also warned him that if the Western Powers did not end dismantling on their own initiative, German resistance would halt it anyway within a few weeks[87]. This helped to persuade the three Powers to delete over 400 synthetic oil and rubber plants and seven major steel plants from the dismantling list, although there were to be no concessions on Category One war plants. Key steps were also to be taken to integrate the Federal Republic into Western Europe: she was to become an associate member of the Council of Europe, to be allowed to establish consular representation abroad, to apply for membership of the International Authority of the Ruhr and to assist the work of the Tripartite Military Security Board, which had been set up by the London Agreements of 1948 to oversee the demilitarisation of Germany. In short, this programme went far to carry out what Brian Robertson had been advocating for the last year and a half. It was appropriate that he was in the chair when Adenauer met the High Commissioners on 15 November to discuss the decisions made at the Conference. As Adenauer's memoirs show, Robertson played a key role in explaining them and making them palatable so that they could form the basis of the Petersberg Agreement which was signed by the Chancellor and the High Commissioners on 22 November. Adenauer was frequently to quote Brian Robertson's assessment that with this agreement the West German people 'had broken out of the ring'[88]. He had come to appreciate Robertson's considerable political skills and a genuine friendship developed between these two rather austere men which lasted until Adenauer's death.

The successful creation of the Federal Republic marked a turning point in the post-war history of Europe. For Brian Robertson, too, it was a period of change and time to return to the Army. In December, he was offered by the new CIGS, Field Marshal Slim, the important command of the Middle East Land Forces. The German Department of the Foreign Office was reluctant to let him go, but Bevin was not willing to stand in his way, particularly as he needed a general in the Middle East in whom he had confidence. Bevin was however adamant that nothing should be said publicly until he had agreed on his successor and was ready for the change-over, as 'a man on the way out never cuts the same ice'.

During his last six months in Germany, Brian Robertson continued to draw on his accumulated experience and prestige to protect the still tender plant of West German democracy from the inexperience of its own politicians, the all too frequent clumsiness of the High Commission and the storms of public protest triggered by the dismantling policies. His weekly reports to Bevin regularly show him in his now familiar role of a calm, benign and usually flexible adviser. In April 1950, for instance, after the High Commission, much to the German public's anger, had first vetoed the Federal Income Tax Law and then on receipt of fresh assurances from Adenauer had withdrawn its disapproval, Brian Robertson went out of his way to try to repair the damage done by appealing to Adenauer to exercise 'greater restraint and greater trust in his relations with the High Commission'[89]. Again, when the Saar Convention, which was concluded between the French and Saarland Governments on 3 March, 1950, momentarily soured relations between Bonn and Paris, and led to threats that the *Bundestag* would not ratify the Republic's accession to the Council of Europe, Brian Robertson counselled moderation. He told Bevin perceptively:

> I doubt whether my advice will have any immediate effect. On the other hand I suspect that Adenauer has deliberately planned his tactics in such a way that although we [sic] will swim with the popular tide at the moment, at a later opportunity of his own choosing he will shift his own position[90].

At times, of course, it was convenient for Adenauer to shelter behind the High Commission. To protect the Republic, Brian Robertson was certainly ready to persuade the High Commission to make unpopular and indeed even harsh decisions. For instance, when the Poles tried to exploit an agreement for repatriating some 25,000 Germans who had relatives in the Federal Republic to send a further 400,000 Germans, Adenauer understandably was not ready to alienate German public opinion and stop this influx. Brian Robertson, however, took the initiative and persuaded the High Commission to send out instructions to the border authorities to let in only those whose names were on the original list. He was convinced that the Communists were hoping to destabilise the West German economy with a tidal wave of refugees[91].

The problem that caused him the most difficulty in his last six months in Germany remained the vexed issue of dismantling. He was under firm orders from London to complete the programme of Category One demolitions, but this deeply alienated German public opinion for little real gain. At the former Hermann Göring steel works at Watenstedt-Salzgitter demolition work was stopped in March 1950 by demonstrations which the police were unwilling to break up. Although Brian Robertson was only too anxious to avoid confrontation, the challenge to the authority of the High Commission was so overt that he could not ignore it. He refused to consider any modifications of the dismantling plan until the ringleaders of the demonstrations had been charged and the police disciplined for their passivity. Furthermore, he was ready to use armed troops to protect the demolition teams[92].

Plans to demolish the Graving Dry Dock, a former German naval installation, at the Blohm and Voss shipyard in Hamburg were even more controversial. The dock had originally been spared destruction in 1946 because it had been a useful berth for Allied shipping. Now, belatedly, the Royal Navy was demanding its destruction. Both the Hamburg Senate and Adenauer pleaded with Brian Robertson to spare it on the grounds that it could be converted to civilian use. The situation was further complicated by the proximity of the Elbe tunnel and the danger that demolition might crack its lining. In the eyes of the Oberbürgermeister of Hamburg, Robertson was rapidly becoming an ogre figure apparently ruthlessly intent on defending British ship building interests[93]. On the front page of *Die Zeit* he was caricatured as a dissolute John Bull destroying both Salzgitter and the dry dock[94]. Test charges took place on 18 March and when their results showed that the explosions had increased the amount of seepage in the tunnel, Brian Robertson quickly seized the chance to appeal to Bevin to accept the alternative plans for the dry dock. This was granted at the end of April. Similarly, once the Brunswick police committee had completed its enquiry into the disturbances at Salzgitter and disciplined four policemen, Robertson was able to accept plans put forward by the Federal Government for an alternative peaceful use of the plant with considerable relief.

Right up to the date of his departure from Germany, Brian Robertson continued to pen his memoranda to the Foreign Office, ease the task of the Bonn government, hold conferences for his staff and carefully watch the situation in Berlin. His last two weeks were inevitably a round of farewell feasts and visits, the grandest of which was a special lunch in his honour organised by the Foreign Office at the official residence of the Foreign Secretary at No. 1 Carlton Gardens. Then, on 22 June, came his final attendance at the Council of the Allied High Commission or, as François-Poncet phrased it, 'the last day when our colleague sits with the knights of the round table'. A week earlier, at a farewell dinner, he had paid Brian Robertson a warm and witty tribute:

> In the Trinity which we constitute – one in three, three in one – I would not decide who, Mr McCloy or myself, is the son or the Holy Ghost. But you undoubtedly were the Father. If we had to elect a permanent

chairman you would have been our choice . . . you have been present at
the various stages of the genesis; you were informed of every precedent,
of every text and never has your memory, your learning, your knowledge
of the problem been at fault.

Then on a more serious note he went on to say:

> . . . You never lost sight of the duty imposed upon us which was to
> restore Germany to normal living conditions, to divert her from the
> hideous excesses which led her to the catastrophe, to bring her back to
> the ways of democracy and peace, to restore her within a united Europe
> to a place which is hers among Western nations linked together by a
> common conception of civilisation and of the fundamental freedom on
> which it rests[95].

With this accolade ringing in his ears Robertson and his family left on the
following day from Cologne railway station. In Germany it is no exagger-
ation to say that he had transcended his role as administrator and become
a statesman of European stature. He was certainly recognised as such
when he was awarded an honorary Doctorate of Laws by Cambridge
University in 1950.

8

COMMANDER-IN-CHIEF MIDDLE
EAST LAND FORCES, 1950–53

Brian Robertson formally took over command of the Middle East Land
Forces when his plane landed in the Suez Canal Zone on 25 July, 1950.
His headquarters were situated in Fayid to the centre of the Zone where
he lived in one of the small cluster of houses inhabited by the senior officers and their families on the shores of the Bitter Lakes. His new residence
was comfortable and equipped with all the necessities for a pleasant existence, including a billiard table, but it lacked, of course, the aristocratic
elegance and dignity of *Schloss* Ostenwalde. He also had ample opportunity to play polo. Within a few months his team had become the most
formidable in the Mediterranean, even beating an apparently invincible
team, of which both Lord Mountbatten and Prince Philip were members,
at Malta in 1951.

The now legendary tales 'of how he ate major-generals for breakfast'
preceded Brian Robertson, but his staff and their families found that he
did not live up to his reputation as a 'man eater'. Indeed, Doris
Humphreys, the wife of his AQMG, recalled her surprise at how friendly
he was when they first met at a dinner party at his house:

> We duly arrived for dinner and were greeted by a charming man at the
> door. I joined our fellow guests. After a time I asked my husband which
> was the 'terrifying' General. He said, 'he met you at the door'. I was sur-
> prised and on sitting next to him at dinner, found him easy to talk to . . .[1]

The Middle East Command was responsible for the rather haphazard
chain of bases radiating out from Suez to Tripolitania, Cyrenaica, the
Lebanon, Jordan and Cyprus, as well as for the troops in the Sudan, the
Trucial States and all the British colonies and protectorates as far south as
Kenya. Furthermore, Brian Robertson had to liaise closely with the pro-
British governments of Jordan and Iraq and assist in building up their
armed forces. The hub of the command was the great base which ran
along the whole length of the Suez Canal, containing a mass of workshops
and depots[2]. In retrospect it can be argued that with the independence of
India and Pakistan, these bases were an anachronism as they were the
communications with 'a now vanished Indian empire'[3]. However, in July,

149

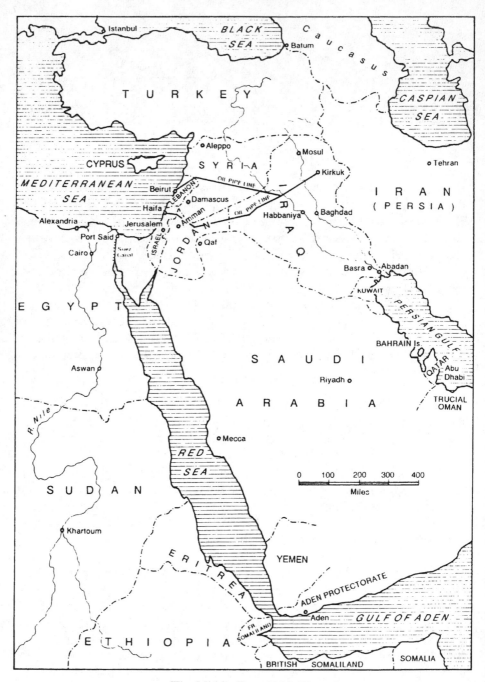

The Middle East, 1950–53

1950, only a month after the outbreak of the Korean War and with the threat of a major war with Russia hanging over the world, this was by no means clear. The role of the Suez base in such a war would still be 'to provide immediate maintenance' for British combat forces and their Arab allies and then to 'receive, equip, train and maintain'[4] the large reinforcements which it was planned to bring in from the Commonwealth to defend the Middle East against a possible Russian attack through Turkey and Iraq. The Middle Eastern Command was also ultimately responsible for defending the oil fields in Kuwait, Iraq and Persia, access to which in war was vital for the West.

The Americans saw the Middle East theatre as very much a British responsibility, yet in July, 1950, Brian Robertson had neither sufficient troops nor the equipment to defend it. Between Tripoli and the Canal Zone, where some 22,000 troops were stationed, there was only the equivalent of one weak division. In addition, five more battalions were scattered around the Middle East. In his initial assessment of the fighting capacity of his command, he was 'very disquieted' to find that a lack of sufficient technical, medical and signal personnel would make it 'impossible to start quickly the expansion of our administrative machine'. Much of the stores and reserve equipment in the base was 'miscellaneous unbalanced stock', which had been hastily moved out of Palestine when the mandate came to an end in 1948. Even more worrying was the transport situation: only about 60 per cent of the vehicles were 'battleworthy' and a much smaller percentage 'desertworthy'. He reminded Brownjohn, who was now back at the War Office as VCIGS, of 'the misery of trying to fight in the desert with an inadequate number of vehicles'[5].

Ultimately, these were technical matters that could in time be rectified by improved organisation and fresh equipment. A greater and more insoluble problem was the very future of British power in the Middle East. By the 1936 Treaty with Egypt, Britain was bound to evacuate the Suez base in 1956 unless an agreement could be negotiated with Cairo to remain. Successive British Governments had sought to bolster their own power in the region by persuading the Arab states to sign a regional pact, to which Britain, America and France would also belong, to defend the whole of the Middle and Near East. Once that was secured, the Suez base would effectively become internationalised and remain open to both Britain and her new allies. It was an excellent idea but not easy to realise as the Arab powers were bitterly divided amongst themselves and saw the Israelis rather than the Russians as their real enemy. The situation was further complicated by the lack of close Anglo-American cooperation in the area. There was no Lucius Clay whom Brian Robertson could assiduously cultivate and work through. In short, it was a command that would test to the utmost all the politico-military talents which he had developed in Germany over the last five years[6].

GRAND STRATEGY

In the context of the Cold War, Brian Robertson's priority was to plan the defence of the Middle East from a Russian attack. In September, the Chiefs of Staff ordered him to work on 'Operation CELERY', the purpose of which was to hold the Russians along the Lebanon-Jordan line[7]. His ADC remembers how, with his staff, he meticulously and slowly chewed over every single detail of the plan and like an artist or scholar became so absorbed in the work that he often 'withdrew into himself'[8]. Once he had carefully analysed the situation he came to the conclusion that the Americans were right and that the only way to hold the Middle East was to defend the 'outer ring' based on Turkey and Persia. He dismissed 'CELERY' as a 'rotten plan' and argued forcefully that

> . . . 'the outer ring' alone provides a continuous position with secure flanks resting on the sea. All other positions involve a large defensive right flank, covered it is true by the lava belt and sand sea, but not impenetrable. This is particularly dangerous in view of our shortage of armour[9].

While he conceded that the British could currently do little more than defend the Jordan-Lebanon line, he was convinced that the proper place for British forces to fight was in Iraq, cooperating closely with the Iraqi Army and the Jordanian Arab Legion. Its lines of communication and, if necessary, of retreat would be the Persian Gulf and the rail and road routes through Baghdad. He thus urged that local forces in Jordon and Iraq should be built up and that any available units of British troops should be pushed forward into Iraq in peacetime. He was also anxious that plans should be drawn up for Commonwealth troops to arrive in the Middle East in the very early stages of the campaign. Nostalgically, he thought back to the days of the British Indian Army and wondered whether the armies of the sub-Continent could still be deployed:

> Indian troops have been fighting in Mesopotamia at intervals during the past century. Pakistan is a co-religionist and practically a next door neighbour to Persia and Iraq. Can nothing be done to liquidate or sta- bilise the foolish Kashmir issue, and to induce one or other of these powerful states to play their proper part[10]?

India of course remained neutral, but ultimately Pakistan did sign a defence agreement with Turkey in April 1954. The Australians readily promised to send three divisions within the first nine months of war, but Robertson was less successful with the South Africans. In May, 1951, he flew down to South Africa, making a detour to stay in Durban to visit old friends and to play polo. He explained Britain's defensive plans in the Middle East to the South African Government and the potential role of South African troops within them. His efforts were, however, unwittingly made more difficult by Sir Frank Whittle, the pioneer of jet propulsion, who was reported in the *Natal Mercury* to have told Malan, the Prime Minister, that Britain would rapidly be overrun in the event of a war with Russia, but wrote a much publicised article stressing how defenceless Africa was. Apparently he was trying to promote plans for large-scale European emigration to Africa, but Brian Robertson found him him 'an unmitigated pest' whose efforts merely encouraged the Union Government 'to devote its resources to home defence[11].

A vital part of Brian Robertson's work over the next two and a half years was aimed at strengthening the defences of Iraq and Jordan. In January, 1951, he met a high powered Iraqi delegation in Cairo where he discussed Iraq's role in a future war against Russia. He emphasised that they should ultimately plan with British and Commonwealth support 'to keep the Russians out of Iraq'. Nuri Pasha, the Prime Minister, then presented him with a formidable list of demands including the speeding up of arms deliveries from the United Kingdom, the training of Iraqi officers and the provision of a battalion of British troops to be used to subdue the Kurds in the area to the north of the Ruwandiz pass, if they should exploit the outbreak of war to attempt to liberate themselves from Iraqi control. To this last demand Brian Robertson 'replied that he would have the matter examined but he made no other comment'. A few months later, he proposed sending a staff officer to Iraq to create the nucleus of a liaison mission which would work closely with the Iraqi high command in wartime. The biggest hindrance to Anglo-Iraqi military cooperation was the tardy deliveries of equipment from Britain. In July, when he again visited Iraq, Nuri Pasha asked him abruptly whether it was British policy to strengthen the country or 'were we content to see Iraqi forces remain static in their present state'[13]. Brian Robertson had constantly to remind the War Office of the importance of Iraq in the outer ring strategy and the need to reinforce the pro-British elements there. He stressed that the Army was 'the one sure stabilising influence and is pro-British' and that by building it up 'we are building up our own position'[14]. He also worked hard to strengthen the Arab Legion in Jordan under Glubb Pasha, who had been his contemporary at Woolwich, by supplying him with equipment from the Suez base, helping him to raise a second armoured car regiment and to find a good officer to command it. In September, 1951, two months after the assassination of King Abdullah, when there was a real possibility that the kingdom might disintegrate, he visited Jordan for a second time and sought to reassure Amman of the loyalty of the British officers in the Arab Legion and the continuation of British financial and military aid. He dismissed insidious rumours that Britain was too weak to play a major role in the Middle East and categorically reassured the Jordanian Government that Britain was capable of supporting her friends in the Middle East and carrying out her responsibilities there[15].

He used tirelessly to fly off in his RAF Valetta to visit the isolated British garrisons under his command and the disparate states for whose defence he was ultimately responsible. These flights were not always without incident. Once, over the Red Sea, one of the plane's engines caught fire and Stephen Anderson, who was his current ADC, remembers the air of calm authority with which Brian Robertson ordered him to inform the pilot of the incident[16]. On another occasion, his Military Assistant, Major Coverdale, committed a 'cock-up . . . of major proportions'. Brian Robertson had decided to pay an official visit to Nairobi and to call in at Asmara in Eritrea on the return journey. Instead his plane was flown straight to Asmara and landed in a sandstorm. There was nobody on the airstrip except a young half-naked corporal. Eventually an ancient jeep was found to take the C-in-C to the British Club only to find that the Chief Administrator had gone fishing! Major Coverdale remembered his own acute embarrassment as soon as he discovered his error:

> I went back to our small bungalow and told my wife of the disaster and suggested that she should pack her bags as, as soon as BHR returned, he would clearly either send me home immediately or refer me to the medics!

Coverdale's worst fears were not, however, realised, since Brian Robertson's reaction was surprisingly generous from a man who usually insisted on absolute efficiency from his staff:

> I met the aircraft on its return to Fayid – in fear and embarrassment! BHR descended the steps onto the tarmac, looked at me, raised his eyebrows and never uttered a word. He knew that I knew I was a complete idiot and apparently decided that there was no point in venting his displeasure! What a man! I cannot think that any other person would have been so charitable[17].

After each of these tours Robertson compiled an incisive memorandum on the military and political weaknesses of the states, colonies and protectorates he had just visited. In the light of the weaknesses he had perceived, he analysed their value to Britain logically in the context of her overall Middle Eastern strategy. If he believed that independence would serve British interests best, he did not hesitate to recommend it. Thus he saw 'no great military advantage' in a continued British presence in the Sudan and felt that it merely complicated relations with Egypt. In Eritrea he was anxious for the local Field Force to be built up rapidly to replace the British troops there. Apart from monitoring the activities of the Soviet Legation in Addis Ababa, Britain had no particular interest in Ethiopia, but he did nevertheless warn the War Office that under the Emperor the country was sliding into anarchy[18]. In the Persian Gulf, he was above all impressed by the phenomenal development of the oil industry but alarmed by its vulnerability to attack. In his report to London he wrote:

> Here lies the most glittering prize in the world for the covetous. Its loss to the free world would be immediately serious in peace, and fatal in a long war. The sudden access of fabulous wealth to these primitive Arab countries is very dangerous. They cannot absorb it, and the fate of Midas hangs over them all. In this situation cooperation between the Americans and ourselves is obviously essential and as obviously missing[19].

Creating an effective alliance system and a viable international command structure in the Middle East which would include not only America and Britain but the Arab states as well was a complex and, in the end, impossible task. Initially, as Brian Robertson was quick to perceive, such a system would have great attractions for Britain. It would co-ordinate the 'hitherto erratic activities'[20] of the United States in the region with British defence policies, ensure the fullest cooperation with Turkey and provide a means for internationalising the Suez Canal base. In October, 1951, Britain, France, Turkey and the United States agreed to set up an integrated command, but by the spring of 1952 the proposal was already running into difficulties because Turkey wanted to join NATO. At a stroke, this deprived the proposed alliance of some 15–20 divisions. This then prompted Robertson to question whether it was worth setting up an allied Middle East Command, which would

> . . . command nothing of any importance, except the troops of the British Commonwealth, and of countries sponsored by us. Is it really desirable for such a purpose to create a pentecostal military headquarters on which Englishmen, Americans, Frenchmen, Turks, Egyptians, Iraquis and possibly even Italians and Greeks jockey each other for important positions?[21]

He argued that instead it would be more practicable to persuade the United States to recognise the British headquarters as 'the interim coordinator of Allied strategy' and attach liaison officers to it. His ideas were given a mixed reception by the Chiefs of Staff[22]. After further reflection, he came up with a complex plan a few weeks later for associating the Middle Eastern command structure closely with NATO[23]. The thinking behind this was motivated more by psychological than military factors. He felt it would appeal both to the Americans for whom with the exception of

Korea everything which 'is not NATO is not important' and for the Arabs and Turks for whom NATO had a unique prestige. Even this subtle and elastic approach was unable to overcome the complexities of Middle Eastern politics and pave the way for a coherent anti-Communist Middle Eastern alliance.

THE CHALLENGE OF NATIONALISM

Brian Robertson and the military planners in London and Washington viewed the Middle East as a potential southern front against Russia and hoped that the fear of Communism would force the Arab states to cooperate closely with the West. Yet their hatred of Israel and the strength of Arab and then later African nationalism complicated this simple equation. To the Nationalists in Persia and Egypt and later in Kenya the main enemy was British Imperialism. Thus, as Commander-in-Chief in the Middle East, Brian Robertson was potentially preparing his troops for two very different types of conflict: one was an all-out war with Russia, the other was a containment of local nationalisms which could assume varying forms. During the years 1950–53, he had to face three main attacks on British power. In Persia the challenge came from a forcible takeover of the Anglo-Iranian Oil Company with accompanying threats to its British personnel by a nationalist government led by Dr Musaddiq; in Egypt the nationalists parties focused their resentment on the British occupation of the Canal Zone; while in Kenya opposition took the form of a protracted guerrilla war against the British settlers and administration.

The Persian Oil Crisis
In the late summer of 1950, the Chiefs of Staff in London asked the Commanders-in-Chief in the Middle East to draw up plans for the defence of the vulnerable oil fields in southern Persia against a possible Russian attack. Over the next few months, the threat materialised, not from the Russians but from the Persians themselves. On 26 December, 1950, the Persian Government, on the advice of its Parliamentary Oil Committee, whose chairman was Musaddiq, rejected the Supplementary Agreement which it had signed with the Anglo-Persian Oil Company in July[24]. The crisis escalated when Musaddiq, whose avowed intention was to nationalise the company, became prime minister in March, 1951. Over the next six months, the Commanders-in-Chief at Fayid were bombarded with constantly changing demands for contingency plans for either seizing the whole of the south-western Persian oil fields, or just the refineries on the island of Abadan or for evacuating the British personnel of the Anglo-Iranian Oil Company. Appropriately, this last operation was to be called 'Operation MIDGET'. Brian Robertson, as Commander-in-Chief, was

not involved in the detailed military planning. This was coordinated by his Chief of Staff, General Packard, but together with the naval and air commanders he was responsible for liaising with London and ensuring that sufficient equipment and reinforcements were sent to execute the plans drawn up by the 1st Division, which was to carry out the operations. Although the relevant records are still closed, it is also likely that when he met the Iraqi Prime Minister, the Minister of Defence and the Prince Regent on 9 July, he discussed plans for using the British air base at Shaiba and the port of Basra as staging posts for troops en route to Abadan.

On 19 June, when the Persian Government abruptly broke off negotiations with the Anglo-Iranian Oil Company, Fayid was warned that the prospects of putting MIDGET into operation had significantly increased. The Cabinet Committee on Persia also asked the War Office to have its plans ready for seizing Abadan and for holding it for an 'indefinite period'[25]. Thus when General Packard flew over to London on 29 June to brief the Chiefs of Staff on MIDGET, he was told, much to his surprise, that the forces used for MIDGET might well have to stay on in Abadan 'in certain circumstances – admittedly most unlikely circumstances'. The Commanders-in-Chief at Fayid, who had hitherto 'resolutely set their faces against any prolongation of MIDGET' had now to ask their staff to work out yet another variation of the original plans[26]. Initially, the new plan was to have been given the decidedly unmartial name of DANDRUFF but this was quickly dropped, apparently on the personal intervention of Brian Robertson, and the more appropriate name, BUCCANEER, was used. On 2 July, the troops were put on a six hour notice for MIDGET, or BUCCANEER 1 as it was now to be called[27], and there began a long period of uncertainty which lasted through to early October when the task force was finally stood down. Brian Robertson, who always believed strongly in briefing his troops on the importance of an operation, was concerned about the potential effect on their morale of the confused reports on the oil crisis in the British press. On 4 July he complained to the VCIGS:

> The trend of the news, as I read it in my clippings from English newspapers, is that nothing very much is happening. Mussadeq [sic] is unyielding but may be thrown out, and the most serious thing that they have to say is that the Persians will not supply the [HMS] *Mauritius* with ice.

On the strength of what he had heard from the General Manager of the Anglo-Iranian Oil Company, he argued that this was obviously inaccurate:

> I am not suggesting that the press should be encouraged to tell lies, but I do think that they ought to be persuaded to paint things in their full colours rather than tone them down all the time. All news is propaganda

in a sense and I submit that we ought at this time to be building up our case and not belittling it[28].

Brownjohn was sympathetic but the Foreign Office was rather more sceptical and pointed out in August that it would be undesirable to increase popular pressure for military action when the Government was still unwilling to authorise it.

On 18 July, the Cabinet decided at last to authorise the Commanders-in-Chief to prepare to implement BUCCANEER with the ultimate intention of landing troops on Abadan to protect the withdrawal of the British staff from the oil fields on the mainland. The task force was put at three hour notice to move and Brian Robertson, who was now anxious to see the operation carried out rapidly, was already making plans to visit Abadan. Then, unexpectedly, the Americans, who were attempting to mediate between Musaddiq and the Anglo-Iranian Oil company, asked for a postponement of the operations because they thought that they were at last making progress towards an agreement[29]. In the middle of the night, Attlee personally phoned Brian Robertson, who had to be woken up by his ADC, to tell him that BUCCANEER was to be delayed for a further 24 hours. He received the information in his usual calm and unflappable manner[30]. Further orders from London postponed the operation indefinitely, although the troops were still kept on a 72 hour alert.

Throughout August and most of September, BUCCANEER was worked on and improved until Brian Robertson and his staff were quite convinced that it would succeed. The most controversial aspect of their plan was the proposal to occupy a ten-mile perimeter on the mainland so as to protect the troops on Abadan from Persian artillery. Although this was rejected by the Chiefs of Staff, GHQ, MELF was given authority to patrol the area 'on a considerable scale', should operations commence[31].

Briefly, at the end of September it looked as if BUCCANEER might still have to be implemented when Musaddiq ordered all the Anglo-Iranian Oil Company's staff to quit Persia. The troops were duly put on a six hour notice with effect from midnight 27/28 September, but the British Cabinet decided instead to refer the whole problem to the United Nations and, on 3 October, the company's staff were ferried out ignominiously by Persian naval launches to HMS *Mauritius*. The following day, the troops were finally stood down.

EGYPT AND THE CANAL ZONE, 1950–52

Short of an all out war with Russia, the most intractable problem facing the British in the Middle East was the future of their base in the Canal

Zone. In 1936, at a time when Egypt needed defending against Fascist Italy, the British Government had signed a 20 year Treaty with Cairo, which allowed Britain to station military forces along the Suez Canal. However, as soon as the Axis powers were defeated, the Egyptians started to press for an early revision of the Treaty, and in 1949 the Nationalist Party, the Wafd, which had led the campaign to expel the British, regained power. Once the British had withdrawn from the Canal Zone, the Egyptians were, theoretically at least, ready to consider some sort of defence agreement, but the British were only ready to move out the bulk of their troops after they had negotiated an agreement which ensured that the base could be quickly reactivated in war. As Robertson succinctly put it, the Egyptians had to accept 'the principle of joint arrangements in peace for joint defence in war'[32]. The outbreak of the Korean War which, so it seemed, might at any point escalate into a world war, made the Army even more reluctant to leave Egypt and face the disruption that this would involve. The future of the Suez base was thus a complex politico-military problem to which there was no magic solution.

Together with his fellow Commanders-in-Chief, Air Marshal Sir John Baker and Rear Admiral Campbell, Brian Robertson was initially highly critical of the pessimistic attitude to an Anglo-Egyptian agreement which was adopted by Sir Ralph Stevenson, the Ambassador in Cairo. Stevenson argued that given the internal situation in Egypt, the only realistic option open to the British Government was to negotiate an agreement with the Egyptians that would enable it at best to erect only 'a militarily weak façade of defence in the south-eastern Mediterranean'[33]. In other words, the British would have to clear out of Egypt and hope that Cairo would allow them back in time of war. Brian Robertson felt that this was positively defeatist, although by the summer of 1953 he himself was to move much closer to Stevenson's position. Optimistically, he believed that the Egyptian élite could be educated in the realities of the Cold War and convinced that their country 'stands at the moment in deadly peril'. When this lesson had sunk home, he felt that a joint approach with America, France and the NATO powers should be made to Cairo, laying down certain basic principles to the effect that an Anglo-Egyptian defence council should be set up and that in war the Egyptian Army would need to be strengthened with substantial reinforcements. This last factor, he argued, above all necessitated Britain's retention of the base. Once this was accepted, 'many things might be possible' like drastically reducing the number of British troops in Egypt and re-equiping the Egyptian Army[34]. With his responsibilities for defending the whole of the Middle East, he was acutely conscious that the Nile Delta and Suez Canal formed its 'solar plexus' which could only be adequately defended by troops in Egypt. It was thus axiomatic to him that 'the evacuation of Egypt in peace would place serious restraint upon our ability to defend the Middle East in war'[35].

Two months later, he was less optimistic about the chances for a settlement and began to fear that the Wafdists were deliberately fermenting trouble to distract the attention of the Egyptian people from 'their own short comings and iniquities'. In November, as a consequence of the increase in the number of demonstrations and defamatory articles in the Egyptian press, he began seriously to think about what measures he would have to adopt in the event of an upsurge of terrorism. These varied from relatively simple measures, such as placing certain areas out of bounds to the troops, to arresting Egyptian officials and ultimately even assuming direct control of the whole Canal Zone. He still recommended negotiations, but he was adamant that Britain should stay put until a successful agreement had been reached [36]. Bevin, however, when he met the Chiefs of Staff on 8 December made it very clear that he wanted a quick settlement, and that after 1956, when the Anglo-Egyptian Treaty came to an end, he was ready to transfer responsibility for guarding and maintaining the base to the Egyptians, retaining only the right for periodic inspection by British experts[37]. The Chiefs of Staff, joined by Brian Robertson and Air Marshal Baker, were duly invited to study these proposals in greater detail. Robertson again stressed the overriding importance of the Suez base in both peace and war and criticised Bevin's proposals for its periodic inspection by British experts. He pointed out that

> There was more to the running of a base than looking after sheds and ammunition dumps. For example, in order that the present base could function effectively in the early stages of a campaign, it was necessary to maintain long lines of communication involving the maintenance of underground cables, etc. Past experience had shown that the Egyptians were incapable of the degree of administrative ability that would be required. Any offer, therefore, that was made by them to look after the base was in his opinion of almost negligible consequence[38].

The 'logical military conclusion' was, of course, to stay in the base come what may after 1956, but he conceded that in those circumstances the Egyptians would have a strong case in the United Nations and no British Government would risk placing itself so blatantly in the wrong. In practice then, he realised that the troops would have to move out by 1956 and GHQ MELF move to Malta, Cyrenaica or Aden, the organisation of which would be 'a tremendous task'. This conclusion was endorsed by Slim and the other Chiefs of Staff.

In January, 1951, there was a brief explosion of violence in the Canal Zone when a military signal box and the filtration plant in Kafr Abdu, which purified the drinking water for the British garrison, were fired upon by Egyptian police or auxiliaries. British tanks had to be used to clear them out from the neighbouring houses. This action was followed by an outbreak of rioting in Suez. The main Coptic church was attacked, its unfortunate caretaker murdered, and his body dragged through the streets and burnt. The violence then rapidly subsided and an uneasy peace returned to the Canal Zone. It was a warning of the troubles to come.

Over the next ten months, the British Government put forward a series of initiatives aimed at finding a solution to the future of the Canal Base. In April, the Government proposed that the base should be run by a joint Anglo-Egyptian control board and kept in working order by British civilian technicians. This was quickly rejected, as were two other proposals in August and October for guaranteeing the security of the Canal Zone. These involved setting up an integrated Middle Eastern Command and a regional pact, to which America, France and Turkey as well as Britain and Egypt would all belong. Essentially, the Egyptians suspected that all these schemes were merely elaborate attempts to perpetuate British control of the Canal. It is possible that if the British had handed over to Cairo the sovereignty of the Sudan, which theoretically they ruled as a condominium with Egypt, although in practice they administered it as if it were a purely British protectorate, the deadlock might have been broken, but this the British were unwilling to do until they had consulted the wishes of the Sudanese. Brian Robertson was convinced that if the Sudanese were offered independence quickly, the pro-Egyptian party would be routed and at the same time a formidable irritant to Anglo-Egyptian relations would ultimately be removed[39].

The complete deadlock in negotiations over the future of the base, combined with Britain's humiliation at the hands of Musaddiq, encouraged the Egyptian Government unilaterally to abrogate the 1936 Treaty and to declare a union with the Sudan under the Egyptian crown on 15 October. This was immediately followed by a wave of violence. British vehicles were stoned, a water pipe damaged and an officer stabbed in Ismailia. Brian Robertson was also confronted for the second time in his career with the challenge of a blockade. The civil telephone system and the Egyptian state railways were closed to British military personnel and most Egyptian labour was withdrawn from the Zone. Militarily and politically, however, the situation was fundamentally different from the Berlin blockade of 1948. The British forces were rapidly strengthened by flying in over three brigades. Far from being hostages to the Egyptians, the British were potentially capable of occupying Cairo and Alexandria. The real problems facing Brian Robertson and his former deputy from Germany, General Erskine, now the GOC of the Canal Zone garrison, were political not military. Neither the Egyptian officials nor most of the population of over 300,000 in the Zone, either from conviction or as a result of intimidation, would cooperate with the British authorities. Unlike the situation in West Berlin the British could employ decisive military force but could not win over the people themselves. Consequently terrorists from the Muslim Ikhwan movement or the Egyptian Socialist Party were easily able to infiltrate across the border where their activities were connived at by the local police.

The powers to arrest terrorist ringleaders and disarm non-cooperative Egyptian police officers and officials were given to Robertson by the British Government in early December. But he also needed sufficient powers to import or retain 'any resource in persons or goods' necessary for the security of the Army and the right to control communications. These powers, he felt, should be implemented through a small civil affairs office set up in the Zone. As an expert who had four years experience of military government in Germany, he was opposed to any official declaration of military government, as that would involve the assumption of complete economic, political and fiscal responsibility for the Canal Zone, which 'would be almost intolerable to us and should only be accepted if complete anarchy is the only alternative'[40]. The Foreign Office was rather sceptical of the distinction Brian Robertson was drawing between his proposals and military government proper. One official minuted that 'whatever we call it, it will sooner or later be military government if we have to take such steps as setting up courts and providing substitutes for Egyptian administration in various fields'[41]. There was no doubt that military government, with its expensive and open-ended responsibilities, was clearly a real possibility and the Cabinet decided in December to set up an inter-departmental committee to prepare for it.

Until February, 1952, the terrorist threat continued to increase and the scale of military measures needed to combat it seemed inexorably to lead to an ever deeper British involvement in Egyptian affairs and possibly even full-scale war, culminating in the occupation of Cairo and the Delta towns. General Erskine was responsible for the counter-insurgency campaign in the Zone, but given the potentially politically explosive repercussions of many of the measures he had to take, he needed constantly to refer back to his C-in-C, who in his turn remained in close touch with London. The water filtration plants, without which the water in the Zone could not be made drinkable, were an obvious target for the terrorists. On 8 December, Erskine improved the security at the plant at the village of Kafr Abdu near Suez by demolishing some 107 houses. The army offered immediate financial compensation to the Egyptian Government to build new houses but the incident inevitably caused considerable resentment and bitterness which Cairo neatly exploited for propaganda purposes[42]. Brian Robertson fully supported Erskine and to help refute criticism in London that houses were destroyed unnecessarily, he sent a report with aerial photographs showing the road to the filtration plant. In retrospect, it has been argued that the whole incident was 'a monumental blunder'[43], but as Sir Thomas Rapp, the head of the Middle East Office recognised, the Army faced a real dilemma:

. . . either some militarily expedient action has to be undertaken without delay although it may evoke a storm of protest, and seemingly still further vitiate the atmosphere, or alternatively it has to be postponed to a more politically convenient season with the attendant risk that lives may be unnecessarily sacrificed and a larger operation eventually necessary at a time no more propitious[44].

On 16 January, the dangers of a clash between the British and Egyptian armies significantly increased when, as a result of attacks on British vehicles on the Cairo-Ismailia road, British troops moved over the Sweet Water Canal and thus beyond the frontiers of the Zone. The Egyptian military authorities were informed and, as Brian Robertson told the Ministry of Defence, 'detailed dispositions' were being studied and care being taken 'that we do not take up such positions, that owing to the proximity of houses and other cover, lead us to a desire to go further forward'[45]. A week later, when British forces were flushing terrorists out of Ismailia, they were given what amounted to an ultimatum by the Egyptian Government and told that if they did not stop, 'forcible measures', would be taken against them. Brian Robertson reckoned that this probably meant that the civil police would be given orders to intervene in Ismailia or else that reprisals would be taken against British civilians in Cairo, but he also feared that there was 'a remote responsibility' that the Egyptians might attack the Canal Zone by air. If this did occur, he planned 'to hit back at once by attacking the Egyptian aircraft at their bases'[46]. He was given clearance for this by the Ministry of Defence and also advised to prepare to update operations for 'FLAIL' and 'RODEO', which were plans for occupying Cairo and Alexandria and evacuating British civilians resident there. Over the next few days, the violence came to a head. In Ismailia, on 25 January, the Egyptian auxiliary police had to be flushed out of their barracks and in the ensuing battle some 42 of them were killed and 800 detained for questioning, while British casualties consisted of three killed and 13 wounded[47].

On the following day, large-scale riots broke out in Cairo. Brian Robertson, as a consequence of the scale of the operations in the Canal Zone and the news that large numbers of Egyptian liberation troops had arrived in the eastern Delta, had revised his opinions about the fighting qualities of the Egyptians. Much to the annoyance of Anthony Eden, he now advised strongly against occupying Cairo. He was emphatic that:

Any idea that we can waltz into Cairo and find some moderate elements whom we could set up to restore order is out of the question. Our former expectation that the Egyptian Army might offer only token resistance will not be realised. On the contrary we must prepare for the possibility that the Egyptian division in Sinai may turn round and attack us.

Thus he recommended that military operations should initially be limited to evacuating British nationals from the cities and that an occupation of Cairo could only be safely carried out once the immediate threat to the Canal Zone had been dealt with, but Eden brushed this advice aside and informed Brian Robertson that he would have to intervene whatever the risks if so ordered[48].

Fortunately, in the late afternoon of 26 January, King Farouk brought in the Egyptian Army to restore order, dismissed his prime minister and asked Ali Maher to form a new government. The violence in the Canal Zone subsided and by the middle of February all was quiet except for isolated cases of sniping. However, as Brian Robertson graphically put it, it was impossible to say 'whether we have passed through the hurricane or are only at its centre'[49]. Thus, throughout the spring and summer of 1952 plans for the possible introduction of military government in the Canal Zone and for the military measures to be taken in the event of another flare up of violence were regularly updated.

During the winter of 1951–2, serious differences of opinion had again arisen between Brian Robertson and Sir Ralph Stevenson. Although he was 'on friendly terms' with Stevenson, he deeply mistrusted his judgement. He felt that Stevenson lived 'in the stratosphere', was out of contact with Egyptian opinion and relied too much on the advice of local British businessmen whose main desire was simply to return to the luxurious life they led before the troubles started[50]. In essence, he suspected that Stevenson wanted a 'quick agreement at any cost' with the Egyptians, whereas he was convinced that:

> Until such time as Egypt accepts the principles of joint defence and is prepared to implement it [sic] we must maintain our position in the Canal Zone intact accepting as inevitable any risks inherent in the internal political situation in Egypt[51].

With the advent of the new government in Cairo, Brian Robertson did see an opportunity for re-starting negotiations. Realistically, he advised the War Office that Ali Maher would have to be offered terms that he could accept without the fear that they would lead to his fall. Thus the original Four Power proposals 'could easily be dressed up in a manner to make it appear as an Egyptian victory'. The future of the Sudan presented a greater problem, but here too he felt that there was room for compromise:

> The King [of Egypt] wants to keep his title, but as he is after the shadow and not the substance, it ought therefore to be possible to find a form of words which would satisfy him without betraying the Sudanese.[52]

Until a satisfactory formula could be found, Robertson felt that Britain should continue to maintain her position in the Canal Zone at least until 1956. At times it seems as if he even envisaged an occupation beyond that date if no agreement with Cairo was forthcoming. He was particularly irritated by the 'querulous and defeatist' tone of the *Times* and by a series of 'ill informed and unwise' articles in the *Economist*, which suggested that the British should confine their occupation of the Canal Zone to the Fayid area and build a 'Mulberry' harbour in the Great Bitter Lake. He suspected that the author of these articles was one Elizabeth Monroe who was later to write the classic history of Britain's involvement in the Middle East[53].

Although both the Foreign Office and War Office were ready to begin negotiations in the summer of 1952, first the unresolved Sudanese issue and then the military coup in Cairo in July effectively delayed their start until the following year. The delay gave the War Office and Fayid valuable time to work out plans for the ultimate redeployment of the Suez garrison. In an era of growing Arab nationalism, it was becoming increasingly difficult to secure alternatives to the Canal Zone. In the long term, Slim thought that 'two firm footholds' in Cyprus and Gaza would have to suffice and Glubb Pasha spoke of 'a chain of Gibraltars' around the Middle East[54], but Brian Robertson had to deal with the immediate and pressing problems of finding alternatives to Suez whilst still retaining Britain's military capacity to fight a war that could break out at any time. At the end of 1951, he produced a short-term and a long-term plan for the redeployment of the Suez garrison. The British headquarters would move to Cyprus but initially there would be no alternative to sending a considerable number of troops back to Britain. As soon as possible, however, he wanted them returned to the Middle East and stationed in Cyprus, Jordan and Libya, with whom Britain was about to negotiate a 25 year financial and military agreement[55]. He warned that unless there were sufficient British reserves already in place in the Middle East, the Levant and Egypt would quickly be overrun in the event of war with Russia. He stressed that if an inter-Allied command under a British Commander-in-Chief was set up, Britain would need to justify her predominant position in it by immediately employing a large number of troops. He also wanted to avoid the Middle East becoming an unpopular 'non-families station' and recommended the rapid building of married quarters in Cyprus and Cyrenaica. To Brian Robertson, the options facing the Government were brutally simple:

The plain fact is that the conclusion of an agreement with Egypt will bring us hard up against the question as to whether we are willing and able to produce a large sum of money to construct elsewhere the accommodation which we shall have lost in Egypt . . . the alternative is to accept the fact that we cannot afford to make such dispositions in peace as will give us any reasonable chance of defending the Middle East in war[56].

Kenya

As Commander-in-Chief of Middle East Land Forces, Brian Robertson viewed British East Africa as primarily a source of reserves in the event of war. Although nominally under his command, the GOC East Africa dealt directly with the War Office rather than Fayid on most purely African matters. However, when the Mau Mau uprising broke out in October, 1952, Brian Robertson had to send down a battalion of Lancashire Fusiliers and liaise with the Governor and General Cameron, the local commander, on counter-insurgency tactics. He dismissed panic stricken comparisons with the Communist guerrilla campaign in Malaya as misleading since there was 'as yet no formidable outside source of support and reinforcement' for the Mau Mau. Initially, he thought that the trouble would take about nine months to eradicate, but he did concede that it could take much longer. He was conscious that 'all Africa' was watching the situation in Kenya and that if not dealt with firmly, unrest could spread. He was, for instance, particularly worried about the Copper Belt in Rhodesia where there were 'some very bad elements among the white population . . . and the possibility of serious trouble'[57].

He optimistically hoped that the Lancashire Fusiliers would so stabilise the situation that by mid-January the local police would be able to take over operations. By the end of November, it was clear, however, that the emergency was already turning into a small guerrilla war. He was critical of the Colonial Government for attempting to deal with the emergency through the 'normal machinery of its colonial administration' rather than handing over executive action within the framework of an approved policy to 'a determined individual'. In response to a request from the Governor, Brian Robertson sent down a Director of Operations to coordinate the work of the administration, police and the Army. He was also to devote especial attention to intelligence gathering and forward planning[58]. He recommended Brigadier Hinde, who had been the former Deputy Military Governor in the British sector in Berlin and then briefly responsible for creating a nucleus of civil affairs officers in the Canal Zone. Hinde, promoted to Major General and initially entitled Chief Staff Officer to the Governor, set up a two-tiered organisation for the prosecution of the emergency but it proved hopelessly cumbersome because of the lack of a single authority. Even when he was later appointed Director of Operations, Hinde had no executive powers except over the Army. Field Marshal Sir John Harding, the CIGS, on visiting Kenya, quickly realised that a more senior man, with full executive powers over both the Army and the RAF and over any police involvement in operations, was essential. General Sir George Erskine was appointed in this role and was able to establish a clear plan of campaign. Meanwhile, Hinde, who had an almost legendary reputation as a fighting soldier, remained in Kenya as Erskine's deputy for field operations, a task for which he was subsequently knighted.[59]

A GLITTERING PRIZE DENIED

Everybody who knew Brian Robertson at all well agreed that his failure to succeed Slim as Chief of the Imperial General Staff in 1953 was a deep disappointment. Brian was an ambitious man and thus naturally coveted a post which would have rounded off a distinguished career and also have resulted in his promotion to the rank of Field Marshal. Yet such was the depth of his disappointment that it cannot be accounted for by mere thwarted ambition. The post was symbolically and psychologically important to him because, by following exactly in his father's footsteps, he would have posthumously vindicated Wully, who as CIGS was peremptorily sacked in 1918 by Lloyd George and his military career thereafter permanently blighted.

There is no doubt that he would have made a first class CIGS. In February, 1951, under pressure from Attlee, Slim had reluctantly agreed to have his appointment extended until November 1952, but he had mentioned Brian Robertson's name to the Prime Minister and in the meantime felt that 'another year in the Mideast' would do him no harm. Brian Robertson was obviously flattered and wrote back:

> I am not concerned on my own account. I like my job out here immensely and I like the life (although rough on the bank balance!). I am human enough to want to succeed you and candid enough to admit it to you. But only a fool would try to anticipate decisions of that sort and I shan't blub if someone else is chosen. In any case as you say, an extra year out here will do me no harm[60].

***

When the Conservatives won the election in October, 1951, Churchill offered first Montgomery and then Brian Robertson the post of Governor General and Director of Operations against the Communists in Malaya. Both turned it down, as indeed did his third choice, General Dempsey. Brian Robertson apparently pleaded that he 'was worn out with all his responsibilities in the Middle East', although this was not the impression of those who worked with him or had recently met him. Montgomery somewhat illogically was very annoyed that Brian Robertson had rejected the appointment and claimed that in Churchill's opinion he had 'had it' as far as his career was concerned: 'He had been asked to undertake one of the most important military missions upon which the security of the British Empire depended. He had refused'[61]. It is difficult to know what lay behind that 'unsoldierly decision', as one historian calls it[62]. It may have been a desire to spare his family the siege conditions of Malaya, although at the time the Canal Zone was also beleaguered. Edith certainly loathed the intense heat and had been frequently ill in Egypt. He may too have felt that a posting to Malaya would have put him out of the running for the appointment of CIGS. It is also possible that he realised that he was the wrong man for the task, which needed, according to Montgomery, 'a soldier with fire in his belly'[63]. Brian Robertson excelled at political and administrative tasks. The accusations that were levelled at Hinde in Kenya in 1953 might have been levelled at him in Malaya on a greater scale.

Montgomery was also opposed to Brian Robertson's appointment as CIGS. He told Slim that he:

> . . . is not a high class soldier in the widest sense of the word. He is first class at administration and would make a good QMG or AG. He is first class at diplomacy and political intrigue and is known in the Army as a political general. In my view he will never make a CIGS. Another point is that you cannot, in these days have a CIGS who has never won a battle, even a Division or Brigade battle. Such a CIGS would cut no ice anywhere today. Robertson is not popular in the Army, and he commands no confidence[64].

In the Canal Zone, this was certainly not the opinion of General Erskine, who found Brian Robertson 'quite marvellous. He takes all the difficult decisions and leaves me to get on with the job . . . he has the lightest touch of anyone under whom I have served'[65]. Slim also took Montgomery's advice with a pinch of salt and in May, 1952, gave Robertson's name together with John Harding's, to Churchill on a short list for the post of CIGS. Churchill chose Harding, who also had the support of Montgomery. Slim wrote immediately to Fayid informing Brian Robertson that:

> My advice to the PM was that both you and Harding were well suited to the job. I recommended you both and beyond that I would not go. Personally I don't mind telling you that for Chief of Staff work I think you would have been better both by temperament and experience, but for the more parochial business of the Army John Harding would be at an advantage[66].

Brian Robertson did not hide his disappointment but wrote immediately a generous letter of congratulation to Harding:

> I was a runner in the race: of that there is no secret between us. The prize has gone to the man for whom I have more esteem and personal regard than I have for any other among the senior officers of our service. This is great consolation for such disappointment as I may feel being human (!) for my own failure to gain it[67].

He reassured Harding that he was ready to serve out his final year in the Middle East. 'Former contacts in the business world' had already been in touch with him, but 'for the time being he had put them off'. His old departmental chief at the War Office, Major General Piggott, advised him not to despair but to set his sights on becoming CIGS in 1955 when he would still be only 59. In the spring of 1953, it was agreed that he would take over the post of Adjutant General when his tour of duty in the Middle East ended in June, and he was already planning his family's move back to England, when he was asked to act as 'Ambassador's Co-delegate' in the resumption of negotiations with the Egyptians[68].

AMBASSADOR'S CO-DELEGATE, APRIL–NOVEMBER, 1953

By early 1953, the prospects for an Anglo-Egyptian settlement had improved considerably. The link between the future of the Sudan and the negotiations over the Suez Base was broken when the new Revolutionary Command Council under Colonel Neguib, which was set up after Farouk's abdication in July 1952, decided that Egypt should waive her formal claims to sovereignty over the Sudan and instead concentrate on winning over the Sudanese political parties to the idea of a political union with Egypt. Both the Foreign Office and War Office also wanted a settlement badly as the present deadlock was keeping 80,000 men in the Canal Zone 'for no purpose except to maintain themselves'[69]. Thus in consultation with the Chiefs of Staff the British Government's negotiating position was drawn up. It offered the phased withdrawal of the Suez garrison from Egypt and a programme of economic and military assistance financed jointly by Britain and America in return for the maintenance of the base with the assistance of several thousand British technicians, so that Allied forces would be able to return to it immediately in the event of war. There would be a joint Anglo-Egyptian organisation for air defence and Egypt would join a new Middle East defence organisation.

At first it was envisaged that Slim would represent the War Office in the negotiations, but by the time they were due to start he had to depart to Australia to take over the Governor-Generalship. Churchill therefore appointed Brian Robertson the 'Ambassador's co-delegate'. He was to give up his command and have a villa taken for him 'as near as possible to the British Embassy' in Cairo. Churchill was also insistent that he must not suffer financially in any way for giving up his command prematurely.

In the voluminous briefs he had to master, the possible conclusion of the negotiations was broken down into three 'cases'. Under 'Case A', the British would keep control of the base installations and keep some 5,000 personnel there permanently to look after them. In 'Case B', only a small technical staff would be left to supervise the installations and in 'Case C', no British personnel, apart from a few inspectors, would be left. His instructions were to aim for 'Case A' with 'if necessary the acceptance of some elements of Case B'. The British delegation was to ensure above all that the garrison should have a minimum time of 18 months to move out of the Canal Zone and that British technical personnel remaining behind would be given an international jurisdictional status which would protect them if necessary from the Egyptian population. Churchill was later to insist that they should wear uniform and carry arms. Finally, there would also have to be satisfactory arrangements for the retention of bulk oil storage and air staging facilities.

The resumption of talks was scheduled for 20 April. Robertson explained to a meeting of officials at the Foreign Office how he envisaged his role:

> After the opening by Sir Ralph Stevenson, he would attempt to explain to the Egyptian side the strategic background of Middle East Defence, and then to show how this underlay the various points of our proposals. He would certainly not wish to 'bang the table' and he would not consider it desirable to force the question of a Middle East Defence Organisation to the fore: in any case, he thought the latter was a matter of political rather than military importance[70].

The talks did not get off to a good start. The Egyptians insisted on clarifying basic principles in advance of the detailed committee work and, or so Brian Robertson believed, deliberately broke off the negotiations just as John Foster Dulles, the American Secretary of State, was visiting Cairo in the hope that he might intervene on their behalf[71]. As far as the British were concerned, the initial Egyptian insistence that 'the present military base in the Canal Zone' should be transferred to 'full Egyptian control' and that the Egyptian Government should also be entrusted with all the equipment left there, was unacceptable. On 12 May, Brian Robertson sent Churchill a personal report on the situation. He was quite clear that 'Case A' was now out of the question and that at the very best the Egyptians would accept the presence of British technicians in the short term only. He gave Churchill an interesting assessment of the dilemma facing the Egyptian leaders:

They are not really prepared for the resort to force in spite of their brave words. They know that they can expect no mercy from the Wafd if they give way. They also know that the only organisation capable of giving them effective political support is the Muslim Brotherhood which demands a price they cannot pay.

He warned him that there was a real danger of the situation drifting until 'an explosion occurs', but nevertheless he did not recommend precipitate action:

> . . . at the moment . . . we should sit tight and do nothing. If they put out a feeler we shall, of course, report it to you without any sort of commitment. If, however, you then decide to do anything about it I do suggest that you send for me before discussions are resumed so that I can explain matters to you personally and receive your personal guidance again[72].

On 30 May, Brian Robertson flew back to London to attend the Coronation and for consultations with Churchill, the Foreign Office and War Office on how to proceed with the negotiations in Cairo. Churchill had accepted his advice about 'sitting tight', but he himself was beginning to have second thoughts about it. Robertson told the Chiefs of Staff that if a resumption of talks was delayed for too long, the Egyptians might 'be driven to take drastic action, the consequences of which were unpredictable . . .'[73] He then wrote for Churchill and the Foreign Office a series of papers in which he tried to reconcile the British 'sticking points' with what the Egyptians would realistically accept. As far as the duration of the agreement went, he produced a formula for it to remain in force either until the organisation of an Arab security pact or, if this never materialised, for a period of five years 'after which either party shall be entitled to request discussion of its revision on the grounds that the condition of principle . . . has been fulfilled'. He sought to overcome the Egyptians' natural reluctance to allow Britain the right to reoccupy the base whenever she thought war was likely by drafting an anodyne clause which referred to Egypt's duties under the Charter of the United Nations. Finally, he suggested a way of overcoming Egypt's objections to allowing the British Government to pass orders directly to the British base commander by proposing that this officer should act officially as a representative of the British Government and formally communicate the contents of these messages to the Egyptian Supreme Commander[74].

Until the end of July, not even the most tentative talks took place between the British and the Egyptians. Apart from a brief trip to Washington, Brian Robertson remained in London to advise the Government. Increasingly, he became more emphatic that an agreement must be concluded on the terms he had already outlined. He felt that two imperatives dictated this: financial pressure drastically to reduce British overseas commitments and the undeniable fact that 'without a measure of Egyptian cooperation our base in Egypt is useless to us'[75]. In early July he offered to explain his thinking to an informal meeting of MPs and actually prepared a talk, which Strang, now the Permanent Under-Secretary of State at the Foreign Office, thought was persuasive and brought 'new and decisive facts to some of our parliamentary critics'[76]. The talk was never actually given, but it was a clear and well argued case for an agreement with the Egyptians. The conclusion is particularly worth quoting:

> To sum up, there are three courses open to us in Egypt. The first is to tell the Egyptians to go to blazes: that means that you gentlemen will have to confront the people of this country with a bill for money and men which to say the least of it, will cause them a very big shock, even indeed if it can be met. The second possible cause is to clear out lock, stock and barrel. Some quite serious minded gentlemen favour this course. I do not, partly because I believe that the strategic importance of the Middle East is something of great permanent value which we should not throw away, and partly because I believe that the effect on our prestige as a great nation would be disastrous . . . The third cause is to reach an agreement with Egypt and I believe that if we pick our way very carefully we may be able to get an agreement which can be accepted only in view of the serious consequences of having no agreement. Even so, of course, there is the possibility that the Egyptians will not stick to this agreement any more than they have honoured the others. I have no complete answer to that: the best we can do is to persuade the Americans to underwrite the agreement, and to keep ourselves as strong a force as we can afford in the Middle East near to Egypt in the hope that this evidence of our strength will induce them to be loyal to their undertakings.[77]

In an attempt to persuade the Americans to put pressure on the Egyptians, Lord Salisbury, the acting Foreign Secretary, flew over to Washington on 10 July with a small British delegation which included Brian Robertson. The terms which he was to explain to them were in essence those drafted by Robertson. Through the State Department, the British were also able unofficially to study Egyptian proposals for breaking the diplomatic deadlock. Brian Robertson was briefly encouraged by an American suggestion that a few US technicians should also work alongside the British in the base workshops, but in the long term nothing was to come of this idea[78].

By mid-July, there were a number of signs that the Egyptians were edging back to the conference table. Brian Robertson returned to Cairo on the 17th, wrote his name in Neguib's visiting book and sent 'the customary cards' to the Minister for Foreign Affairs. The first unofficial contact between the two sides took place at a dinner party in the house of the Pakistani Chargé d'Affaires on 31 July. Brian Robertson initially let the Egyptians know informally what British policy was. The Cabinet had approved his formula for an agreement on the key question of the availability of the base with one important modification. It had dropped his anodyne formula proposing that Britain should only be invited to re-occupy the base in the event of war 'if such action should be required of Egypt by her obligation under the Charter of the United Nations . . .', and instead insisted that Britain's right to re-enter the base should be automatically reactivated if a major war broke out or if there was an attack on or a threat of aggression against Egypt or any of the other Arab countries, including Turkey and Persia[79]. In persuading the Government to revert to his original formula, Robertson showed the suppleness and grasp of reality that made him a first-class negotiator. He conceded straight away that a sovereign nation could only commit itself in advance to a course of action in the event of the threat of war if it was convinced that the threat was a reality. Thus unless there was an all-out Soviet attack on Turkey and Iraq, which would be a self-evident threat to Egypt, he felt that some provision for prior consultation between the Egyptians and the British would be needed. Similarly, he understood Egypt's unwillingness to concede too many rights specifically to Britain and quickly accepted Dulles's advice when he was in Washington that 'we should if possible pick up the wording suggested by the Egyptians'. He was therefore prepared to take seriously an Egyptian proposal that the base should be made available to 'Egypt's allies and to allies of Egypt's allies', although he was aware of the ambiguity of this formula. He was unsure, for instance, what would then happen if Britain ceased to be an ally of Egypt.

> On the other hand, the Americans at Washington made it clear to us that they regard the formula as a genuine and somewhat ingenious attempt by the Egyptians to meet us: this alone is a reason why we should look at it carefully and not reject it out of hand[80].

Over the next two weeks, in a series of four meetings, detailed discussions with the Egyptians at last resumed. No immediate breakthrough was achieved as the Egyptians proved to be formidable negotiators, but the Foreign Office still hoped that they could be brought a long way towards meeting Britain's demands. In the midst of these exhausting negotiations, Brian Robertson's own plans were radically and suddenly changed. On 5 August he received a telegram from Churchill asking him:

> How would you like to be Chairman of the British Transport Commission [BTC] with interests of a million men in your hands instead of becoming Adjutant General? In either case you would have to finish your Egyptian work first.

In a second telegram, he learnt that the post involved the control of a number of rather ill-assorted nationalised transport industries ranging from the railways to a large road haulage fleet[81]. He asked Edith to find out from the Permanent Secretary to the Ministry of Transport, Gilmour Jenkins, whom he had known well when he was Permanent Secretary of the Control Office in London, whether the post would be adversely affected by the new Transport Act. Although it was not quite the kind of civilian job he ultimately envisaged for himself, it had 'undoubted attractions' for him – not least the salary of £8,500 a year which was then a relatively generous sum that could support a comfortable standard of living. The War Office did not stand in his way. Harding immediately telegraphed him:

> Much as I would have liked to have worked in close association with you, I am persuaded that it is in the National and Your own interests to accept new offer, which I consider that you can do without any compunctions about your indebtedness either to the Army or me personally. Would like you to feel absolutely free to do what you yourself consider best.[82]

Thus when it was confirmed – somewhat erroneously as it turned out – that the job would not 'be affected by political change', that Gilmour Jenkins himself was anxious to work with Robertson and above all that Edith approved of the change[83], he accepted the post. The immediate problem then was to find time to fly home to be briefed about his future responsibilities at the BTC. In Cairo, as Brian Robertson told Jenkins, the negotiations were 'just approaching the crisis of the present informal discussions where means have to be found to bridge [the] gap between the Egyptians and ourselves'[84].

It was not until the second week in September that Brian Robertson was able to fly back to London. After accepting the freedom of Gillingham on behalf of the Royal Engineers, whose Colonel Commandant he had become three years earlier, taking the salute one evening at the Edinburgh Tattoo and discussing his future work with Ministry of Transport and BTC officials, he was free to turn his mind to Egypt again. Before returning to Cairo, he candidly discussed the prospects of an agreement with the Egyptians with Lord Salisbury. On balance he still thought one likely but he painted a bleak picture of the military consequences if the talks broke down: the British Army would either have to occupy the Delta or be sitting targets for terrorist attacks[85].

Over the next two months, he did all he could to bridge the still formidable differences between the Egyptians and the British negotiating team. On both sides, the situation was exacerbated by a hostile press and outspoken speeches by the politicians. Brian Robertson observed ironically to one Foreign Office official that normally when two states negotiated an agreement there was at least the pretence of cooperation. With Britain and Egypt he feared that even this 'formal courtesy [would] be lacking on both sides on this occasion'[86]. He did all he could to urge restraint on the Egyptians and to educate British MPs and journalists in the realities of international politics. He advised, for instance, that the Minister of Defence, Field Marshal Alexander, would be the best Cabinet Minister to sell an eventual Anglo-Egyptian agreement 'to the more conservative newspapers and public'. He also sent the Foreign Office a draft memorandum on the whole question of press guidance in the event of an agreement being concluded. He spelt out with an almost brutal clarity that whilst it would be far from perfect it 'at least faces the facts; it is a workable agreement, given goodwill on both sides, and by its terms it does not make goodwill impossible'[87].

Previously, like most Englishmen of the time, he had been dismissive of the Egyptian leaders and regarded them as 'miserable fellows'[88], but over the last six months he had developed a considerable respect for the new rulers of Egypt. He was anxious to make clear to his fellow countrymen that:

> They are ruthless young men and they have done many things which we condemn as bad or foolish. On the other hand, they have shown a determination and capacity to exact obedience; they live austerely and are not enriching themselves; they work hard and they put the interests of Egypt before their individual interests. They can make this agreement work if they wish to do so . . .[89].

By the end of October, it was clear that the Egyptians were in no hurry to resume negotiations until the elections in the Sudan, which were due to take place on 29 November, were over. After the meeting of 21 October, when the British delegation put forward proposals for what it hoped would be the final compromise of all outstanding issues, no further sessions were arranged and the Egyptian Government went out of its way to avoid contacts with the British Embassy. The crucial question of the availability of the base in war still remained unsolved. The second phase of the talks was obviously now over and on 19 November Brian Robertson was at last able to fly back to London to start work at the Transport Commission.

On the evening of 17 November, he made one last vital contribution to the ultimate success of the talks. In a farewell talk with Colonel Nasser, he won his trust and spoke to him very much as he had done to Adenauer some four years earlier. He disarmed him by treating him as a responsible person, who like himself understood the complexities and compromises necessary in politics and diplomacy. Thus over the vexed question of the availability of the base he told Nasser:

Both sides should seek a way out of the difficulty. It would be most irresponsible, when no difference of substance existed, not to carry matters to a successful conclusion . . . he appreciated a soldier's impatience at the delay (he himself felt such impatience and even irritation after the last meeting of the delegations) but having assumed political responsibility Colonel Nasser and his colleagues had to go through with it.[90]

When Nasser spoke of the hostility within Egypt to the agreement, Brian Robertson went out of his way to reassure him that once it was signed his regime would be able to claim the credit for getting the British out of Egypt. He also elicited from him the vital statement that 'Egypt unlike Iran, was bound to be on the side of the West in the event of a major war.' The Embassy in Cairo was delighted with this interview, which it believed had 'clearly done much good'[91]. Nasser, too, was pleased by it. The following day, as Brian Robertson was about to board his plane for London, he was given a parcel from Nasser. He assumed that it was merely some Egyptian sweets, but when he opened it at home he discovered that it was an antique silver salver.

Largely as a result of the power struggle between Neguib and Nasser, negotiations were not resumed until the following summer. The Heads of Agreement were signed in Cairo on 27 July 1954 and the subsequent treaty concluded on19 October. In essence it was the agreement which Brian Robertson and the Cairo Embassy had prepared a year earlier: its duration was seven years, the base was to be maintained by British and Egyptian technicians, and it was to be reactivated in the event of an attack on Egypt, the Arab League or Turkey.

Brian Robertson's crucial role in the initial negotiations was not forgotten by either the British or Egyptian Governments. Eden told him that 'we could never have done it without you'[92], while Nasser in his speech to the British delegation went out of his way to praise Brian Robertson for 'his friendly attitude towards Egypt' and sent him a personal telegram in appreciation of his efforts 'in helping to reach a new era of good relations between both our countries'[93]. The positive impact that he had made on the Egyptians was confirmed by Anthony Head, the War Minister, who had signed the initial agreements in July. He wrote to Brian Robertson telling him

. . . how impressed I was by the universal respect and admiration felt towards you by the Egyptian delegation. Your name was constantly mentioned and I can well understand what a very profound impression you have made upon them during the long negotiations in which you took part . . .[94]

Robertson was delighted by the recognition he received, and was cautiously optimistic about the success of the agreement. He told Head that 'any agreement with Egypt must always be a gamble' but 'that if one must gamble [Nasser] is a reasonable horse to carry the money!'[95] Overall he felt that the agreement could work, 'given a modicum of common sense on both sides'. Alas, that is just what it was not to receive!

THE EVACUATION – A POSTSCRIPT, JUNE, 1956

In June, 1956, Brian Robertson visited Cairo for the last time. He had been invited personally by Nasser to attend the ceremonies planned to mark the final withdrawal of British forces from Egypt[96]. Originally it was decided in London that no official representative from London should attend the celebrations which, it was feared, might degenerate into an anti-British demonstration. However, the Government was persuaded by Trevelyan, the Ambassador in Cairo, that if Brian Robertson accepted the invitation on a strictly personal basis, he might have a calming affect on Nasser and behind the scenes influence Anglo-Egyptian relations for the better. He would, too, be something of a counterweight to the presence of Shepilov, the Soviet Foreign Minister[97]. Such a visit was bound to be controversial and inspire hostile attacks in the Conservative press and in the Commons. Nevertheless, Brian Robertson reluctantly agreed to go provided that the Government made it clear that he went 'with the blessing of HMG'.

He flew over to Cairo on Sunday 17 June and on the following day met Nasser, whom he found 'considerably changed . . . more reserved and pleased with himself, a bit pompous and apt to talk down to people . . .'[98] Then there followed an enormous and somewhat chaotic dinner at the [Egyptian] Officers' Club, where Trevelyan 'had to intervene . . . to ensure [him] a suitable position during the standing buffet . . .' The atmosphere was not made any easier that day when Nasser delivered a 'turgid, demagogic speech' which infuriated the British press. On the Tuesday, the British party toured the former Canal Zone and had lunch with the General Managers of the Suez Contractors at the Fayid Club, noting particularly a MiG fighter on the airfield. On their return to Cairo, Brian Robertson called on General Hakim, the Commander of the Reserves, and impressed upon him the 'necessity for constructive reference to Anglo-Egyptian relations by Colonel Nasser' in the major speech he was scheduled to deliver that evening. It was a considerable tribute to Brian Robertson's influence that this advice was heeded in Nasser's subsequent speech. On Wednesday, the climax of the celebrations, the military parade, took place, which he found 'interminably long and boring'. No effort was made to organise the smooth departure of the guests and the British party had to wait 'about for a long time' until their cars 'could fight their way to the stand'. Later that day, he had tea with Nasser, who clearly wanted to keep off politics, but Brian Robertson did manage to elicit from him that he wanted 'a period of detente and a cessation of mutual abuse in the press'.

He flew back to London on the following day. The Ambassador was delighted by his contribution and was convinced that it might even succeed in persuading Nasser to moderate his hostility towards Britain. Robertson did not visit Egypt again. During the Suez Crisis he maintained a diplomatic silence which, as his children and friends all confirm, he never broke, even within the privacy of his own family.

CHAIRMAN OF THE BRITISH TRANSPORT COMMISSION 1953–61

When Brian Robertson's appointment was announced, he was inundated with requests for jobs at the BTC and letters of congratulation from former colleagues, old friends and acquaintances. All agreed that the Chairmanship of the BTC was a formidable task, which was perhaps even a 'tougher nut' to crack than the Control Commission in Germany. Brigadier Edmonds, the military historian, wrote him a flattering letter comparing him to Wolseley for the sheer scale of his talents, while Adenauer not only observed that the new task suited his organisational gifts, but that it would also bring him back to Europe where he would be able to see more of him[1]. Inevitably he had some second thoughts about the post. Ideally he would still have preferred to have remained in the Army and to have been seconded to an 'international job'[2]. Nevertheless, the challenge of the post attracted him. Churchill appointed him specifically to provide the Commission's workforce of 850,000 men with what it had hitherto lacked: leadership. On his appointment, Lennox-Boyd, the Transport Minister, wrote to him again emphasising this point:

> During the 15 months that I have been minister, I have found the lack of leadership on the Railways the most disturbing feature but I feel confident the men will respond if given proper encouragement[3].

Brian Robertson's reservations about the appointment were in hindsight to be amply confirmed. The British Transport Commission was a huge conglomerate rather than a 'civilian army', which even his fabulous administrative skills could not turn into an efficient organisation although his impact on it was to be both radical and dramatic.

THE 'ROBERTSON REVOLUTION', 1954–55

When Brian Robertson moved into his office at the BTC's new headquarters at 222 Marylebone Road in late November, 1953, he was convinced that there was 'something in the nature of an Augean Stable requiring attention'[4]. To his staff he seemed an aloof and Olympian figure – indeed the General Manager of the Eastern Region rather unfairly went so far as to observe that he was 'the most fair minded and impartial man I have met. He hates us all equally'[5]. They awaited his first moves with an apprehension mixed with resentment that he did not know one end of a locomotive from another. His personal office staff, who were used to the staid ways of his predecessor, Lord Hurcomb, were taken aback by Edith Robertson's determination to choose new curtains and wallpaper from from Sanderson's and to order sophisticated modern electric light fittings from Germany[6]. As soon as he was established in his office, Robertson insisted on attempting to visit every officer 'of standing' in the building. Michael Bonavia remembers how:

> . . . he came to my room preceded by Sydney Taylor, who was then Chief Secretary. One got up from the desk . . . He was pleasant and brusque [and asked] 'what exactly do you do in the organisation? Any particular thoughts about how a railway should be going?' And looked at a coat of arms on the wall . . . 'I don't much care for that lion and wheel device. I think we should have something more correct in heraldic terms'[7].

Gradually, his senior staff, like their predecessors in Berlin and Fayid, rapidly discovered that beneath his detached and cold veneer there was a more human side to him. This impression was succinctly summed up by one officer of the Commission, Arthur Pearson, who observed, like many before had done: 'Nothing to worry about with this chap. He's just shy that's all'[8].

Brian Robertson took over the chairmanship of the BTC at a crucial stage in its short history. The BTC had been created by the Transport Act of 1947 and was supposed to preside over an integrated transport system. It was not only responsible for the railways, together with the shipping services, docks and hotels which the old railway companies had formerly controlled, but also for London Transport, inland waterways, road haulage and passenger bus services. These were administered by Boards or Executives responsible to the BTC. However, when the Conservative Government was elected in 1951, this whole organisation was put under review and drastically revised in May 1953, by a second Transport Act, the rationale behind which was to decentralise power to the regions and encourage competition. Thus, with the exception of the London Transport Executive, it swept away the whole centralised Executive structure in October, 1953, which, it laid down, should be eventually replaced by 'area authorities' that would take over the operating responsibilities. The Commission's role was not clearly defined but the Act seemed to suggest that it should continue as a policy making body, while the area authorities dealt with the day-to-day management. Long-distance road haulage was to be denationalised and encouraged to compete under private ownership with the railways[9].

Robertson's first task was therefore to draw up a complete new scheme for reorganising the BTC according to the terms of this inchoate Act. It was made infinitely more complicated by the Government's determination to decentralise and to ensure that the Executives did not re-emerge under a new guise. Not surprisingly, it took him some three months before he found a way of reconciling the instructions from Lennox-Boyd and Churchill to provide strong leadership with the spirit of the act. For the officers at Marylebone, this hiatus was a period of both chaos and paralysis – one officer, for instance, had nothing to do for six months but read the *Times*.

Brian Robertson initially concentrated on the powers and constitution of the new area authorities, which were seen by the Conservatives as the hallmark of decentralisation. He decided to set up Area Boards for each of the six existing railway regions. At first he tried to avoid defining their actual powers and relationship to the Commission too closely. Rather, he wished to retain a certain flexibility and draft what amounted to 'an enabling instrument'[10] which would allow him to hold the balance between centralisation and decentralisation. On the question of the appointment of chairmen to the Boards, for instance, he insisted that the Commission should have the power to nominate one of its members from time to time, but, as he wrote to Lennox-Boyd, this was a right that would be exercised only sparingly[11]. In the accompanying memorandum explaining the general principles behind the plan, Brian Robertson tried to allay the Minister's fear that it was a camouflage for continued central control. Essentially, he stressed, the BTC was 'a policy forming body', but the Area Boards were also policy forming and supervisory bodies at regional level and were, as he later characterised them, 'projections of the Commission' which could make decisions in their own right[12]. Nevertheless, the BTC had to be the focus for some administrative decisions, such as the management of wagon stock or the negotiation of national contracts with large firms. He then went on to point out that inevitably there would be a constant two-way contact between the BTC and the Chief Regional Managers. Indeed he positively welcomed this as:

> . . . new policy itself is not often born by a process of immaculate conception within the august body responsible for producing it, but more frequently is initiated by discussion between those responsible for the daily operation of existing policy.

Lennox-Boyd was at first highly critical of Brian Robertson's plan and in a draft letter, which was never dispatched, complained that it was 'quite a shock to find how little in the way of positive binding provisions the scheme contain[ed]'[13]. He even feared that it might not prove to be *intra vires* under the terms of the 1953 Act. Nevertheless, on second thoughts he decided to accept the scheme, provided that the Commission supplemented it with further explanatory material. It was then sent out for scrutiny to various consultative bodies like the TUC, FBI and the Local Authority Associations. The TUC attempted to insist on a right to representation on the Area Boards, but the BTC was determined not be fettered by special interests and to retain complete freedom to chose the best people available[14]. Although both Brian Robertson and Lennox-Boyd were anxious that the organisation of the Area Boards should be approved before the Summer Recess, it was not until October that the White Paper containing the details of the scheme was debated. Despite considerable scepticism on the Conservative backbenches about the Commission's willingness to make the Area Boards as autonomous as possible, it was approved and introduced by Ministerial Order on 25 November 1954.

The restructuring of the headquarters organisation did not require parliamentary approval. By July, 1954, Brian Robertson was able to explain its essence to Lennox-Boyd with the help of a hastily 'scrawled' sketch, but it was not until December that it was unveiled with an accompanying battery of diagrams to the rather apprehensive senior officers of the BTC. His exposition was so lucid and clear that 'at the end he received a spontaneous round of applause'[15]. For perusal at leisure they were also given copies of the 'Grey Book' – or 'Bible' – in which the new organisation was described in minute detail. In the accompanying press statement Robertson stressed that his aim was:

> . . . to leave management of the Commission to subordinate organisations, to keep the organisation for control clear and simple, and to restrict within practical limits the numbers of bodies and people with whom the Commission normally deals direct[16].

However, the consensus of opinion, both at the time and later, was that he had in fact failed to do this and had drawn up a complex and cumbersome scheme or a 'creaking dinosaur' which was to be the subject of constant criticism until its abolition by the 1962 Transport Act. At the top level, the Commission was served by a plethora of advisory bodies, committees and sub-commissions. Below this came the core of the BTC organisation: the Central Services, which were responsible for such matters as research, advertising and the Transport Police and the Six Divisions each covering an aspect of the Commission's activities. Then there were the Area Boards and the London Transport Executive. The whole organisation was cemented by what the historian of British Rail has called 'the controversial General Staff'[17]. The name was unfortunate in that it gave ammunition to those critics who were only too ready to accuse Brian Robertson of turning the Commission into a bastard military organisation. When he appointed first General Sir Daril Watson and then, in early 1955, Major General Llewellyn Wansborough-Jones to be its Secretary-General, he appeared to confirm his critics' observations, but he himself always insisted that the term 'General Staff' did not derive from military usage; it was merely an accurate description for the general transport advisers of the Commission[18]. In many ways the General Staff was his 'kitchen cabinet', which coordinated the mass of memoranda and information which came from the various sections of the Commission. Under Wansborough-Jones's effective but not always popular direction it processed a vast amount of information and was undoubtedly of enormous help to the Chairman in providing him with positional papers and vital data. However it was not just a kitchen cabinet. It was also senior to the Central Services. It was disliked by the members of the Divisions and the key railway officials out in the regions, as it formed a barrier between the Chairman's office and themselves. They all too frequently found that Wansborough-Jones and his colleagues put their own stamp upon policy as it passed through the General Staff office. Their own ideas, as one member of the Commission put it, lost 'their savour in the process'[19].

The technical railway press gave a reserved and critical reception to the new organisation. The *Railway Gazette*, for instance, characterised the new organisation as:

. . . top heavy and too complex; it bears the mark, as is perhaps inevitable, of a military mind. Something simpler might have been devised, which would have been much more suitable for a group of undertakings run, like nationalised transport, on a commercial basis[20].

The conclusion that the organisation was top heavy particularly irritated Brian Robertson. He argued that the Commission's headquarters staff of 400 compared favourably with the number of officials in the War Office, whilst controlling an organisation twice the size of the British Army[21].

In retrospect, however, it can be seen that the main fault in the new structure of the BTC lay in the lack of a clear organisational focus for the railways. The London Transport Executive and the other divisions had a reasonably clear management structure, but the railways were trapped in an administrative muddle at headquarters. There was quite simply 'no one body under an effective head answerable to the BTC for British Railways as a whole'[22]. Thus if a Regional General Manager needed permission to implement a particular policy, before it reached the Commission it would have to be examined by the Area Board, the relevant officers of the British Railways Central Staff, the General Staff of the Commission, the Railway Sub-Commission and the Committee of the Commission[23].

How was it that the 'Prince of Administrators' failed to work his usual administrative magic for the BTC? Part of the reason was undoubtedly that the 1953 Transport Act had left him with what the Comptroller of the Commission called a 'first class English mess'. It had, as Brian Robertson observed in 1960[24], compelled the Commission:

> . . . to fulfil two separate roles. The first is their proper role as headpiece to a great public transport organisation. The second role they have been forced to play as a result of the abolition of the Railway Executive, is that of the headquarters and Board of the British Railways.

After six years of trying to run the BTC he came to the conclusion:

> . . . that the proper organisation for British Railways is to have a British Railways Headquarters and Board with wide and firm powers over policy and finance, but decentralising to the regions and below them the executive work of running and selling the services.

In 1960 he felt that this solution was 'probably politically unacceptable'. In 1953 it would almost certainly have been seen by the Conservatives as an attempt to revive the much hated Railway Executive. Perhaps, in retrospect, he should have created a holding company with subsidiaries on ordinary commercial lines.

Whilst the BTC was painfully undergoing an organisational revolution, it was also embarking on a radical modernisation programme which was undoubtedly 'one of the most controversial elements in the history of nationalised railways'[25]. The outline of a modernisation plan had already been drawn up in 1953 but a detailed discussion of it was interrupted by the Transport Act and the subsequent problems of reorganisation. In April 1954, Robertson, who saw modernisation as the cornerstone of his policy for the railways, set up a planning committee under General Watson to submit at the end of six months a detailed plan 'for the modernisation and re-equipment of the railways' based on the assumption that the Government would provide a loan of some £500 million. It was to be launched within five years and completed within fifteen. By August it was clear that an immediate electrification of the majority of the main lines would be too expensive and thus the Planning Committee was informed by the Commission that it was 'prepared to look sympathetically at a proposal for a bold programme for the trial of diesel locomotives'[26]. The Committee's proposals were duly presented to the Commission in late October and, in a slightly altered form, to the new Minister of Transport, John Boyd-Carpenter, in December. It was an ambitious programme involving the upgrading of much of the track, the introduction of new colour light signalling and the replacement of steam locomotives by

diesels and electrification. Nine hundred miles of line were to be electrified and 3,600 diesels were gradually to be introduced by 1974. New
marshalling yards were to be built and continuous brakes were to be fitted
to the total wagon stock. Its overall cost was estimated at £1,240 million.
The whole project was buttressed by the optimistic forecast made by the
financial committee set up by the Commission in November that it would
'ultimately attract a return amounting to at least £85 million a year'[27].

The plan was ambitious, exciting and well presented. It was common
knowledge that the railways had long been starved of capital investment
and adverse comparisons were frequently made with the progress being
achieved in Western Europe where, thanks to massive investment programmes, countries were rapidly rebuilding their railways. The sheer scale
of it caught the imagination of Alison Munro, the Assistant Secretary
who first examined the plan in the Ministry of Transport. To acquaint
herself with its technical complexity, she spent several weeks travelling up
and down the system with railway officers and quickly became aware of
the antique state of Britain's railways. She was in no doubt that they
needed a 'grand design' and that the plan needed to be approved in its
totality. In 1994, she recalled her enthusiasm for its 'sheer boldness' and
regarded it as 'one of the most brilliant things Brian Robertson ever did'.
Somewhat disappointed by the scepticism of her Under-Secretary she
then discussed it with Boyd-Carpenter, who, already persuaded of its
necessity, needed little further convincing. Reflecting on the rapidity with
which it was accepted by the Government, Mrs Munro stressed forty
years later that, in the early Fifties, decisions of this magnitude rested primarily on policy judgements and broad economic arguments, and that the
techniques for sophisticated micro-economic appraisals had not yet been
developed:

> I think everyone was aware that it was a gamble but it was of a kind with
> which the country had grown familiar during the war and there was lit-
> tle doubt that it was one worth taking[28].

Neither the Treasury nor the Ministry of Transport raised any serious
obstacles to the modernisation plan even when Brian Robertson revealed
that, as a result of the wage spiral in 1954, the financial outlook for the
Commission for 1955 was 'bleak'[29]. By the terms of the Transport Act of
1953, the Commission was supposed to break even, 'taking one year with
another'. In early January, 1955, Robertson proposed to Boyd-Carpenter
that this should be interpreted liberally so as to allow the Commission to
carry forward a larger deficit than previously 'one would have dared to
contemplate'. Ultimately, he believed that there would have to be a major
reconstruction of the Commission's accounts[30]. Both the Treasury and
the Ministry of Transport were sympathetic to the Commission's financial

predicament and were quite prepared to believe that the modernisation programme would prove to be the ultimate key to profitability. Boyd-Carpenter then sent the Cabinet's Economic Policy Committee a memorandum urging the acceptance of the Plan, emphasising strongly that the proposals were 'sound in their conception' and would ultimately make 'the railways an efficient, economic and adaptable unit capable of meeting the country's requirements for many years to come'[31]. The Cabinet itself considered the memorandum and, despite some concern about the long-term viability of the railways in the face of competition from road and air, it nevertheless gave permission for the Commission's plan to be published.

It was launched by Brian Robertson on Monday 24 January at a press conference at 222 Marylebone Road. In the evening, he answered questions about the plan on the BBC news programmes. His theme throughout was to stress the novelty and the scope of the programme. Above all, he tried to convince not only the railwaymen but the whole country that the British railways were not 'a decaying anachronism'[32]. The plan was enthusiastically defended in the Commons by Boyd-Carpenter in early February and there was little difficulty in gaining parliamentary approval. At the end of March, a Bill extending the borrowing limit from £275 to £600 million was also approved.

The Plan was initially well received, but *The Economist*, however, struck a sombre note warning that 'grim experience suggests that there are at least three ways in which it could go wrong – poor railway management, road competition and lack of cooperation from the railwaymen'[33]. Unfortunately, as will be seen, this analysis was to prove accurate. Yet the Plan, for all its shortcomings, did ultimately drag British Railways into the second half of the twentieth century. Psychologically, it had been presented at the right time. Had Brian Robertson not steam rollered it through in 1954, the deterioration of the nation's finances, combined with the ever-growing strength of the road lobby, would have stifled much of it at birth.

LABOUR RELATIONS, DECEMBER, 1953–JUNE, 1955

In principle, Brian Robertson was well disposed towards the trade unions. In the British Zone in Germany, the trade union movement had proved to be an invaluable stabilising force at a time when there was no democratic government and he had enjoyed a considerable rapport with Hans Böckler and the other German trade union leaders. He believed strongly too in the beneficial effect that nationalisation would have on industrial relations. He was convinced, somewhat naively perhaps, that the workers would see themselves as partners in the industry and would thus be ready to cooperate all the more closely with management[34]. The state of labour relations in the railway industry was thus to be a rude awakening for him.

The reorganisation of the BTC and the subsequent launching of the modernisation plan had to be carried out against a background of increasing industrial unrest on the railways where labour relations were in many ways a microcosm of those of the nation as a whole. The Commission had to deal with three unions, the National Union of Railwaymen (NUR), the Associated Society of Locomotive Engineers and Firemen (ASLEF) and the Transport and Salaried Staffs Association (TSSA), who were naturally all intent on gaining the best deal for their members.

The NUR and ASLEF, which were in many ways rival unions, tended to leapfrog over each other with their wage claims. His problems were compounded by frequent government intervention in the negotiations between the unions and the BTC, the unions' own hostility towards the Transport Act of 1953[35] and their initial aversion to being led by a General in an era when Generals were unpopular. Industrial relations were, of course, conducted by the Commission's Manpower Adviser, but whenever a major strike seemed imminent which threatened to paralyse the nation's railways, both the Chairman and the Government speedily became involved in what usually became almost a ritual national drama. Brian Robertson was confronted with his first industrial relations crisis within days of taking up his post at the BTC, the origins of which went back to December, 1952, when the three unions, after winning a mere seven shillings a week increase, put forward further claims of up to 15 per cent. On 3 December, the Railway Staff National Tribunal offered only a small increase of four shillings and both the NUR and ASLEF decided to strike, but over the weekend, in what the Cabinet minuted as 'a remarkable combination of firmness and understanding',[36] Brian Robertson won over ASLEF and TSSA by offering to have the whole wage structure of the railways examined with a view to ironing out anomalies and where necessary providing new incentives. Yet this was rejected by the NUR which then called a strike scheduled to begin at midnight on 20 December. Faced with an embarrassing disruption of Christmas traffic and post, the Cabinet put pressure on the Commission to make further concessions, despite its warning that the cost of a settlement would be heavy and in the short term impossible to recoup. The Commission agreed to paying out four shillings immediately and to follow it up with a further three shillings in February. Brian Robertson was not a confrontationalist and his instincts were to compromise, but a combination of government pressure and 'the obvious power of the NUR'[37] combined to push him much further than he wished to go. The settlement appreciably worsened the finances of the BTC as every shilling added to the pay of the lowest grades of the railwaymen increased the Commission's costs by some £1½ million a year.

The review of the wages structure was completed in the summer of 1954, but then, in October, ASLEF insisted on further rises at all levels and took its demands to arbitration. It eventually accepted the National Tribunal's recommendations, but just as the round of wage bargaining seemed to be over, the NUR, intent on ensuring that its members were not left behind, leapfrogged over ASLEF and in November revived its original demand for 15 per cent, first made in July, 1953. This was rejected by the Commission and on 21 December the Executive of the NUR duly decided to call its men out with effect from 9 January, 1955. Neither the Cabinet nor the Commission were spoiling for a fight with the NUR. Brian Robertson was quite ready to pay more if the Government agreed to the Commission running up a larger deficit, while the Government feared the impact of the strike on the economy. Consequently, in an attempt to escape from its dilemma, the Cabinet set up a court of enquiry headed by Sir John Cameron which, in its interim report on 3 January, endorsed the NUR's claim in full. The NUR thus won a considerable victory and the Cabinet had no alternative but to accept it. On 6 January, Walter Monckton, the Minister of Labour, presided over a meeting between Brian Robertson and Jim Campbell, the General Secretary of the NUR. Like a soldier negotiating an armistice after a defeat, Brian Robertson was terse and to the point. He assured them that he would

> . . . eschew vague expressions because there is no need for them. I will be absolutely clear and blunt. We have . . . to conduct these negotiations in accordance with the recommendations of the Court, and I give my word that we will do that in letter and spirit . . . I won't haggle. I will do quick business . . .[38]

The Union then called off the strike and within the next fortnight the railwaymen were given virtually everything they had demanded.

This brinkmanship focused the attention of the national press at the turn of the year on the affairs of the railways and Brian Robertson became something of an 'Aunt Sally'. His reorganisation of the Transport Commission was ruthlessly caricatured as a system for finding relief for retired blimpish generals. The *Star*, for instance, observed:

> No wonder the hierarchy of the Transport Commission is to be known in future as the General Staff and the six area groups as Divisions. Under the supreme command of General Sir Brian Robertson the whole set up is now stuffed with top brass[39].

Much of the press, while sympathetic to the claims of the railwaymen, paradoxically had a field day in criticising the railways as an organisation.

The *Sunday Chronicle*, for instance, dispatched some reporters on a tour of inspection of the railways within a 40 mile radius of London and took great delight in subsequently revealing 'an Emett world of Gothic inefficiency'[40]. In early January, *The Times* particularly must have made uncomfortable reading for him, even though it exempted him personally from its criticisms. On 8 January, in a leading article on the rail settlement, it perceptively commented:

> British industry, of which the nationalised undertakings are now so substantial a part, would either be self-supporting, efficient and dependent on productivity or the alternatives would have to be faced of ever increasing inflation or a straitjacket of controls. However it may be, the plain truth is that in the first week of 1955, a firm step has been taken on the worse path.[41]

In Germany, of course, Brian Robertson had been used to being the subject of journalistic controversy, but at that stage he could always rely on the staunch backing of Ernest Bevin and the loyalty of the British Element of the Control Commission. At the BTC he had to defend himself from constant criticism from the unions, whose leaders tended to see him as a creature of the Conservative Government intent on turning the clock back to the 1930s. As a soldier for whom it was axiomatic that group loyalty was essential, he found union hostility particularly difficult to understand. He did not see himself as a remote figurehead, but rather as a person deeply involved in bringing about the renaissance of British railways. Thus the bitter attacks from Campbell in January 1955 were something of a stab in the back. His feeling of discomfiture was further compounded by the ambivalent attitude of his political masters, who were faltering and lukewarm in their support during his negotiations with the NUR in January, 1955. He must have drawn some comfort from the way the regional managers rallied to him in protest against the 'unfair and very spiteful press attacks'[42]. Nevertheless the experience so depressed him, that his friend Cuthbert Bardsley, the Bishop of Croydon, was moved to write to him later in the month:

> I think I know something of what you are going through at the moment. I also know that one cannot cure this tiredness and depression from one's own effort. It must be lifted from us by prayer. It can be. I know for I have experienced this amazing phenomenon. It is when the fog suddenly disperses. I shall ask some very wonderful women – women in an Anglican community – to pray for you. Lack of appreciation and the disloyalty of friends are, I suppose, the two hardest burdens to bear. I have a feeling that you are bearing these two loads now[43].

While Bardsley's letter was of considerable spiritual comfort to Brian Robertson, the prayers of the Anglican nuns had no immediate impact on ASLEF. On 21 January, intent on restoring the traditional wage differentials afforded to its members, it took a new claim of eight shillings for arbitration to the Railway Staff National Tribunal. When it was turned down in Decision No. 17, ASLEF responded by announcing a strike with effect from 1 May. This time the Government was ready to be much tougher and, if necessary, to risk a strike.

Thus when Brian Robertson met representatives of ASLEF on 27 April, he was able quite bluntly to tell them that 'until the strike threat was removed and decision No. 17 was accepted, the BTC could not enter into any fresh negotiations'[44]. Labour fears that a strike might damage its chances in the coming General Election and last minute intervention by the TUC temporarily averted the stoppage on 30 April, but further talks between ASLEF and the Commission still failed to produce a settlement and the strike went ahead on 28 May and was to last until 14 June.

In its early stages, Brian Robertson was laid up at home recovering from a polo injury. By the time he had returned to London, it looked as if the Commission would be able to win the strike. Public opinion was now for the most part hostile to ASLEF and the regional managers were able to keep a skeleton service going in most areas as the NUR drivers did not come out in sympathy. The Commission's cause was also assisted by the BBC's controversial decision to allow Lord Samuel to broadcast an appeal to the railwaymen to think again on 2 June. Brian Robertson's old friend, Ian Jacob, who was now the Controller General, was convinced that Samuel was a 'spokesman for sentiments widely and keenly felt'[45].

Behind the scenes, both Walter Monckton and the TUC were working for a settlement. Brian Robertson, who had no desire to inflict a humiliating defeat on his own men, was quite ready to reopen talks with ASLEF. However, as an experienced negotiator, he realised that an element of mutual confidence needed to be restored first between the two sides. He therefore wrote to Monckton suggesting 'a very early meeting' at the Ministry:

> . . . at which Mr. Baty [General-Secretary of ASLEF] and I, accompanied by as few colleagues as possible, should endeavour to put ourselves right with each other in regard to this matter of mutual confidence. If when the time comes to talk, there is still an issue of bad faith between us, discussions are not likely to go very well[46].

Baty was responsive and was ultimately ready to negotiate more flexibly. The two sides first met on 9 June and held exploratory discussions which were chaired by the Chief Industrial Commissioner, Sir Wilfrid Neden. This time, Brian Robertson was determined not to be pushed by either

Neden or Monckton into making premature concessions. When Neden remarked that the aim of the meeting was to get the strike called off, he sharply interposed, 'Not at any cost'. Nevertheless, he assiduously attempted to find areas of 'common ground' which could progressively be expanded until agreement was possible. Early on in the meeting he told Hallworth and Baty that:

> . . . the common ground to which I refer is that the Society, in various ways and at various times, had put forward the principle that there should be rewards, and they hold that they should be higher than they are at the moment for real skill and special responsibility. That is the sort of principle that we could work upon provided it is interpreted to mean what I think it means.

Brian Robertson was insistent that he could not agree to wage rises right across the board as that would 'merely reduce the thing to the lowest common denominator'. When this was angrily rejected by the Union leaders, the meeting came to an abrupt end.

The following day, before the second meeting began, Neden confidentially warned Brian Robertson:

> . . . that we have Downing St. on our collar and the Prime Minister wants to know how things are going and keeps on wanting to know, expecting much more rapid progress than is possible and if there is any sign of what he calls a breakdown he wants to know at once.

Brian Robertson refused to be browbeaten. While he assured Neden that he would not break up the meeting himself, he emphasised that he could not give way on what he considered fundamental points. He had also to keep in touch with the NUR to ensure that any agreement did not trigger a new bout of leapfrogging. He told Hallworth and Baty half-humorously that:

> If we do not set something down in the settlement to satisfy them that this process of leapfrogging or the equal is going to stop, well, I do not know what they will say about me but it will not be polite. I do not mind that so much, except that I do mind the thought that it would be justified[47].

Over the next four days, the outline of a settlement slowly emerged, despite an initial deadlock over pay increases for firemen and cleaners. Brian Robertson was particularly adamant that there should be no increase in the rates of pay for either category. He argued convincingly that the cleaner was 'virtually an apprentice'[48] who would rapidly move on to become a fireman or driver, while the firemen would benefit financially from the BTC's proposal for mileage payments. On 14 June the strike was called off when Baty agreed to Brian Robertson's proposal that the thorny question of engine drivers' rates should be submitted to arbitration. Eventually they were awarded small increases of up to three shillings.

Brian Robertson and the Commission had certainly handled the negotiations with considerable skill and had managed to engineer a moderate settlement that did not cost it too dearly. Yet the strike was in many ways a disaster. The BTC lost £12 million pounds in revenue and valuable freight traffic was diverted to the roads. Neither did it prevent the continuation of escalating wage claims. In retrospect, it is clear that the Government and the BTC should have stood firm in January against the strongest of the three unions, the NUR.

THE HIGH NOON OF THE ROBERTSON ERA, JANUARY, 1956–OCTOBER, 1959

By the end of 1955, Brian Robertson had reorganised the BTC, launched the railway modernisation plan and achieved a temporary respite from strikes. Apart from the ever-present threat of a Government U-turn, he was now free to run this unwieldy organisation in his own way. It was not an easy task, but it did have its compensations. It enabled him, for instance, to buy an attractive house at Iles Green, Far Oakridge, near Stroud, where his family could at last have a real home that was not just an official residence. Unless there was a particularly acute crisis which required his attention over the weekend, he was able to leave Marylebone Road at 4.30 in the Commission's Austin and catch the 4.55 to Kemble, any particularly urgent correspondence being signed en route to Paddington. Once at Iles Green, he was free to relax. He was, as one family friend observed, often gently teased by Edith and his daughters:

> to which he reacted with the benign tolerance of a lion whose cubs were playing with its tail. Similarly, he tolerated the dogs which occupied most of the most comfortable spots on the sofas, chairs and beds in the house[49].

On the occasions that his son, Ronald, came home on leave from his regiment, the Royal Scots Greys, Brian, would also listen stoically to the latest horror story about travelling on British Railways! On Sunday afternoons he would often work in the garden stripped to the waist, while his gardener, dressed in his Sunday best, would oversee his labours. Or else he would play polo at Cirencester. Edith frequently organised house parties made up of a mixture of old friends from the Army, the Control

Commission days and his new colleagues from the BTC. On one occasion, Brian Robertson's secretary was entrusted with the task of bringing down a bag of newly shot grouse for dinner, which much to her embarrassment bled copiously between Paddington and Kemble. The guests were often taken shopping to Cirencester where Brian Robertson would sometimes deliberately parody his reputation as a genius in logistics and set each one of them an objective and then the time at which 'forces should be regrouped' at a chosen rendezvous.

On Monday, he would return to London, arriving at Paddington at 10.35. The main event of the week was usually the meeting on Thursdays of the members of the Commission to review current problems and to make policy decisions. These meetings, which in their plenary sessions were attended by some 50 people, were conducted by Brian Robertson in a formal and businesslike manner, but contrary to the impression initially conveyed by the popular press, he did not impose his view ruthlessly on his colleagues. He ruled a vast ramshackle empire in which his senior managers had strong views about how policy should be implemented. He was dealing with senior railway managers who had a long tradition of working in the pre-war companies and who could be very outspoken. For instance, at a Plenary Meeting of the Commission in January, 1957, Robertson vigorously stressed the need for the Regional Managers to delegate and decentralise. Brusquely he told them that enough attention had already been paid to 'tranquillity' and that 'rigidity' could only lead to inefficiency. This apparently triggered such violent expostulations from Keith Grand, the formidable Manager of the Western Region, that his Area Board Chairman sought later in a confidential letter to Brian Robertson to excuse his behaviour by placing it within the context of the fierce tradition of independence that still survived at Paddington. He conceded that Grand was too often looking back to the past, but believed that if he could only be granted an 'honour of sorts' this would 'provide a sort of psychological uplift which will induce an eagerness to row in a team'[50]. The Chairman of the BTC was hardly in the position to shower honours on difficult colleagues, however sterling their character might be, nor indeed to sack them unless he wished to alienate the regions and plunge the Commission into turmoil. Inevitably then, Brian Robertson had frequently to compromise with these regional barons when it came to a detailed implementation of policies. Wansborough-Jones, or 'Mr. Fixit' as one officer of the Commission called him, and the General Staff were adept at working out such compromises.

Since Robertson administered by compromise rather than *diktat*, there were those who dismissed him as a weak chairman, but he did have a very definite philosophy of leadership, which he pursued in a quiet and unostentatious way. He believed firmly in devolving power to the regions and in creating a structure which allowed managers to manage and to have time to think, although in practice he was not very successful in this. He was also constantly reiterating the message that it was the responsibility of management at all levels to look after their staff and to ensure that they were 'fully informed of facts and reasons for changes planned'. Like the conscientious officer he himself had been, he reminded his managers that:

> Those who had authority over men had also a responsibility for keeping in touch with them, for knowing their attitude of mind, for smoothing out difficulties from time to time, and generally for ensuring that industrial relations were as good as they could be[51].

He practised what he preached. He believed strongly that the Chairman had to put himself across to the 'officers and men' of the Railways, and that 'if he fails to do this, he will fail altogether'. He had to be 'a leader of men', but emphatically not 'a bully'[52]. When he went on tours of inspection, he made a point of talking to the ordinary railwaymen or lorry drivers, with whom he had a considerable rapport. The men realised that he was interested in their problems, which he considered his duty to take seriously, and was not just putting on an act. In Liverpool he once met one of his wartime drivers and at Bank Hall locomotive depot he was delighted to run into an elderly railwayman who had served with him in the First World War. At the King's Cross Goods Yard, however, he inadvertently entangled himself in a situation which went completely out of control. He had requested the Goods Agent to call an impromptu gathering of men and group themselves round him in a semi-circle so that he could address them 'army style', but then the plan went rather wrong:

> . . . he quickly found himself surrounded by motor drivers, goods porters, and yard staff . . . Instead of addressing his men, he was obliged to listen to a sardonic tirade from Evans [a goods checker] and then to answer questions and counter questions . . .

When he was eventually allowed to leave the yard he remarked to the General Manager that 'he would take care never to be shanghaied again'. But he had not flinched from the questions nor shown any irritation or apprehension, 'points not lost upon these men, whose respect for him – afterwards and out of earshot – was unqualified except for the use of the descriptive and colourful adjective'.[53]

Robertson's desire to improve labour relations and establish better links with the railwaymen was illustrated by the unexpected friendship he developed with the London Secretary of the NUR, the relief signalman, Sidney Hoskins, who was both an admirer of Red China and of the Moral Re-Armament movement. In the aftermath of the ASLEF strike in June,

1955, he invited Brian Robertson to visit him and his wife for supper in Hendon to discuss the problems facing the railways, but he was to come ' not as the head of an industry, but as a fellow worker'[54]. After making discreet enquiries about Hoskins, Brian Robertson took up his invitation to go up to Hendon for supper provided the visit was accorded complete secrecy. Unfortunately, there is no record of the subsequent discussion around the supper table, but for the next five years Hoskins remained in touch with him, sending him his observations on the current state of labour relations. Once or twice he was invited to Brian Robertson's flat in Chiltern Court, off Baker Street, for drinks and at one juncture Hoskins also invited him to see a play he had written, which apparently had a bearing upon the endemic problem of labour relations.

At managerial level, Brian Robertson was particularly anxious to foster and reward talent and pressed for the introduction of a system of confidential staff reports, which would enable the Commission to spot 'unusually promising staff'. He was fond of quoting Napoleon to the effect that in war three quarters of the time it was personal character and relationships that mattered, while the balance of manpower and *matériel* accounted for only the remaining quarter[55]. He set up a staff college in Woking in 1959, which in retrospect he thought was the most valuable initiative he had launched at the BTC, and he was insistent that the General Managers and the Divisions should appoint their best men to attend 'however inconvenient it might be'. He never missed visiting a course in progress and made a point afterwards of mixing informally with staff members and listening to what they had to say. He also organised regular officers' conferences each year where such pertinent subjects as 'The Commercial Outlook' or 'The Future Pattern of Traffic' were discussed. He used to chair these meetings himself and sum up lucidly at the end of the sessions.

He was in many ways an enlightened employer. After the abortive Hungarian revolt of 1956, he was, for instance, anxious to employ Hungarian refugees on the railways and have provision made for them to learn English. He was also quite ready to appoint a woman to a position of responsibility, provided that she was genuinely the right person for the post, but he set his face resolutely against 'positive discrimination', arguing that 'The emphasis should be on employing women where they were the most suitable [person] for the job rather than on employing them because they were women'[56].

After the upheavals of 1953–55, Robertson was determined to protect the BTC from any further government interference so that its new organisation would have time to shake down and its modernisation programme could proceed unimpeded. When Lord Falmouth suggested in the Lords that a government commission should be set up to look at the railways, Brian Robertson was horrified and informed him immediately that:

I would do a great deal to save this vast enterprise from being thrown once more into the melting pot by the institution of an enquiry, public or private, into its organisation. It has an enormous job on hand and I feel that it would be really tragic to upset it now. Napoleon, in spite of being a soldier and a politician, said a number* of sensible things. Amongst them he once said something to the effect that it is a good deal better to make a plan and go ahead on it with determination than to spend endless time casting around for the ideal plan . . . [*Joke only!][57]

In early 1956, Brian Robertson was still sufficiently optimistic to feel that Britain in its 'own odd way' was 'instinctively stumbling towards' the right balance between public and private transport. His heartfelt but ultimately vain plea was that this whole area should be treated as 'a scientific problem, and not as a conflict of political ideologies'[58].

As can already be seen from the history of his first 18 months as Chairman of the BTC, the railways dominated the work of the Commission. This was inevitable because they were by far the largest part of its organisation, and were running at such a loss that they dragged the Commission's finances deeply into the red. The other Divisions, with the exception of the inland waterways, were profitable and were run relatively efficiently by their own managers. Brian Robertson, of course, kept a watching brief over their progress but their problems occupied little of his time. At the weekly Commission meetings their progress was somewhat perfunctorily monitored. In January, 1959, he quite candidly informed the Commission that he had devoted most of his annual review to the railways simply because they were the largest Division and created the most problems, and told the other Divisions that 'to be left alone could be taken as a compliment'[59].

Nevertheless, if a crisis did arise in a Division their managers could be sure of his support. During the long London bus strike in the summer of 1958, he strongly supported Sir John Elliot, the Chairman of London Transport Executive. He also threw himself energetically behind Elliot's proposals for building a new tube line, 'Route C', or the Victoria Line, as it was later called. He first persuaded Boyd-Carpenter in 1955 to allow the Commission to promote a private Bill in Parliament to gain authorisation in principle for the construction of the line, even though work would not begin for several years. Then, at the end of 1956, the Commission permitted London Transport to spend some £500,000 on preliminary work. Over the next year, Brian Robertson tenaciously kept up the pressure on the Ministry of Transport to ensure the Government's commitment to the line's construction. Countering possible criticism from the road lobby, he argued forcefully that:

The Victoria Line can in many ways be regarded as an underground road and consequently as a major contribution to the solution of

London's traffic problems. In such a context, it would be reasonable to agree, as in many other great cities of Europe and America, that some financial assistance should be given towards its construction[60].

In July, 1958, the Government announced its support for the project in the Commons and a year later it authorised the grant of the first million pounds.

While in no way forgetting Elliot's vital role, the Victoria Line can be regarded as one of Brian Robertson's more uncontroversial legacies to the travelling public. Unfortunately, his far greater project for modernising the railways was to be dogged by controversy and acrimony from its inception onwards. When the Plan was first announced in January, 1955, Elliot warned Robertson that 'the tightest grip' would have to be kept upon it and that it would have to be driven through to its completion 'quite ruthlessly'[61]. Brian Robertson was only too aware of the need for this and the General Staff, through the Modernisation Committee, tried to coordinate the work of the 16 specialist panels responsible for such crucial matters as traffic, electrification and the introduction of diesels. The Ministry of Transport was somewhat sceptical of this 'mammoth organisation' and believed that the Commission should concentrate the work in the hands of a few key individuals. Possibly in response to this criticism in July, 1956, Robertson set up the 'Chairman's Conference on Modernisation' to discuss major technical problems with the relevant experts before the final decisions were taken[62].

The execution of the modernisation programme was dependent upon crucial decisions of principle which the Commission had to take concerning electrification, the type of continuous brake to be adopted for freight wagons, and above all the future pattern of traffic flows, which would determine the siting of new marshalling yards and the design of freight wagons. By November, 1955, the Commission was ready to adopt the 25,000 volt alternating current system after Brian Robertson had studied its operation in France. It was costly to install and suffered from teething troubles but in the long term it proved the right choice. Unfortunately the Commission did not act with the same logic in the crucial question of continuous brakes. After being impressed by the obvious superiority of the air brake, it plumped for the inferior vacuum brake as the Area Board Chairmen and General Managers insisted that it would be cheaper and easier to fit, an argument that was authoritatively backed in *The Times* by Sir Charles Goodeve, the Director of the British Iron and Steel Research Association[63]. In retrospect, this can easily be seen to have been an expensive mistake, which had to be reversed in the 1960s. Indeed, Gourvish, the historian of British Railways, castigates the Commission for embarking 'on a spending programme before the technical and commercial implications had been fully investigated'[64].

The Commission, however, was confronted with a serious dilemma. It was convinced that the modernisation plan 'alone would be the saving of British Railways'[65]. It had to satisfy both the public and Parliament that rapid progress was being made in order to secure the continuation of the necessary funding. Inevitably, this imperative dictated an almost reckless tempo of modernisation carried out on insecure foundations. This was particularly apparent in the Commission's dieselisation policy. Initially, in 1955, it ordered some 134 locomotives from several different manufacturers with the intention of testing them out over a three-year period, but as financial pressures intensified, the Commission moved on to a policy of eliminating steam traction as rapidly as possible and started ordering large quantities of diesels from a diverse number of British firms in 1957. By 1962, British Railways had a diesel fleet containing some 41 different types of locomotive, some of which were hopelessly inefficient[66]. In retrospect, this can be seen to have been another serious miscalculation. Yet in the context of the late fifties it was one that did make some sense. Although it was uneconomic to replace steam so quickly, the modernisation programme appealed to the Treasury precisely because it would lead to an appreciable saving in good quality coal at a time when oil was cheap. The problems of ordering 'too many unproved types' of diesel was fully explored at the Chairman's Conference, where it was also stressed that if the trials took too long, then many of them would be redundant before their life was expired[67]. Diesels were, after all, seen only as a stopgap until the whole network could be electrified. In 1957, it could hardly be foreseen that the Government would severely prune the number of electrification projects in three years time. Stewart Joy, who was later the chief economist of the British Rail Board, accused the Commission of pursuing a 'Chauvinist policy' of buying only second rate British models. Ideally, Brian Robertson, after visiting America in the autumn of 1957 would have preferred to order a large number of diesels from the United States where General Motors had an excellent track record in producing locomotives whose 'reliability is absolutely proven'[68], but both the economic and political obstacles to this course were formidable. The Government was loath to lift its restrictions on dollar spending and General Motors were initially unwilling to allow a British firm to undertake the construction of their diesels under licence. By the time these problems had been overcome, the Commission had already awarded contracts to British firms.

Ernest Marples was later to accuse Brian Robertson of being technically incompetent[69]. He was, of course, no railway engineer, and was thus like Marples himself, dependent on expert advice. He made many mistakes because the advice coming to him was often contradictory or not thought through. In retrospect he should, for instance, have stamped firmly on demands from the Western Region in 1957 for a diesel locomotive fleet with hydraulic transmissions, which later proved to be an expensive failure, but at the Chairman's Conference he was faced by a formidable alliance of Hanks and Grand, who quoted the experience of the *Bundesbahn* to back up their case. Even the advice of the co-opted Continental expert, Dr. F Q den Hollander, from the Dutch railways, was ambiguous: whilst being sceptical about German experience in the higher powered units, he did confirm that a number of Continental railways 'were about to embark on proposals for developing this form of transport in the lower powers'[70].

The implementation of the modernisation Plan was accompanied by a sharp deterioration in the finances of the BTC. Until the autumn of 1959 Brian Robertson was able successfully to convince the Ministry of Transport that the progressive modernisation of the railways would earn an extra £35 million pounds by 1961/2 and £85 million by 1970 and thus stave off any severe pruning of the programme. In March, 1956, the new Minister of Transport, Harold Watkinson, seized on the application of the BTC to raise its freight charges to demand a reassessment of the Commission's economic and financial future. In the meantime, he added considerably to their financial problems by pressing during a period of inflation for only very low rises in railway freight, dock and canal charges and for the postponement for six months of any increases in passenger and London Transport fares[71]. Technically, Watkinson's intervention was *ultra vires* of the Acts of 1947 and 1953, and some of Brian Robertson's colleagues believed that he should have made a stand on the issue, even threatening to resign if necessary[72]. It is, however, open to debate whether the eruption of a violent row just at the point when the Commission was negotiating for further financial assistance from the Government would have helped their case.

The Commission's reassessment, which was included in the White Paper, published in October 1956, was an optimistic document, which produced figures that apparently confirmed that there would be a profit in revenue of £85 million by 1970. It made some very rash assumptions that it would be allowed to adjust charges to cover costs and that labour costs would not outstrip inflation. In many ways the forecast was more wishful thinking than accurate financial analysis, but it was accepted by Watkinson, and the Finance Act of 1956 duly empowered the Ministry of Transport to lend money to the Commission. In the three years 1956–58 some £221 million were advanced. Brian Robertson was, however, probably right when he observed that for the Government 'to give us adequate relief involved no more political difficulty than giving us less than we needed'[73].

The second half of the 1950s was a paradoxical period for the railways. On the one hand, the Commission was investing record sums in modernisation, while on the other, it was accumulating a record deficit, the principal causes of which were the precipitate decline in freight coupled with the sharply rising wages of the railwaymen. In 1956, the deficit was £57.5 million, while by 1958 it had risen to £90 million. There was then the very real danger that the modernisation programme, which all saw as the ultimate key to profitability, would be halted by a Government tired of pouring money into a bottomless pit. In January, 1958, Watkinson warned Brian Robertson that 'a lot more questions are going to be asked about the worthwhileness of all you are planning on the freight side and about the likelihood of your being equipped in time to stop the rot that at least some people think has set in'[74]. Watkinson personally, however, continued to back the Commission and its borrowing powers were extended by another £600 million, but at the cost of further government scrutiny in the shape of a second White Paper, which was published in July, 1959.

Throughout these years, the Commission had attempted to contain the deficit through a mixture of economies, cross-subsidisation in its various branches and attempts to reverse the decline in its freight traffic, until the completed modernisation plan, like the US cavalry of old, would come to its assistance. An obvious economy, which the Ministry of Transport favoured, was the withdrawal of uneconomic railway services. In March 1956 Brian Robertson urged the Commission to pursue this policy vigorously, but in the course of the next six months, after several senior rail officers had argued that these branch lines were often lucrative feeders to the main lines, it switched its emphasis to keeping them open, but using small diesel trains, 'new operating methods, the substitution of halts for stations with staff, ticket issuing by train staff, and other simplifications designed to reduce the cost of the services to the minimum'.

If even a slimmed down railway was ever to be profitable, the decline in freight had to be reversed. Brian Robertson constantly urged his managers in their quest for more freight orders to show 'a greater sense of offensive, not defensive'[75], and he himself did not hesitate to act as a salesman when he visited the Chairman of the Port of London Authority in October 1956. Yet apart from a brief respite brought about by the Suez Crisis in the aftermath of which the Government cut oil supplies by 10 per cent, the volume of freight carried by the railways continued to fall. In February 1958 Brian Robertson set up a small committee under A J White, the Assistant-General Manager of the Eastern Region, to analyse the problem and produce a 'cohesive freight policy' rather than, as hitherto, trying 'to deal with individual features as they came along separately and disjointedly'[76].

By the autumn of 1958, the Commission was ready to embark on a more vigorous policy to cut costs, boost profits and speed up the modernisation programme. Although Brian Robertson stressed in September that 'it was not a matter of paring or slashing the railways but of streamlining them in relation to modern requirement', the scale of the projected cut-backs in many ways foreshadowed Beeching's ruthless pruning of the railways some three years later. He envisaged swingeing cuts in maintenance facilities, rolling stock and antediluvian goods depots and also urged that the closure of unwanted branch lines 'should continue to be pressed forward strongly'[77].

A month later, White presented to the Commission a 'planners' document' for a more compact and streamlined railway system and a more aggressive strategy for winning freight contracts. Both White, Brian Robertson and later Beeching were convinced that as the coal industry was in decline and mineral traffic static, it was in increasing their share of general merchandise that the railways' best hopes lay. The assumption was that modernisation with its containers and pallets and a new pricing policy would persuade businessmen and industrialists once again to use the railways. Unfortunately, despite an elaborate publicity programme, which proposed planting references to new freight services for farmers in 'The Archers' and an interview by Robin Day with Brian Robertson on television, the annual tonnage of freight carried continued to fall steadily. For general merchandise, lorries were undoubtedly both cheaper and more effective.

The financial problems of the Commission were further exacerbated by the repeated wage rises which were extracted from it by the unions. In January, 1956, the three railway unions were offered a 7 per cent rise, some 15 months later a further 3 per cent was awarded with an extra 2 per cent added subject to productivity. At first it was hoped that this link between productivity and wage increases would usher in a new era in labour relations. Optimistically, Sir Cecil Weir, Brian Robertson's former colleague in Germany, who had joined the Commission as a part-time member in 1955, congratulated him on setting 'a pattern of good understanding from which all industries will derive the benefit . . .'. The chairman was also so heartened to hear from Sidney Hoskins that the agreement was received with relief by 'many thousands of railwaymen' that he forwarded the letter to Watkinson[78]. Yet, essentially, the unions remained convinced with some good reason that their members' wages were slipping back not only in real terms but also in comparison with other industries. In May, 1958, a strike threat by the NUR was only averted by Government intervention. The unions were given a 3 per cent award accompanied by a promise that an enquiry, to be chaired by CE Guillebaud, Emeritus Reader in Economics at Cambridge, would be set up to look into the wage structure of the railways and its comparability with other industries.

***

While Guillebaud was pursuing his slow but meticulous investigations, the Commission was able to win a brief reprieve from further wage claims, but when by January, 1960, he had still not reported, the pressure on the leadership of the NUR, now in the hands of the more moderate Sidney Greene, intensified. On 5 January, the London District Council ignored Hoskins' appeals and planned a local strike for 1 February, and the Manchester branch pushed for a national stoppage. Brian Robertson argued forcefully, when he met the unions, that they should await the Guillebaud report, but he was willing to backdate any rises recommended by it to 11 January 1960. This was rejected by the NUR which wanted an immediate interim payment, and on 29 January Greene again threatened a national strike unless the payment was made. To the Commission, the behaviour of the NUR in particular seemed to be suicidal. Reggie Hanks, for instance, complained bitterly in a private letter to Brian Robertson that 'You and I and the rest of us struggle to save the railways and we meet union opposition at every turn', and he advised him 'to make a stand and do what you know to be right as an act of faith'[79]. The Chairman, however, was more cautious as a strike would only plunge the Commission's finances still further into debt. Consequently, after intervention by both Edward Heath, the Minister of Labour and the TUC, the Commission and the NUR agreed on an interim payment of 5 per cent. In March, 1960, Guillebaud at last completed his report, and his recommendation of increases of between 8 per cent and 10 per cent was acted upon in June.

Throughout these years, British Railways faced a torrent of destructive criticism and abuse from public opinion, the press and often the backbenches of the Commons. Labour unrest and the apparent slowness of the modernisation scheme to conjure an efficient and modern rail system 'out of the ground like magic mushrooms'[80] to replace the grimy and run-down post-war railways with something infinitely cleaner and more efficient, caused considerable impatience and disillusionment. Quite often Brian Robertson, who was usually portrayed as 'the Army's . . . £8,500 a year boss of the British Railways'[81] was personally a target for criticism. A particularly virulent attack on him was mounted in December 1959 by 'Cassandra' of the *Daily Mirror*. 'Cassandra' had been a journalist in Italy during the 1943–45 campaign and had been bitterly critical of military censorship, and was thus probably paying back old scores on the CAO who had kept such a close watch on his reporting. Brian Robertson was, however, not without his champions. One of his former batmen in Italy, who was now farming in Yorkshire, immediately wrote to Cassandra asking him 'to lay that pistol down' and informed him that Brian Robertson was 'the greatest man' he had ever met[82]. In the New Year, Cassandra returned to the attack. He congratulated Brian Robertson on not writing his memoirs, calling him 'a military Trappist', and conceded that he had done 'a wonderful job' in Italy, but then he plunged in the dagger:

And he has done to my immediate first hand knowledge a lousy job at Marylebone Station and all points West, South, East, and North[83].

Up to a point, Brian Robertson could be philosophical about such attacks, but as he explained in a lecture to the Royal United Services Institute, he was all too aware of its negative impact on the morale of the Commission and its staff:

The people of this country have always enjoyed poking fun at their own institutions. The present condition of the railways, which results from past neglect, is too good an opportunity to be missed. It would be foolish if we were to be hyper-sensitive or resentful about criticism up to a point. Beyond that point it seems fair to say that it does not fortify morale or discipline to tell the men that they are a crowd of miserable slackers and that those in charge of them are a bunch of blithering idiots. Incidentally neither the one nor the other is true[84].

In countering the attacks on the BTC, his leadership was seen at its best. He was not a charismatic or slick leader, but he tenaciously defended the Railways and the policies which he and his colleagues had collectively arrived at. He never lost a chance to bolster the morale of his managers and the hundreds of thousands of men under them by emphasising 'that they were a wonderful body of men', who deserved good leadership[85]. He used skilfully to orchestrate a blaze of publicity immediately a particularly significant modernisation scheme was completed. When, for example, the Kent Coast electric express was inaugurated in June, 1959, it was given considerable coverage in the national and London papers. The *Evening Standard* featured a long article by Brian Robertson with a Foreword by Watkinson, and the Queen was persuaded to travel in the new rolling stock, attached to the Royal Train from Portsmouth to Waterloo[86]. He also made extensive use of film production units and outside public relations services to wage, as he saw it, 'a form of psychological warfare to counter the constant and heavy attacks which were being made on the railways as such'[87]. Skilfully, these films sought to implant in the minds of the public a potent moral point, which would later appeal to the 'Green' lobby, namely that 'it was wrong in principle for heavy freight traffic to be conveyed on roads besides which people lived and walked and on which they drove their private cars'. Even if such messages did not stop the progressive transfer of the freight business from the railways to the roads, they did eventually sow in the mind of the public the vague idea that railways were 'environmentally friendly' and should not be too badly abused by the Government!

THE TRIPLE INQUISITION

1959 was a watershed in the affairs of the BTC. First Brian Robertson lost an important ally in the Ministry of Transport when Sir Gilmour Jenkins retired in April and was replaced by Sir James Dunnett, an advocate of a leaner and much more cost-effective railway system. Dunnett then proceeded to bring over another advocate of strict financial control, David Serpell, from the Treasury, as his Deputy Secretary. Shortly after the General Election of October, 1959, Watkinson was moved across to the Ministry of Defence, and Ernest Marples became the new Minister of Transport. Marples was an ambitious and energetic politician who was determined to push Britain into the motorway age. He himself had set up his own road construction business, Marples, Ridgeway and Partners, and not surprisingly had little sympathy with the railway lobby. What really excited him was the problem of coming to terms with the motor car. Essentially, he saw the future of the railways within the context of their impact on the country's road system. He conceded that the railways did have some part to play in the future transport system of the country, but there is no doubt that in his heart he felt that they were an expensive anachronism in the motor age.

At first, Brian Robertson made a determined attempt to establish friendly relations with Marples as he had done with his predecessors. In October, 1959, he invited him to a small dinner party to meet the leading members of the BTC, but the occasion was not really a success. After dinner, Marples stood up and introduced himself. In an amusing address, he gave a brief account of his career in which at one point, with many suggestive gestures, he talked as if he were a junior office boy appraising the attractions of the junior office girl. The crudeness of this approach appalled Brian Robertson and one colleague noticed a look of 'supreme disgust' pass across his face[88]. Over the next few months, it soon became clear that there was a deep personal antipathy between the two men.

Marples lost little time in submitting the BTC's investment plans for 1960–62 to a close scrutiny. His officials recommended immediate cuts of some £35 million and pointed out that it was most unlikely that the railways would generate sufficient profits to service the new capital necessary for financing the modernisation plan. In December, Marples informed Macmillan that he would like to appoint a committee along the lines of the Herbert Commission, which had looked into the affairs of the electricity supply industry, to consider the future of the railways, although at that stage he was wary for political reasons of provoking the resignation of the Chairman. Macmillan emolliently suggested that if it was emphasised that one of the aims of the committee was an attempt to get 'the right relationship between Parliament and the British Railways', it might give him less offence[89].

While Marples was considering how best to proceed with the reorganisation of the BTC, in November, 1959, the Commons Select Committee on Nationalised Industries decided to make its own investigation into the Commission's activities. It was now clear that 1960 was indeed, as Brian Robertson remarked in January, 'to be a year of decision' for the Commission[90]. The Select Committee convened at the end of January and after interviewing Dunnett and other senior Ministry of Transport officials, summoned the Chairman himself for a cross-examination. While the Committee did indeed ask him searching questions, it was fundamentally well disposed towards the BTC and Brian Robertson in particular. It was chaired by Sir Toby Low, who remembered him as a formidable CAO in Italy, and Austen Albu, who had worked with him on the Control Commission in Germany, was also a member. Brian Robertson performed brilliantly and in a series of lucid replies explained – and defended – the workings and policies of the Transport Commission. His performance so impressed Sir Alexander Spearman that he was moved to observe:

> . . . I do not think since I have been on this committee that we have ever had a witness who has to answer questions ranging over such an immensely wide field, and I would like to pay tribute to the skill, patience and immense knowledge Sir Brian has showed[91].

When the Select Committee reported in July, 1960, it did censure the Commission for not applying effective costing procedures to its modernisation projects and for failing to rationalise the rail network and evolving a profitable freight strategy, but overall its criticism was muted. Cecil Weir found it positively encouraging. He wrote to Brian Robertson observing that:

> Obviously, looking at matters as they have done some years after the events and with the benefit of hindsight, they have said certain things which they might not have said had they been in our places at the time we embarked upon the projects, but by and large it is a fair minded report which gives reasonable credit to the Commission for the work it has done in the past six or seven years under your leadership[92].

In the meantime, Marples and his officials were drawing up their own plans for the future of the BTC. Essentially, the Commission was to be broken down into its component parts, which would then be formed into separate companies with their own boards[93]. The Commission would become just a holding company empowered only to hold the shares and properties of the former BTC. Brian Robertson's own future was bleak. Ultimately, Marples was quite convinced that he would have to go, but in the short term he still had some use for him. He was to negotiate with the

unions a phased acceptance of the Guillebaud report and continue to run
the BTC until the new organisation was in place. Ironically, he was also to
be charged with working out the details of the new plan, the broad lines
of which were to be laid down by the Government, so that a Bill could be
introduced into the Commons in November. Somewhat condescendingly,
Marples then informed Macmillan that:

> If General Robertson will agree to this concept of the next 12 months,
> he will have earned, and should receive, the thanks of the nation[94].

While the rumours of impending change flew round 222 Marylebone
Road, and indeed the whole rail network, unsettling managers and workers alike, Brian Robertson tried to allay their fears. At a Commission
meeting in March, he stressed, for instance, that no organisation the size
of BTC could ever be static and asked the heads of the Divisions to tell
their senior officers:

> . . . not to worry over what they might read in the newspapers, much of
> which was either rumour or conjecture, and often not even intelligent
> conjecture. If there were to be any changes affecting them or their part
> of the organisation, they would learn of them from him long before they
> were likely to take effect[95].

On 10 March, 1960, Macmillan announced in the Commons the
Government's intention both to remodel the railways and the Commission
and to set up a preliminary 'planning board' to advise the Ministry of
Transport on how this was to be done in detail. After considering Reay
Geddes, the Managing Director of Dunlop, and Eric Coates, another of
Brian Robertson's old colleagues from the Control Commission, Marples
managed to persuade Sir Ivan Stedeford, the Chairman of Tube
Investments, to head what became called the Special Advisory Group. He
was joined by Dr. Beeching from ICI, an accountant, Henry Benson,
from Cooper brothers and Frank Kearton from Courtaulds.

Inevitably, Stedeford's Group was regarded with considerable suspicion
by the Commission, but Brian Robertson emphatically informed his
Board that there was no option but to cooperate:

> . . . Any other attitude by the Commission would be quite unthinkable.
> Not only would it be wrong to do otherwise but it would also be dam-
> aging to the interests of the organisation and those who serve in it[96].

The Special Advisory Group very early on came to the conclusion that
the Commission's commercial policy was 'simply the provision of the
best possible railway system they could buy without reference to

economics'[97]. Thus, for the second time in a year, there had to be a re-appraisal of the BTC's finances. The costs of the modernisation programme had to be re-examined and all projects over a quarter of a million pounds justified. In June, the Committee recommended that the sections of the plan on which work was still not too far advanced should be temporarily halted pending further scrutiny. Throughout these disheartening proceedings, Brian Robertson cooperated patiently, yet he also fought a skilful rearguard action to defend the modernisation scheme. He stuck to the principle that

> . . . the British Railways system, contracted to any extent that may be considered wise and socially acceptable, must be a modern system. Otherwise our railways will never cease to be a drain upon the Exchequer, nor will they give satisfaction to the country[98].

He also constantly stressed how the railways' financial position was so often critically influenced by factors outside the Commission's control. He pointed out to Stedeford for instance that in the budget of 1959 the Government, by cutting duty on commercial vehicles, made things 'more difficult for the railways'. Yet, apart from urging a 'solution, which is flexible enough to contain these imponderables', he freely confessed that the BTC had no easy answer to the intractable financial problems of the railways:

> Our men have lived with this problem a long time . . . They have no *idée fixe* as to how it should be solved (I almost wish they had). They are only anxious to discover an answer which will both solve the problem and gain governmental acceptance. It is comparatively easy to do one without the other, but very difficult to do both.

He invited the Advisory Group to discuss 'the problem and its possible solution' with the financial staff of the BTC, 'not as inquisitors, but as fellow seekers after the light'[99].

Robertson sought to exploit the divisions that opened up in the Advisory Group between Beeching and Stedeford, in an attempt to safeguard as much of the modernisation programme as was possible and to influence the shape of the new post-BTC organisational structure. From its first meetings in April, it was clear that the Group was split into the hawks led by Beeching and the doves by Stedeford, who wanted to cooperate with the Commission. Beeching, on the other hand, adopted a much more radical approach not only to organisational matters but also to the modernisation plan. The Commission soon learnt of these differences from sympathetic civil servants in the Ministry of Transport[100]. These leaks inspired Wansborough-Jones while on holiday in Scotland to make 'a military appreciation' of the situation. He argued that Stedeford himself 'who wants to stick to the broad view' was clearly the key to the situation and that the Government, having begged him to become the chairman of the Group, could not easily disregard his recommendations[101]. Brian Robertson was well aware of this and had already suggested to Stedeford that they meet informally for a chat over dinner, a suggestion which Stedeford quickly accepted. Shortly afterwards, Robertson handed over a memorandum to Stedeford containing his own ideas, which have already been quoted (see p 184), on the reorganisation of the BTC.

The Commission fought particularly hard to salvage their plans for the electrification of the Euston line to Manchester, Liverpool and Birmingham. In a lengthy and well argued letter to Stedeford, Brian Robertson pointed out that the project had nearly passed the point of no return as some £40 million had already been spent or committed to it. To abandon it at this stage would lead to confusion and demoralisation which mere figures could not convey. He then bombarded Stedeford with every possible economic argument for electrification that he could think of: it would save on imported oil, create a demand for coal (by using electric power) and ultimately perhaps benefit from cheap atomic power. Drawing on the French experience of the Paris–Lyons and Paris–Lille lines, he argued that an efficient Euston line would act as a magnet for traffic from the Paddington-Birmingham line and would in due course lead to considerable economies. Finally he nailed his flag defiantly to the mast and declared that ' If the Commission had their original decision to make again, they would decide again in favour of electrification of this line'[102].

When the Advisory Group drew up its report, it was clear that Brian Robertson's policy of cultivating Stedeford did not quite bring in the dividends for which he had hoped. A particularly unwelcome development was the Group's Recommendation No. 2, proposing the setting up of the 'Continuing Body', which would conduct a more leisurely investigation into the future of the railways in general and the BTC's modernisation plan in particular under the chairmanship of Marples himself. After the Select Committee and the Advisory Group, the proposal for yet another enquiry was seen by the Commission as adding insult to injury. As Cecil Weir observed, it demonstrated 'a complete lack of trust in the Commission, which contains the most experienced railwaymen in the country'[103]. Weir urged the Commission to fight the proposal, but Robertson rejected this advice and stoically accepted yet another inquisitorial round. His tenacious and skilful attempts to defend various apparently unremunerative projects of the modernisation programme irritated Marples immensely, who in a minute to Macmillan commented testily:

> . . . as usual when a General is in command he seeks to claw back at the conference table (on the armistice and peace terms) what he lost in the

battle. I intend to soldier on with determination but will be in touch with you and Lord Mills before I smell a crisis[104].

In these stressful and often humiliating negotiations, Brian Robertson did win one major concession thanks to the influence of Stedeford, when in January, 1961, Marples finally reprieved the Euston–Manchester–Liverpool electrification scheme.

The Advisory Group could not agree on the crucial question of the shape of the organisation that was to replace the Commission. In their Recommendation No.8 two sets of proposals were drawn up – one by Kearton and Stedeford and the other by Beeching and Benson. The former had considerable similarities to the ideas outlined by Robertson in June as it envisaged the conversion of the BTC into a holding company similar to the model established by the Electricity Council in 1958, while the latter was more streamlined and made the original divisions of the BTC directly responsible to the Minister.

In the ensuing arguments between the Ministry of Transport, the Advisory Group and the Commission it soon became obvious that Wansborough-Jones and Robertson had been backing the wrong horse. It was Beeching rather than Stedeford who had Marples' ear. Thus it was essentially his scheme for reorganising the Commission that Marples chose, despite the strong, even vehement opposition of Brian Robertson. In the closing months of 1960, Marples made up his mind about the changes he wanted and pressed on with drawing up the White Paper on the reorganisation of the BTC. He was convinced that Brian Robertson was 'incompetent both technically and financially' and in November told Macmillan that he would like 'to get Mr. [sic] Beeching as Chairman of the [proposed] Central Railways Board'[105].

While the officials at Marylebone Road worked overtime on memoranda and accounts for this triple inquisition, the day to day management of the Commission had to continue. The familiar problems of staff morale, dismissive articles in the papers, freight policy and the performance of diesel locomotives continued to press upon the Commission. There were, too, the usual crop of embarrassing incidents which afforded the superficial or jaundiced observer ample opportunity to laugh loudly at the Commission's expense. On 11 January, 1961, for instance, a Type 3 Brush Diesel locomotive broke down while drawing the Royal Train to Sandringham. Also the new electrified suburban services in Glasgow developed so many 'teething troubles' that they had to be withdrawn and temporarily replaced by steam again, much to the nation's amusement and the Glaswegians' irritation.

On the one hand, the Commission was branded by 'Young Turks' like Correlli Barnett as unable to think in a revolutionary way and act in a dynamic manner[106], yet when it did try to be ruthless in sweeping away the old in favour of the new it was equally criticised. Its decision to demolish the Doric Arch and the Great Hall at Euston station met with a storm of criticism from the London County Council, the Victorian Society and a protest campaign led by John Betjeman and Woodrow Wyatt. Betjeman rightly pointed out that they were 'magnificent architecture and the first great railway buildings in the world'[107]. The Commission. however, insisted that the Arch would have to be removed as they planned to build a new escalator and booking office immediately below it. Brian Robertson was agreeable to its removal and reconstruction elsewhere, but was adamant that the Commission would not pay for it. Unfortunately the Government refused to find the necessary money and this 'great museum piece' as *The Times* called it was destroyed[108]. An act of vandalism certainly, but it was also understandable that a bankrupt Commission harried by Marples would be reluctant to dig into its pocket to preserve redundant historical relics.

By the end of 1960, Brian Robertson's role in the Commission was reduced to being a caretaker smoothing the way for 'the men who are to occupy the key positions in the new organisation'[109]. It was a potentially difficult situation, but he approached it as a highly professional public servant, informing Marples:

> I have pledged myself to cooperate in introducing the new organisation as quickly as possible. I can help the chairman of the British Railways a lot, and am prepared to do so while giving him every possible freedom in the pursuit of his own policies. But cooperation is a two way business. While I remain I must carry the ultimate responsibility . . . and my position would become quite impossible if the new man deliberately refused to work in with me . . .[110]

He also gave Marples his opinion on the choice of his successor. He personally favoured the appointment of a professional railwayman like Keith Grand, but conceded that 'a new man from outside' might be the right choice. Marples had informed him unofficially that he had already approached Beeching. Brian Robertson viewed this move with considerable reserve and warned the Minister:

> I know him to be a man with a first class brain. You have every right to appoint a man of your choosing . . . I only venture to advise that you should be sure before coming to a final decision that he really does possess the qualities which are necessary for this post. Brilliance of intellect alone will not be enough. As you yourself agreed, it will be a very difficult choice for the organisation to accept. Is it the only possible choice?[111]

Marples was unimpressed by this advice. On 15 March, he announced Beeching's appointment with the princely salary of £24,000 per annum. He was first to be Chairman of the BTC Commission and then, after its demise, to chair the new British Railways Board. He was to take up his appointment on 1 June but until then he was to be a part-time member of the Commission.

Brian Robertson disliked pathos and drama and continued his work at 222 Marylebone Road with the minimum of fuss right up to 1 June. Over the course of his last year at the Commission he won, perhaps for the first time, the real affection of his colleagues and of large numbers of the ordinary railwaymen, some of whom on his retirement, as a mark of the respect they had for him, presented him with models of engines which they themselves had made[112]. Most of his colleagues admired, as Cecil Weir put it, the 'patient, thorough and tactful way' in which he dealt with the Commission's inquisitors[113]. They felt, too, that he had been unfairly treated by Marples, and of course dreaded what a new broom in Beeching's hands might bring. The strength of their feeling was very evident when he chaired his last BTC officer's conference at Balliol College in April 1961. At the end of the conference there was a formal dinner after which Brian Robertson gave what was in effect his farewell speech. When he finished, he was given a prolonged and genuinely moving ovation. He formally handed over the poisoned chalice of the Chairmanship a few days after he had presided over his last meeting of the Commission on 25 May, where significantly he was thanked for his unfailing courtesy and kindness. Shortly afterwards, some amends were made for the humiliating treatment meted out by the Government to a great public servant when he was created an hereditary baron.

Perhaps, in retrospect, Brian Robertson would have been wiser to have become a successful Adjutant General rather than take on the Sisyphean task of the BTC. In the opinion of one distinguished railwaymen he was miscast as Chairman of the BTC. He was led by Churchill and Lennox-Boyd to believe that it was 'a civilian army' requiring firm leadership from the centre, yet really what it needed was a much more drastic decentralisation of power to its individual divisions than he in fact gave it[114].

Strictly by the financial terms he set in the modernisation programme, he did fail. The railways had lost so much money by 1959 that the Government was forced to question the modernisation plan and insist on stricter accounting and a reorganisation of the Commission. Could this financial debacle have been avoided? With hindsight it is all too easy to stress the errors and wrong decisions. Of course, a tighter and more financially accountable organisation should have been created and both a ruthless closing of branch lines and rigorous pruning of labour carried out long before the Beeching era. It is not hard to paint the Robertson era as a distressing catalogue of errors, yet not to qualify this would be a travesty of the truth. At every step he was subject to government pressure to hold down fares and freight rates, while leapfrogging demands from the unions steadily increased the annual wage bills. Brian Robertson did take the essential step of launching an ambitious and controversial modernisation programme. Under enormous pressure from the Government and public opinion to produce, almost overnight, a futuristic rail system, the Commission inevitably cut corners and sometimes made embarrassing and expensive mistakes, yet it did stick tenaciously to its aim of modernising the system. There were, too, plenty of bold and technically advanced decisions taken. The much maligned BTC followed closely railway developments on the Continent and in America and was ready to cooperate with the French to build a Channel tunnel. It pressed for the building of the Victoria Line and supported the development of that sturdy work horse the Route Master London bus, as well as planning a Railway Technical Centre at Derby, which opened shortly after Brian Robertson's retirement. It often took the right decisions, for instance over branch line closures, but implemented them too slowly. At the BTC, Robertson presided over a period of rapid transition from post-war austerity to the affluent age of the car and the motorway in the 1960s. Inevitably, social and economic changes on this scale had a radical impact on the finances of the BTC, which had not been easy to gauge in 1954.

AN INDIAN SUMMER?

In his prime, Brian Robertson had been what today would be described as a 'workaholic'. He was essentially a man who throve on responsibility and the constant pressure of hard work. He had been at his happiest in Germany where his workload was of positively ministerial proportions. He did not therefore enjoy the long periods of enforced leisure which awaited him after 1 June 1961. Neither did he enjoy growing old, although in his speeches in the House of Lords he often joked about his 'great' age. He was a man who had derived considerable pleasure from physical exercise – tennis, polo and skiing, which he continued to do up to the age of 70. He hated having to give up these sports, but he was, of course, able to play bridge, which, as his manservant observed, was 'breakfast, lunch and dinner' to Edith and himself[1].

Unlike most of his military contemporaries he remained a 'Trappist', to use William Connor's expression. Unfortunately, he felt no urge to write his memoirs, even though as far back as 1953 Collins, the publishers, had approached him with an offer to do so. He preferred instead to concentrate his energies on what was still a formidable number of activities, despite the fact that they did not fill up his time. He was on the Board of Dunlop's and the Wagon-lits Sleeping Car Company. Every month on a Thursday evening he used to catch the night sleeper to Paris for the monthly Wagon-lits Board meeting, often staying with the François-Poncets. A pleasant by-product of these visits was the chance to sample the excellent fish cuisine which in those days all good Catholics still ate on Fridays. When the Pope lifted the ban on meat, Brian Robertson had to eat what he regarded as dishes of revoltingly half-cooked lamb at his friends!

At home he was a member of the General Advisory Council of Independent Television, but, increasingly, his main interests were educational. He much regretted the abolition of National Service in 1960, which he was convinced was 'extremely good for the youth of the nation'[2], but realised that no government would dare bring it back. He thus looked to the youth clubs to fill what he perceived to be a vital gap in the education of much of the nation's young men. Here he spoke from experience because he was himself Chairman of the Gloucestershire Association of Boys Clubs. In 1959 the Association had asked him whether they could acquire the small redundant railway station at Kerne Bridge. The request interested him and he arranged for Jim Thomas, the Association's Organising Secretary, to meet his train one Friday evening at Gloucester and then show him a couple of the clubs at work. Thomas took him to a small village in the Forest of Dean, where as a result of the closure of the local coal mines there was a very high rate of unemployment. Here he sat down for two hours in a cold and drafty hall, warmed only by an old-fashioned tortoise stove, and observed what was going on. He put the boys at their ease so that they felt free to talk about their hopes for the future and how they lived at present[3].

Brian Robertson was so impressed by what he saw that he agreed to join the Committee of the Gloucestershire Association of Boys Clubs, and in September, 1961, was elected Chairman, a post which he held for the next six years[4]. He used his influence to raise funds at a time when the local authority was cutting back its grants and to interest prominent local businessmen in the clubs. He gave as much encouragement as he could to the Organising Secretary and his young and (only) full-time assistant. He frequently visited clubs and was especially interested in the industrial and business training courses which the Association ran. Once a week, Jim Thomas would report to him at his house at Iles Green where either over a whisky or while eating crumpets, which were toasted on the fire in his study, he would listen patiently to a review of the current problems. Under his chairmanship, the Association acted as a magnate which attracted the membership of a considerable number of independent clubs. At the AGM in September, 1967, he was, for instance, particularly pleased to note that the 'Cossacks' of Cheltenham, a club composed of 'erstwhile ton-up boys' had affiliated itself to the association.

Robertson was also a member of the Council of the National Association of Boys Clubs and used his membership of the Lords both to protect their interests and to focus attention on the nation's youth. When an article in the *Sunday Times* suggested somewhat inaccurately that the Government was conducting 'a three prong' campaign to replace traditional boys clubs with mixed clubs, Brian Robertson immediately tabled a question in the Lords. Privately he was sceptical about the value of mixed clubs, as he felt that they made the boys unmanageable, but publicly he argued for a plurality of clubs and that the Government should not cut its funding to single sex clubs while assisting mixed organisations[5].

Twice – in 1965 and in 1968 – he introduced debates in the Lords on the state of the youth of the nation[6]. Despite his keen interest in the economy, foreign policy and labour questions, he was convinced that devising the right post-school education 'for the general run of our boys . . . long hair, sideburns, "winkle pickers" and all'[7] was perhaps the most important question confronting the country. In March, 1965, he informed the Lords:

> This country of ours stands today rather disconsolate, perhaps, and a bit bewildered about her future. We are very concerned about our economy, about our foreign affairs, about our defence, and debates on these subjects take place often . . . But is it not wise every now and then to remind ourselves that, however important these subjects are, what matters above all for our future and our future prosperity is what is going on among our youth and how their character is developing[8].

In both debates he was highly critical of the Government's neglect of youth services and lack of any imaginative thinking. He wanted the Government to seize 'hold of this whole problem and translate it to a higher sphere, and make some really bold decisions and inspired planning'[9]. His own suggestions were an interesting assortment of proposals. He wanted the Government to help the parents fulfil their responsibilities, if necessary through a 'Counsel Service or other means', to launch a vigorous campaign for the promotion of voluntary service for the community and to give the department that dealt with the youth question, that 'lies buried away somewhere within the vast Ministry of Education and Science', both a higher profile and more money. More controversially, he also picked up a suggestion, which had been made by the Warden of Toynbee Hall, that there should be a compulsory saving scheme on a PAYE basis for all young wage earners. Finally, he advocated lowering the age of voting to 18 in order to give young people more civic responsibility at an earlier age[10].

Youth and Education were also the main themes of his work in the Salters' Company. In 1918, the Company had set up the Institute of Industrial Chemistry which aimed mainly through the granting of scholarships to students at university and the holding of 'schoolmasters conferences' to increase the number of 'first rate industrial chemists in Great Britain' and to encourage young chemists to enter industry[11]. Brian Robertson had been elected an honorary member in 1949, but it was only after his retirement from the BTC that he was able to devote much attention to the Salters'. In June, 1965, he was elected to the Mastership for a year. He spent much of that year ensuring the future revenues of the company by carefully planning how best the Company could exploit its ownership of the island site in the City 'bounded by Cannon St., Bow Lane and Bread St.', which if redeveloped would be worth some £2½ million[12].

In the midst of the iconoclastic fervour of the 'Swinging Sixties', he sought to secure the future of the Salters' Company by emphasising its links with the real world of science. In his report to the General Court of Livery at the conclusion of his Mastership in June 1966 he observed:

> . . . you will, I hope, appreciate that our over-riding motive has been to maintain and later to increase the amounts which we devote to charity

and education. We hear from time to time those who are ill disposed towards us speak in a denigrating way of those rich city companies; if we could get them to understand and to judge without prejudice the policies which we follow in administering our resources, they might take a rather different view.[13]

Brian Robertson went on to remind the Court that a recent Private Member's Bill 'To Abolish the Corporation of London' had attracted 140 votes, and to stress that he, together with the Masters of the other major companies, had been working on plans for improving their public image.

This same realism and refusal to take a sentimental view of the past infused his speeches to the Lords where he was careful to speak only on matters to which he could contribute an informed opinion. He refused to take a party whip and remained a cross-bencher. This enabled him to speak his mind freely on the subjects which interested him. Appropriately, his maiden speech was on the crisis triggered by the building of the Berlin Wall in August 1961. In early November, General Clay, who had been sent to Berlin as President Kennedy's special representative, had invited Brian Robertson to visit him as a guest of the American Government. There he associated himself closely with Clay in order to evoke the heroic days of Western Allied unity in 1948. On 2 November, both Generals insisted on driving into East Berlin, and neither were stopped at the checkpoint. Once back home, he chose a debate on international affairs shortly before Christmas to make a few comments on the situation in Germany. He prepared his speech carefully as he found the Lords the most critical and well informed audience he had ever encountered and he shook like a leaf as he delivered it[14]. His main message was a familiar one:

> I think all your Lordships would agree that in framing our foreign policy we should be guided by our head rather than by our heart. I say that because, that there should be so many people in this country, who in their hearts are unable to forgive Germany for what she did to the world in two terrible wars is readily understandable, but surely in their heads reason must tell these people that we need the cooperation of Germany in these days. We need her cooperation not only for the defence of Western Europe as a member of NATO but in the organisation of Western Europe to enable it to stand up to the political and economic threats which come from the East . . .[15]

All his speeches over the next nine years contained this same element of blunt realism. He was unsentimental about defence reorganisation and advocated the reform of the House of Lords[16]. He was also 'passionately in favour'[17] of Britain's entry into the Common Market because he had become convinced that 'in this modern world these islands are too small to stand alone'. He criticised his countrymen sharply for their 'psychological insularity' and even belaboured the officers and men of the Rhine Army for imprisoning 'themselves in their own insularity and self-sufficiency'[18]. When the Brussels negotiations broke down in January, 1963, his support for British membership did not waiver. On the contrary, he felt that Britain should answer de Gaulle's accusations of insularity by giving 'some practical, concrete evidence, however small, that this reproach is no longer true' by, for instance, converting her weights and measures to the metric system[19].

The cruelty of the Berlin Wall and then, seven years later, the Soviet re-occupation of Prague affected him deeply and reinforced his belief in European integration. In an emotional speech to the Lords on 26 August, 1968, he castigated the Soviet leadership of Russia for being 'implacable brutes' and urged the Government to build up the country's defences[20]. He was also moved by the plight of that 'poor, silly old man' Rudolf Hess, and in one of his last interventions in the Lords strongly urged his release, yet he realised that only Four Power agreement could achieve this[21].

One of his most interesting and reflective speeches was made when the Lords was debating the departure of South Africa from the Commonwealth. Brian Robertson conceded frankly that he had been proud to wear the South African uniform and reminded the House of that former Dominion's excellent war record:

> . . . I remember the formations with which and in which I served and how magnificent they were at El Alamein and elsewhere – rough, tough chaps, but bonny fighters, like the football teams they send over from time to time. I remember the wonderful comradeship that existed between South Africa and the British troops. I recall how within a few days of the destruction of the Guards Chapel here in London by enemy action, £5000 was raised in the South African Armoured Division from the Officers and men; that works out at about 10s a head.[22]

Yet he did not skate round the thorny question of apartheid. He readily conceded that 'certain aspects' of it offended 'against my conception at least of Christian behaviour'[23]. His solution for South Africa's racial problems was to urge the adoption of Smuts' policy, 'South Africa for the South Africans' not just ' this lot of South Africans or that lot . . ., but for all South Africans'[24].

In domestic policy his main interests, apart from the youth question, were inevitably the railways and labour relations. He gave a cautious welcome to the Beeching report on the future of a slimmed down British Railways, but defended himself from the criticism that such a report should have been produced years earlier by arguing that if it had been, 'it would have been promptly consigned to purgatory and its author along with it'[25]. He also showed considerable concern for the redundant rail-waymen and begged the Government to set up a special organisation to help retrain them and find them work. Essentially he was sympathetic to workers rights and he consequently welcomed the Contracts of Employment Bill in 1963, but he was also emphatic that the workers and the trade unions had responsibilities too[26]. He thus approved of the Labour Government's White Paper on industrial relations, 'In Place of Strife' in 1969, as an attempt to curb the 'tyrannical power' of the unions. He looked to Germany as an example of constructive labour relations and was proud of the fact that British officials had played some part in help-ing to lay the foundation for this[27]. Jack Straw, the Labour politician, was probably right when he wrote in 1989 that he would have been sympa-thetic to the European Social Charter[28], and the extension of workers' councils to British firms, but he would have first expected the unions themselves to act responsibly. This was a rash assumption in the 1960s and he had seen little evidence of it.

Throughout these years, Brian Robertson remained in touch with Konrad Adenauer, who was always delighted to see him[29]. By the 1960s their friendship was not of great diplomatic import, although Sir Frank Roberts, the British Ambassador to the Federal Republic, did at one juncture attempt to improve relations between London and Bonn, which had suffered as a result of the Franco-German Treaty of Friendship and the collapse of the Brussels negotiations in January 1963, by inviting Adenauer specifically to meet Robertson at the Embassy[30]. When Brian Robertson dined with Adenauer, who was then writing his memoirs, at his villa on Lake Como in September, 1964, he was asked to find out in London the name of the Colonel in the Royal Army Educational Corps who had interviewed him so sympathetically after he had been dismissed from the post of *Oberbürgermeister* of Cologne by General Barraclough in October, 1945. Brian Robertson took the request seriously and wrote both to General Erskine, his former Chief of Staff in Germany, and Sir Harold Caccia, the Permanent Under-Secretary of the Foreign Office, in an unsuccessful attempt to track down the elusive colonel. As he told Caccia, he was particularly worried that Adenauer would write

. . . with considerable bitterness about the Barraclough incident. If he was then able to follow this up with some friendly and amusing refer-ences to the incident which he has described to me, it could tone down the anti-British element which he will otherwise give to this period[31].

When Adenauer died in 1967, the Robertsons flew out to attend the funeral in a special plane in which the only other passengers were Edward Heath, Harold Macmillan and Harold Wilson.

Brian Robertson was justly proud of his work in Germany and the successful integration of the Federal Republic into Western Europe, which he had done so much to make possible. On the twentieth anniversary of the *Bundesrepublik* in July, 1969, he was asked how he viewed the future of the Republic. He gave a glowing report on all that the West Germans had achieved and attributed much of their success to the efforts of his now deceased friend Adenauer, but he was inclined to be critical about the formation of the Grand Coalition, which included both the two main political parties, the CDU and the SPD, as he felt that a strong and active opposition was essential for a healthy democracy. He also advocated the British system of direct voting rather than the German system of proportional representation because it discouraged splinter parties and usually gave clear majorities[32]. He himself was quite sure that there had been a miracle in the Biblical sense in West Germany. He told the Royal Institute of International Affairs in a speech which is testimony to his deeply-held Christian beliefs:

> There are those today who tell us that God does not intervene in human affairs, and that it is wrong to expect Him to do so. When, with my simple mind, I look back to Potsdam, 1945, and forward to Western Europe in 1965, it just seems to me that a cleverer hand has been at work than any hand of man[33].

All in all, Brian Robertson remained a formidable presence on the national stage even in retirement, but in 1969, at the age of 73, he began to develop cardiac complications, although he did not have an actual heart attack. The doctors and Edith banned him from undertaking any strenuous activity such as mowing the lawn or digging the garden. This did not stop him, however, from making further speeches in the Lords and becoming Acting Chairman of the Gloucestershire Association of Boys Clubs, when his successor, Martin Cadbury, died in office. Yet to his family the spark seemed to have left him. He felt that as his father had died at 73 from thrombosis, inevitably he himself had little time left.

Wully died instantly and painlessly while ordering his morning tea. His son did not have the same good fortune to escape life quickly and with dignity. Beginning in December, 1970, he had a series of severe strokes, which left him stricken in both mind and body. In November, 1971, he was just able to make his last public speech to the Anglo-German Association, the Presidency of which he had taken over from Field Marshal Alexander. Then in May, 1972, he suffered a further major stroke and could only move about the house with the help of a nurse. Days would pass without any communications from him, but there were occasionally glimmerings of his old intelligence. In the autumn of 1972 Cuthbert Bardsley, who was then Bishop of Coventry, came over to lunch at Iles Green with his wife. Brian Robertson was brought down and appeared to have little strength and no comprehension, but then the discussion turned to the Bardsleys' retirement plans and their need to live near motorways, airports and a good train service, so that they would not be cut off from their friends. Mrs Bardsley remembered how then:

> Lord Robertson seemed to come alive, his eyes bright and his face became trim and he nodded powerfully. I thought then and have continued to do so that I had seen that great and powerful man as he had once been . . . One even felt that the shrewd and brilliant brain had come alive again for a few moments[34].

In the last few months of his long and humiliating ordeal his mind frequently went back to his great organisational triumphs in the Desert and his manservant was sometimes ordered to dispatch imaginary convoys and to provide them with moto cycle escorts[35]. His suffering came to an end when he died on 29 April 1974.

There was first a quiet family funeral at Far Oakridge. On 13 June a Service of Thanksgiving in Westminster Abbey was held at which his old friend Cuthbert Bardsley gave the address and appropriately the Last Post was sounded by a Trumpeter of the Corps of the Royal Engineers. As the service progressed and the singing of the familiar hymns and Psalm 23 echoed around the Abbey, his former colleagues and friends had the chance to reflect on the life and work of the great public servant the nation had lost.

Brian Robertson had more than lived up to his father's formidable example. For much of his life he had been virtually unknown to the public at large because he had worked in a subordinate role, often behind the scenes, first supplying the armies in Africa and Italy and then as Deputy Military Governor in Germany attempting to bring some order to the chaos in the British Zone. The West first began to get some inkling of his quality when he became Military Governor in 1947. Then he really did bestride Germany, the central theatre of the Cold War, like a colossus. He steadied nerves at a time of acute danger during the Berlin blockade and sought to conciliate rather than alienate. Above all, he displayed considerable vision about the future of Germany. He grasped long before most of his countrymen that one solution to the German problem was to integrate or 'dissolve' Germany into Western Europe as a whole. He, the most conventional seeming of men, had, as his colleague François-Poncet stressed, 'a disposition to understand and to recognise even what is not British[36]. The politicians of the fledgling *Bundesrepublik* and Colonel Nasser and his advisers were in a position to appreciate the truth of this observation.

Brian Robertson was essentially a late British Imperial figure. For most of his life British power based upon the Empire and Commonwealth was a reality. Even after terminal decline set in after 1947, he was one of those men who managed through sheer strength of character and diplomatic skill to create a mirage of power and influence. At what point in the 1950s he realised the futility of this is hard to guess, although it is likely to have been after the Suez Crisis. He did not indulge in nostalgia for a vanished world. At the BTC he was the champion of modernisation, while later in the Lords his speeches on education, industrial relations and the EEC were concerned with the present and future rather than the glories of the past. At work he often appeared an Olympian and rather frightening figure, but in reality, as Cuthbert Bardsley stressed in his address, 'his "inner man" was very humble, unassuming, almost diffident'[37].

CHAPTER NOTES

Chapter 1

1. For accounts of William Robertson's life see: W. Robertson, *From Private to Field Marshal*, (Constable, London, 1921) and the biography by V. Bonham-Carter, *Soldier True. The Life and Times of Sir William Robertson, 1860–1933* (Muller, London, 1963).
2. Mildred to W. Robertson (from now on referred to as W.R.), 16.1.00 (W. Robertson Papers). All the Field Marshal's personal letters quoted in this chapter are in the keeping of the present Lord Robertson.
3. W.R. to Brian Robertson (hereafter B.H.R.) 17.6.00.
4. Lady Vincent's interview with author, 11.10.91.
5. For instance, one of his ADCs in Germany, Hugh Browne, while out riding with Brian Robertson, once dared tell him the following anecdote he had heard from his mother: Wully had opened a bathroom door to find a woman bathing there. He extricated himself by bowing and saying 'Excuse me, sir'. This annoyed Brian Robertson immensely and he cantered off saying 'My father would never have done that'. (Interview with author, 19.7.91.)
6. W.R. to B.H.R., 20.8.05.
7. The Tanllwyfan correspondence and reports are in the W.R. Papers.
8. R. Graves, *Goodbye To All That*, (Penguin, Harmondsworth, 1960), p.38.
9. G.D. Martineau, '1910–1914' in: *The Charterhouse We Knew*, edt., W.H. Holden, pp. 51–64, (British Technical and General Press, London, 1950,) p. 54.
10. B.H.R. to W.R. (undated, but almost certainly Dec. 1913), (W.R. Papers): on 19.1.43 he wrote to his wife: 'There is no school in England which I would sooner send Ronald [his son] to than Charterhouse. This is merely because I know it, was there myself and consider on average it turns out good fellows'. Later in 1952 he joined the old Saunderites Association. (B.H.R Papers).
11. E.G. Larkworthy to author, 24.4.92. Also telephone conversation of 7.5.92.
12. Martineau, p. 61; B.H.R. to W.R., 28.11.10, (W.R. Papers).
13. *Annals of Charterhouse Cadet Corps*, 1903–, (Charterhouse Archives). B.H.R. to W.R., 22.2.12, (W.R. Papers).
14. Graves, p.42.
15. *Carthusian*, March 1913, p.87.

16. *ibid.*, Dec. 1913, p. 22. (See also draft speech, prepared for Jan. 1969 in B.H.R. Papers). In fact he delivered a shortened version of this speech on 12 December 1968, as most of its content was pre-empted by Lord Wigg). Parl. Debates (Lords), Vol. 298, cols 650–651.
17. Warner to Roberts, 23.11.13, copy in W.R. Papers.
18. W.R. to B.H.R., 25.11.13.
19. For a description of contemporary life at Woolwich see A. Shepperd, *The Royal Military Academy, Sandhurst and its Predecessors*, (Country Life Books, 1980).
20. *RMA Magazine*, Vol. XV., No. 57, Aug. 1914, p. 5.
21. *RMA Magazine*, Vol. XV., No. 58, Nov. 1914, p. 33. For the report see W.R. Papers.
22. W.R. to B.H.R., 18.11.14.

Chapter 2

1. W.R. to Mildred, 24.11.14, (W.R. Papers).
2. Manuscript of the Diary of Field Marshal Earl Haig (WO 256/7), 17.3.16.
3. He took over compiling the XI Corps War Diary on 24 .9.16, (WO 95/881).
4. 'Minutes of a Conference' . . ., 9.1.18, (WO 95/ 4211).
5. The Memoirs of Lt. Col. K.F.B. Tower, p.30, (IWM, p.142).
6. Haking to General Tamagini, CO Portuguese Expeditionary Force, 19.7.17, (WO 95/882).
7. C.E. Carrington, *Soldier from the Wars Returning*, (Hutchinson, London, 1965), p. 102.
8. See WO 95/882.
9. Memoirs of Major General C.A. Hawes, p. 56, (IWM,. 87/ 41/2).
10. 24–27.12.16, (WO 95/881).
11. *London Gazette*, 15.5.17.
12. *ibid.*, 1.1.18.
13. B.H.R. to W.R., 28.1.18, (W.R. Papers).
14. B.H.R. to W.R., 25.2.18, W.R. Papers. Bonham Carter, pp.313–351.
15. 177 Bde War Diary (WO 95/3022) 'Minutes of a Conference, held at HQ 177 Inf, Bde, 23.9.18.
16. *ibid.*, 'Appendix XLVII', dated 23.10.18.
17. *London Gazette*, 3.6.19.
18. Brian Robertson's activities can be traced regularly through *The Royal Engineers Monthly List*, copies of which are in the Royal Engineers Library at Chatham. Only one of Brian Robertson's letters (undated) from this period seems to have survived in the W.R. Papers. In it he congratulates his father on 'his latest honour' – probably the baronetcy – and gives him some news of his course at Aldershot in 'communication schemes'.
19. The major source on Brian Robertson's years in India is his father's

weekly letters, bound in five volumes for the years 1921–5. Brian's activities are reflected in his father's comments. (W.R.Papers). (See also C. Richardson, *From Churchill's Secret Circle to the BBC*, (Brassey's, London, 1991), pp. 9–15).

20. W.R to B.H.R., 4.1.22.
21. Author's interview with Sir Ian Jacob, 25.5.91.
22. Jacob to author, 6.6.91.
23. Author's second interview with Jacob, 25.1.92.
24. W.R. to B.H.R., 17.5.22.
25. The best history of the Waziristan campaigns is *The Official History of Operations on the North West Frontier of India, 1920–35*, (Delhi, 1945). For the road itself see 'The Isha Razmak Road', *Royal Engineers Journal*, Sept, 1925, pp. 361–379.
26. Jacob to author, *op.cit.*
27. 'Sartor Resartus. The story of Ghulab Khan's camels', *Owl Pie*, Christmas, 1926, pp. 41–2. (The article is anonymous but could only have been written by B.H.R. whilst a student at the Staff College.)
28. *London Gazette*, 30.5.24 & 13.3.25.
29. W.R. to B.R., 4.3.25.
30. Bond, p. 33.
31. *Owl Pie*, Christmas, 1927, p. 43.
32. An after-dinner game in which an officer would sit on a colleague's shoulders and fight a similarly mounted rival.
33. Bond, pp. 38–44.
34. Major General F.S.G. Piggott, *Broken Thread*, (Gale & Polden, Aldershot, 1950), p. 220.
35. 'Report of the Visit of Major B.H. Robertson, General Staff to South America', FO 371 13457, fos 194–246. For a 'Baedecker' account of his travels see Piggott *op. cit.*, pp. 220–23.
36. For the FO minutes and memorandum on the Report see particularly FO 371 13457 fos., 190–2, 253–4, 260–3.
37. Piggott, p. 223.
38. W.R. to B.H.R., 10.9.30, (W.R. Papers).
39. *ibid.*, 21.9.30.
40. For further details see WO 106/379.
41. On 11.2.30 he wrote to B.H.R.: 'Both King and Country, I think, dropped me after the War and I do not wish to be revived again as a public figure'. (W. R. Papers); Bonham-Carter, p.382.
42. 'Interview between Major Sir Brian Robertson and Admiral von Freyberg, German Delegation at the Hotel Beau Rivage on 13 October, 1933', (WO 32 /4099).
43. Author's interview with Sir Ian Jacob, 25.5.91.
44. See *Observer*, 8.12.46.
45. B.H.R. to Reay Geddes, 26.2.63, (B.H.R. Papers).
46. B.H.R. to Mildred Robertson, 22.10 33, (B.H.R. papers).

Chapter 3

1. R. Overy, 'Hitler's War Plans and the German Economy' in ed. R. Boyce and E. Robertson, *Paths to War*, (Macmillan, London, 1989), p. 97. For instance in his speech as Chairman of the Rubber Growers Association on 8.1.37 B.H.R. stressed that 'rubber with gold was an essential war material', *Natal Mercury*, 9.1.37.
2. Unfortunately most of Dunlop's archives have not survived either in Britain or South Africa. Only the Annual Directors' Reports and Accounts are available in the Greater London Record Office. The best history of Dunlop is: J. McMillan, *The Dunlop Story*, (Weidenfeld and Nicolson, London, 1989). For its international policy see G. Jones, 'The growth and performance of British multinational firms before 1939: the case of Dunlop' in *Economic History Review*, 2nd. Ser. Vol. XXXVII, 1.2.84, pp. 35–53.
3. B.H.R. to Mildred Robertson, 25.8.35, (B.H.R. Papers).
4. Parliamentary Debates (Lords), 12.4.62, Vol. 239, Col. 602.
5. *Natal Mercury*, 14.8.35.
6. B.H.R. to Mildred Robertson, 8.9.35, B.H.R. Papers and information from Eric Page, B.H.R.'s valet and chauffeur.
7. *Dunlop Gazette*, April 1938.
8. H.L. Naylor to author, 10.9.91.
9. *ibid.*, quoting his colleague G. Sandison.
10. Author's interview with Sir Reay Geddes, 13.9.91.
11. Conversation with Robertson family, 15.5.91.
12. B.H.R. to Mildred Robertson, 8.9. & 3.9.35.
13. B.H.R. to Mildred Robertson, 19.9.38.
14. Natal Chamber of Industries, Report of the Executive, 1938–9, p. 31.
15. Conversation with Robertson family. 15.5.91.
16. Quoted from S. African Military College certificate in B.H.R Papers.

Chapter 4

1. For accounts of the East African campaign see S.O. Playfair, *The Mediterranean and Middle East*, (H.M.S.O., London, 1954–6), Vols. I & II (hereafter referred to as *Official History*); N. Orpen, S*outh African Forces, World War II*, Vol I, *East African and Abyssinian Campaigns*, (Purnell and Sons, Cape Town, 1968). See also CAB 44/411 & 427.
2. Sir Archibald Wavell, 'Generals and Generalship,' The Lees lectures, delivered at Trinity College Cambridge in 1939. Reprinted from *The Times*, Feb. 17, 18 & 19, 1941, p. 2.
3. B.H.R., 'Draft. Administration' , (Sent to Montgomery, 29.8.43), (WO 204 /7679).
4. *ibid.*
5. B.H.R. to Edith (hereafter E.R.), 5.3.43, B.H.R. Papers. See also Parl. Debates (Lords), Vol. 239, Col. 601, 12.4.62.
6. Quoted in Orpen, p. 48.

7. See 'Q' Branch War Diaries', (WO 169/ 699 &2875 (Dec. 40–Jan. 41)).

8. B.H.R. for General Sir Alan Cunningham, 'Note on S. African Forces . . . 2.2.67, B.H.R. Papers and 'Notes on Tour of 11th and 12th African Division, 15. Jan. 1941 . . .', (WO 169/2875).

9. B.H.R. to Mildred Robertson, 20 Jan. 1941, (BHR Papers).

10. *Official History*, Vol I. pp. 411–2.

11. 'Administrative Instruction No. 30', 2 Feb. 1941 & 'Administrative Notes on the Advance from Tanna to Jubba', 12th Div. 'Q' Staff War Diary, WO 169/ 2875 & 2898.

12. B.H.R. to Cunningham, 2.2.67.

13. Orpen, Vol.1, p. 212; 12th Div. War Diary, May 1941 and 'Administrative Notes on operations during period, 8 Feb–31 March, 1941'. (WO 169/2898).

14. B.H.R., 'Draft. Administration', (WO 204/ 7679).

15. 'E.A. Force, Report on Operations from 1.11.40–5.4.41, Copy in the Papers of Lt. Gen. Sir Harry Wetherall, (P.388, IWM).

16. B.H.R. to Mildred Robertson, 23.9.41, (B.H.R. papers).

17. *ibid*. See also B. Pitt, *The Crucible of War Western Desert 1941*, (Cape, London, 1980), p. 339.

18. Mrs. Miller to her mother, enclosing copied extracts from her husband's letters, 5.2.42, IWM, 78/20/2.

19. C.H. Miller, 'Administration in the Western Desert Campaign, 1940–41', *ibid.*, 78/20/1.

20. Eric Page to author, 6.4.92.

21. See War Diary of 8th Army 'Q' Branch, Sept–Nov., 1941, (WO 169/1012) and *Official History*, Vol. III, p. 11.

22. *ibid.*, p. 11.

23. See War Diaries, Nov. 1941–Jan. 1942, (WO 169/1012 & 3939).

24. Miller, 'Administration . . .'.

25. War Diary, 24.11.41, (WO 169/1012) and letter to author from Lord (Ronald) Robertson, 10.12.94.

26. Miller, 'Administration . . .'.

27. Diary of Brigadier C.H. Miller, 5.1.42, (IWM 78/20/2).

28. War Diary, 13.1.42, (WO 169/3939).

29. *ibid.*, 'Eighth Army Requirements', 18.1.42.

30. Miller, Diary, 17.1.42.

31. See 'Q' Staff War Diaries, February–May, 1941, (WO 169/3939).

32. *ibid.*, '8th Army Administrative Instruction, no. 54', 30.3.42 and War Diary, 26.3.42.

33. Miller, 'Administration . . .'.

34. Wimberley, '*Scottish Soldier*', Vol. II, p. 29, (IWM PP/MER/182).

35. Miller, 'Administration . . .'.

36. Pitt, *Alamein*, p.151.

37. B.H.R. to E.R., 6.9.42, (B.H.R. Papers).

38. *ibid.*, 17.11.42.

39. *ibid.*, 6.9.42.

40. *ibid.*, 3.9.42.
41. *ibid.*, 6.9.42.
42. Carver, M., *El Alamein*, (Batsford, London, 1962), p. 74.
43. See 'Note on deception measures carried through during the preparatory phrase for Operation LIGHTFOOT, October 1942, (IWM, Montgomery Papers, BLM 27 PP/MCR/C30) and Carver, pp. 93–4.
44. B.H.R. to E.R., 23.10.42, (B.H.R. Papers).
45. *ibid.*, 17.11.42.
46. *ibid.*
47. 'Administration of Eighth Army, Part 2'– B.H.R.'s lecture at the 'Bathbrick' Conference, Feb. 14 1943. Copy in the Lymer papers, (IWM PP. MCR./ 131).
48. War Diaries, Nov–Dec. 1942, (WO 169/ 3939). See also the comprehensive 'Notes on the maintenance of the 8th. Army and the supporting RAF by land, sea, and air from El Alamein to Tunisia', (IWM, BML 62, PP/MCR/C30').
49. Robertson, 'Administration . . . Part 2'.
50. B.H.R. to E.R., 17.11.42, (B.H.R. Papers).
51. Robertson, 'Administration . . . Part 1'.
52. *ibid.*
53. ME Joint Planning Staff: 'Operations in Tripolitania' (JPS ME./118), 17.12.42 & minute by Lindsell (LGA/36/17), Surtees papers, (IWM, 81/40/1); 'Notes on the Maintenance . . .', p. 42.
54. 'Operations in Tripolitania'.
55. Interview with author, 10.7.91.
56. *Official History*, Vol. IV, p. 233.
57. Robertson, 'Administration Part 2'. Carter Paterson was a road haulage company.
58. B.H.R. to E.R., 19.1.43, (B.H.R. papers).
59. *ibid.*, 2.2.43.
60. *ibid.*, 16.3.43.
61. *ibid.*, 5.3.43.
62. *ibid.*, 16.3.43.
63. *ibid.*, 5.3.43.
64. B.H.R. to Rev. F. Lt Hughes, 29.4.43, (WO 204/7679).
65. B.H.R. to E.R., 2.2.43.
66. *ibid.* and author's conversation with the late Sir Edgar Williams, 11.7.91. He was equally touched in June when George VI spoke 'very nicely of Dad', B.H.R. to E.R., 21.6.43, (B.H.R. Papers).
67. B.H.R. to E.R., 26.6.43.
68. Copies of the lectures, extracts of which have already been quoted are in the Lymer papers. See also Hamilton N., *Monty: Master of the Battlefield*, (Hamish Hamilton, London, 1983). pp. 141–151.
69. B.H.R. to E.R., 5.3.43, (B.H.R. Papers).
70. *ibid.*, 26.2.42. The note itself has not survived.
71. *ibid.*, 8.2.43.

72. *ibid.*
73. Interview with author, 11.7.91; Hamilton N., pp .263–272.
74. Miller, Diary, 4.5.43, (IWM 78/20/1).

Chapter 5

1. *Official History*, Vol. 5, p. 402.
2. *The Times*, 23.9.43.
3. The Diary of General Penney, 3.8.43, (3/2, LHCMA).
   (See also *Official History*, Vol. V, Ch. 12 & CAB 106/416, 'Operations of British, Indian and Dominion Forces in Italy, 3.9.43–2.5.45, Section G. Principal Administrative Aspects', Chs. I &II).
4. The Diary of Lt. Gen. H. Gale, 16.8.43, (II/9, LHCMA).
5. de Guingand to B.H.R., 19.9.43, (WO 204/7679).
6. 'The Campaign in Italy', 2nd. Phase, p. 6, Montgomery Papers, (IWM BLM 45/4).
7. 'Section G'. Ch. VI, (CAB 106/416).
8. 'Notes on Conferences', HQ 15 Army Group, 11–12 Oct 1943, (WO 204/542).
9. B.H.R. to R. Butler, 22.11.54, (CAB 106/779).
10. B.H.R. to Gale, 10.10.43, (WO 204/542).
11. Diary 5.11.43, Gale II, (LHCMA).
12. B.H.R. to Dowler, 16.12.43. (WO 204/7680).
13. B.H.R. to Gale, 5.12.43. (Appendix HH, CAB 106 /417).
14. Diary, 28/9.12.43, Gale II/12, (LHCMA).
15. Alexander to Eisenhower, 30.12. 43 and B.H.R. to Alexander, 5.1.44. (WO 214/8).
16. Contemporary Notes, 4.1.44, Penney, 8/1, (LHCMA).
17. Cunningham to AFHQ, 28.2.44, (WO 214/29).
18. Alexander to AFHQ, 23.2.44. (WO 204/550).
19. Penney to B.H.R., March 1944, (13/9, LHCMA).
20. *ibid.*, 'Notes by Commander Ist. Division', 21.4.44, (8/33, LHCMA).
21. Mackeurtan (B.H.R.'s ADC). I am also grateful to the Curator of the George Marshall Foundation, Lexington, for sending me a photocopy of B.H.R.'s letter to Gen. Truscott, 25.4.44. Lucian Truscott Papers, Coll. H.20 6/40.
22. C. D'Este, *Fatal Decision*, (Fontana, London, 1992), p. 42.
23. B.H.R. to GOC, 4th. Indian Division, 7.3.44, (WO 204/6701).
24. *ibid.*
25. B.H.R. to Gen. George Clark, 18.3.44, (WO 204/6706).
26. 'Subject: Desertion', 19.5.44, (WO 204/6701).
27. For details of the various conferences and administrative plans see WO 204/ 660 & WO 214/33.
28. See, for example, War Diaries (A Branch, H.Q.A.A.I.), May & June 1944, (WO 170/82).
29. Admin. Instruction No. 36, 28.6.44, (WO 204/6853).

30. *ibid.*, 'Accommodation Policy, Rome', 28.6.44. See also Mark Clark's Diary, Vol 7 p. 161, The Citadel Archives, Charleston, South Carolina. I am grateful to the Director for sending me a photocopy.
31. Lavinia Orde, (then Junior Commander Holland Hibbert).
32. CAB 44/168, pp. 95–6.
33. 'Effect of ANVIL's Withdrawals', 2.7.44, (WO 214/34).
34. CAB 44/168 pp. 95–6.
35. Mackeurtan.
36. B.H.R., 'Subject: Morale Committee–AFHQ', 4.10.44, (WO 204/6701).
37. B.H.R. to Gen. George Clark, 29.9.44, (WO 204 /6701).
38. *Official History*, Vol. VI, Part II, p. 31.
39. Mackeurtan.
40. CAB 44/169, p. 110.
41. *Official History*, Vol. VI. Pt. II pp. 373–4. 'Morale Report', 4.12.44, (WO 204/6701).
42. Lavina Orde, *Better Late than Never: The Diaries of a Born Optimist*, (published privately), p. 239.
43. B.H.R. to Major General Gruenther *et al.*, 1.12.43, (WO 204/7680).
44. Minutes of AFLR (Italian) Board, 29.11.43 (WO 204/5201).
45. *Daily Telegraph*, 28.4.44.
46. Noel Charles to FO. (no. 57), 23.7.44, FO 371/ 43863. H. Macmillan, *War Diaries*, (London, 1985 (Papermac)), p. 493.
47. Minutes of 9th Meeting of AFLR (Italian) Board, 10.4.44, (WO 204/5201).
48. Charles to Sargeant, 29.8.44, (FO 371/43864).
49. MGRE (Brig. Edwards) to CAO, 29.11.44, (WO 204/590).
50. Macmillan, *War Diaries*, pp. 551 & 656.
51. B.H.R. to Ellery W. Stone, (draft, Jan. 1945) (WO 204/590).
52. B.H.R. to Secretaries, Combined Chiefs of Staff, 20.2.45. (FO 371/49814).
53. Macmillan, *War Diaries*, p. 640. Gen. Scobie's Diary, 3.4.45, (IWM 82/17/1).
54. B.H.R., 'Note for Chief of Staff 13.1.45, Harding D.O. Correspondence, 1944–45, Harding Papers, (8908–144–4, National Army Museum).
55. B.H.R. to Graham, 24.2.45, Gale 1/4, (LHCMA).
56. B.H.R.'s minutes on 'Local resources in N.W. Italy', 7.4.45, (WO 204/5234).
57. See for instance tel. from 13 Corps to AFHQ, 6.5.45 (MC IN 4648) (WO 204/621). For this crisis and the subsequent repatriation of the Cossacks, see N. Tolstoy, *The Minister and the Massacres*, (Hutchinson, London, 1986); A. Cowgill, T. Brimlow, C. Booker, *The Repatriations from Austria in 1945, The Report of an Inquiry*, (London, 1990). (This is accompanied by an invaluable collection of 'key papers' or documents in a second volume, *The Documentary Evidence*), C. Mather, *Aftermath of War*, (Brassey's, London, 1992).
58. Macmillan, *War Diaries*, p. 757.
59. *ibid.*, p 758.

60. Cowgill, *Report*, pp. 27–8.
61. *ibid.*, pp. 36–7. *Doc. Evidence*, (KP 107).
62. *ibid.*, pp. 49–63, (KP 53).
63. WO 170/4184. See also *ibid.*, (KP 103).
64. See for example Tolstoy's criticisms of Macmillan and Lord Aldington (Brigadier Toby Low) and the subsequent legal proceedings.
65. Cowgill, *Report*, pp. 56–7.
66. *ibid.*, p. 10. Doc Evidence KP 41 & 49. Also 'Note by Lord Aldington' for the author, 19.1.96, which stresses that the Eighth Army only reached Austria on 8 May.
67. *ibid.*, p. 39 and KP 125.
68. *ibid.*, pp. 150–2, (KP 316 & 317).
69. WO 106/4059, also *ibid.*, p. 70. KP 146.
70. *ibid.*, pp. 70–74, (KP 146, 154, 155).
71. *ibid.*, p. 103, (KP 222).
72. *ibid.*, pp. 99–139. See also pp. 43–44.
73. Minutes of AFHQ-SHAEF Conference at Bolzano, 14–15 June, 1945 (WO 204 /6700).
74. Mackeurtan.
75. Lemnitzer to B.H.R., 26.8.45, (B.H.R. papers).
76. Ashfield to B.H.R., 28.9.45, *ibid.*

Chapter 6

1. Profile, *Observer*, 8.12.46.
2. Interview with the author, 28.8.91.
3. Author's interviews with the late Sir Patrick Dean, 9.7.91 & 11.2.93. See also E. Bullock, *Ernest Bevin, Foreign Secretary*, London, 1983, p. 98.
4. Sir Edward Playfair to author, 3.7.91.
5. B.H.R. to Strang, 6.5.50, (FO 1030/253).
6. Author's telephone conversation with Miss Faith Porter, 4.8.91.
7. Interview, 28.8.91.
8. The late General Sir John Cowley to author, 4.8.91.
9. Author's interview with Mr. Harry Collins, 29.7.91.
10. Interview with Lady and the late General Sir John Cowley, 12.10.91.
11. *Observer*, 8.12.46.
12. *Sunday Graphic*, 18.6.50.
13. See for example 'The statement . . . handed to the press', 22.12.47, (IWM Bishop papers, 164/ Box 1). I am grateful to the Classics Dept. of Highgate School for the translation.
14. Transcript of Oral History Interview with B.H.R. conducted by T.A. Wilson, for the Harry S. Truman Library, 11.8.70, p. 10, (B.H.R. Papers).
15. B.H.R., 'A Miracle? Potsdam, 1945–Western Germany, 1965'. *Royal Institute of International Affairs*, 41, (3) July 1965, p. 403. See also D.G. Williamson, *The British in Germany, 1918–30*, (Oxford, 1991), pp. 348–49.

16. For text of Protocol see *Foreign Relations of the United States: The Conference of Berlin (The Potsdam Conference)*, 1945, Vol. 2 (Washington, Govt. Printing Office, 1960), pp. 1478–1498.

17. B.H.R., 'A Miracle?', p.403.

18. *British Zone Review*, 27.10.45, Vol. 1, No. 3, p. 1.

19. The descriptions of chaos are numerous, but see especially W. Strang, Diary of a Tour through the British Zone, 1–6 July 1945, (FO 371 46933). See also D.C. Watt, *Britain Looks to Germany*, (Wolff, London, 1965), pp. 68–9 and H.E. Collins, *Mining Memories and Musings*, (Garden City Press, Letchworth, 1985), p. 28.

20. For a precise definition of his duties see Montgomery to WO, 5.10.45, (FO 371/ 46974).

21. 'Notes for DMG for Corps Commanders Conference', 14.12.45, (FO 1030/322).

22. B.H.R. to Corps Commander, Dec. 1945, (FO 1030/322). See also Montgomery to Street, 19.12.45 and 'The Future of the Rhineland and the Ruhr', 18.12.45, in Montgomery Papers, (IWM BLM 170/15).

23. 'Minutes of Military Government Conference . . .' 12/13 Oct. 1945, (FO 371/46951).

24. Montgomery, *Memoirs*, pp. 403–405; Executive Meeting of DMG, 1.12.45, (FO 371/4693); Author's interview with the late General Sir Charles Richardson, 10.7.91.

25. 'Notes . . .' 14.12.45, (FO 1030/322).

26. Mackeurtan, April 1993.

27. Author's interview with Mr. Wallis Hunt, 24.4.92.

28. 'Notes . . .' 14.12.45.

29. E.g. Herda Gotthelf to Dennis Healey, 31.8.46, (Labour Party Archives LP/ID/ Box 2, National Museum of Labour History, Manchester).

30. Ritchie Calder to Secretary of State, 31.8.45, (FO 371/ 46973) & Strang to Bevin, 14.11.45, (FO 371/ 46969).

31. B.H.R. to Corps Commanders, 19.11.45, (FO 1030/322).

32. B.H.R. to Control Office, 14.12.45, (FO 371/46975).

33. B.H.R. to Street, 20.12.45, (FO 371/55586).

34. *ibid.* Enclosed memorandum by the British Element.

35. B.H.R. to Montgomery, 25.1.46, (FO 1030/323). See also Montgomery to Permanent Secretary, Control Office, 19.12.45, (IWM BLM 87/23). For an analysis of the British administration in Germany see ed. I. D. Turner, *Reconstruction in Post-War Germany*, (Oxford, 1989), pp. 359–376.

36. B.H.R. to Corps Commanders, 29.1. & and 23.2.46, (FO 1030/322). (See also correspondence between Stokes and Hynd, Sept–Oct. 1946, (FO 938/113).

37. A. Kramer, 'British Dismantling politics, 1945–49' ed. Turner, pp. 131–34.

38. B.H.R. to Montgomery, 22.1.46, (FO 1030/323).

39. *ibid.*, Montgomery to B.H.R., 23.1.46.

40. Ed. J.E. Smith, *Papers of Lucius Clay*, Vol. 1, (Bloomington and London, 1974). p.155.
41. Information and text provided by the late Mrs. A. Handley–Derry.
42. Press release, 28.3.46, (FO 1030/315).
43. B.H.R. to Corps Commanders, 23.2.46, (FO 1030/322).
44. Press Interview, 7.3.46. 'The Food Situation in the British Zone', p. 8, (IWM BLM 170/11).
45. B.H.R. to Corps Commanders, 26.3.46, (FO 1030/307).
46. 'Appreciation of the Effects of a Further Reduction . . . of Imports of Food . . .', 5.5.46, (FO 1030/303).
47. B.H.R. to Corps Commanders, 26.3.46.
48. D.M.G.'s Address to Zonal Advisory Council, 6.3.46.
49. *Collins*, pp. 39–44, B.H.R. to Street, 26.3.46, (FO 1030/303).
50. B.H.R. to Corps Commanders, 26.3.46, (FO 1030/307).
51. B.H.R. to Street, 28.3.46, (FO 1030/ 303).
52. B.H.R. to Regional Commissioners, 15.7.46, (FO 1030/307).
53. 'Verbatim Report of General Robertson's Speech to ZAC, 14.8.46, FO 1014/126.
54. Information given to me by the Hon. Mrs. Fiona Chapman, 21.7.95. Lord Pakenham, *Born to Believe*, (Cape, London, 1953), p. 178.
55. B.H.R. to Regional Commissioners, 28.8.46.
56. 'Memorandum by the Sec. of State For Foreign Affairs' (CP (46), 6.9.46, (FO 800/466).
57. Bullock, p. 310.
58. Address by Deputy Military Governor to the Members of the Staff of the Control Commission for Germany (BE) at Berlin and at Lübbecke, August 1946, (FO 1030/315).
59. Note by B.H.R., 30.6.46, (FO 371/55588). See also J. Farquharson, '"The Essential Division". Britain and the Partition of Germany', in *German History*, 9(1), 1991, pp. 23–45.
60. 'Note on Interview between the British and American Secretaries of State . . .' 3.12.46, (FO 371/55946). Bullock, pp. 342–3.
61. Note by Orme Sargeant on conversation with B.H.R., 13.12.46, (FO 371/55594).
62. B.H.R. to R. Dixon, 16.12.46 and note by Sargent (17.12.46), (FO 800/466).
63. *The Economist*, 18.1.47.
64. 'Verbatim Notes of Speech by DMG to Staff on 31.7.47', p. 4, (FO 1030/329, p. 1).
65. *A Miracle*, p. 407 and *ibid.*, p. 4.
66. 'Report on the Visit of a Delegation of British Churchmen to the British Zone of Germany, Oct. 16–30', 1946, (FO 938/266).
67. Victor Gollancz, *In Darkest Germany*, (Gollancz, London, 1947), p. 107.
68. See, for example, the article in the *Daily Mirror* of 8.7.46: '£160 Million a year to teach the Germans to despise us'.
69. *Financial Times*, 3.1.47.

70. 'Verbatim Notes . . .', p. 8.
71. B.H.R. to FO (8), 2.1.47, (FO 371/70571). L. Clay, *Decisions in Germany*, p. 174.
72. Statement by General Robertson at Coordinating Committee on 5.2.47 (FO 1049/711), Strang to FO 25.2.47, CFO 371/64161).
73. Diary of Michael Holland-Hibbert, (ADC to B.H.R. 1947–48 and later Viscount Knutsford) 8.3.–11.3.47. (Hereafter Diary).
74. This draft is in FO 1030/4. For Molotov's speech, see Bullock, p. 284.
75. The minutes of these committees are in FO 371/64194–64202.
76. 'Verbatim Notes . . .' 31.7.47, p. 5.
77. *ibid.*
78. Diary, 19.4.47.
79. B.H.R.'s note for Secretary of State (Annex 1), 28.4.47, (FO 1030/169).
80. Clay, I. p. 338.
81. 'Record of Meeting Held at Sir William Strang's House . . .' 28.4.47, (FO 1030/169).
82. Bevin's memorandum for P.M., 14.5.47. (FO 800/466). Diary 13.5.47.
83. Author's interview with Brigadier Hugh Browne, 19.7.91.
84. Diary, 13.6.47.
85. Note for Bevin (Ger/47/30), June 1947, (FO 800/466).
86. Weir to B.H.R., 11.6.47, (FO 1030/341).
87. 5.7.47, (FO 1030/341).
88. A. Albu, *Back Bench Technocrat*, p. 111.7, unpublished manuscript.
89. 'Verbatim Notes . . .', 31.7.47, (FO 1030/329).
90. Diary, 18.8.47.
91. Brownjohn to Regional Commissioners, 13.9.47, (FO 1010/20). 'Note of A Meeting held in the Regional Commissioner's Office, on 16.9.47', (FO 1013/98).
92. Information from Viscount Knutsford and Mr. Lederer, his interpreter.
93. 'Verbatim Notes . . .'
94. B.H.R. to Regional Commissioners, 14.8.47, (FO 1010/20).
95. DMG's Conference with the Trade Union Leaders . . . 18.10.47, (FO 1030/346).
96. *ibid.*, Conference of DMG with Minister President, Minister of Economics and Minister of Labour at 0930 hrs.
97. B.H.R. to Gilmour Jenkins, 13.10.47 (Appendix C), (FO 1030/169).
98. 'Anglo-United States Conversations, 18.12.47', (FO 800/466).
99. 'Statement . . . handed to the Press, 22.12.47, (IWM, Box1/164 Bishop Papers).
100. 'Military Governor's Christmas Broadcast', recorded at Bush House on 18.12.47 and broadcast on 24.12.47.

Chapter 7

1. *Illustrated London News*, 31.1.48.
2. Details in FO 1013/1040.

3. 'Policy in Germany' (CP (48) 5), 5.1.48, (FO 371/70571); Bullock, pp. 514–5.
4. B.H.R. to Strang, 22.1.48.
5. I.D. Turner, 'Great Britain and the Post-War German Currency Reform', *Historical Journal* 30 (3), 1987, p. 699.
6. B.H.R. to FO (202), 8.2.48, (FO 371/70489).
7. Resumé of Discussions in FO (German Section), 17.2.48, (FO 371/70489).
8. P.H. Dean to B.H.R., 10.3.48, (FO 371/70582).
9. Text of Speech given by Mil. Gov. . . . 7.4.48, (FO 1049/1474).
10. Mil. Gov to FO (494) 31.3.48, (FO 371/70490).
11. Mil Gov. to FO (510), 2.4.48. In 1965 he wrote: 'There are a number of bottle necks on the road through the Russian Zone to Berlin and my first objection to the proposal was that the operation might well be unsuccessful.' B.H.R to W. Harris, 13.1.65, (B.H.R. Papers).
12. *ibid.*, (510).
13. *ibid.*, Mil Gov to FO (519), 2.4.48.
14. The only other time was when his groom forgot to feed a cage full of birds and they died. Information from the Robertson family, 15.5.91.
15. A. and J. Tusa, *The Berlin Blockade*, (Coronet, London, 1989), p. 156.
16. 'Memo. by CIGS as a Result of Visit Paid to Germany, 7.4.48', (FO 1030/125).
17. Diary, 7.4.48.
18. FO to Mil. Gov. (714), 8.4.48.
19. *ibid.*, Bevin to B.H.R. (723), 9.4.48.
20. Papers of Lucius Clay 2, pp. 620–621.
21. Mil. Gov. to FO, 8.5.48 (851), (FO 371/70493).
22. W. Strang, 'Situation in Berlin', 28.4.48, (FO 371/70492).
23. 'Memo by CIGS . . .'.
24. *ibid.*
25. B.H.R. to Kirkpatrick, 6.4.48, (FO 371/70491).
26. 'British Position in Berlin . . .', 23.4.48, (FO 371/70492).
27. 'Situation in Berlin . . .'.
28. Memorandum addressed to Secretary of State, 28.4.48, (FO 371/70492).
29. Bullock, p. 554.
30. 'Position of Western Powers in Berlin', 28.4.48, (FO 371/70493).
31. *ibid.*, Berlin to FO (850), 8.4.48.
32. 25.5.48, Note for Strang from B.H.R., (FO 371/70591).
33. R. Steininger, 'Wie die Teilung Deutschlands verhindert werden sollte. Der Robertson Plan aus dem Jahre 1948', *Militärgeshichtliche Mitteilungen* 33 (1), 1983, pp. 53–4.
34. See Francomb to FO, 16.6.48, (FO 1030/76).
35. Diary, 16.6.48; Clay 2, p. 686; Information from Mrs Nancy Taylor, 23.5.95.
36. Diary, 19.6.48.

37. O. Pflanze, *Bismarck and the Development of Germany*, Vol. 1, (Princeton, 1963), p. 239. Interestingly Weir referred to a West German politician, 'now a minister in the FDR', who compared Robertson to Bismarck, as he was 'firm and far seeing'. C. Weir, *Civilian Assignment*, (Methuen, London, 1953), pp. 116–7.
38. Bullock, p. 579.
39. Mil. Gov to FO (1165), 24.6.48, FO to Mil. Gov (1333), 24.6.48, (FO 371/70495). The note was despatched on 26.6. (FO 1049/1509).
40. Mil. Gov. to FO (1229), 30.6.48, (FO 371/70498); Frankfurt to FO (9), 1.7.48, (FO 371/70500).
41. Bullock, p. 576. This information is based on an interview with B.H.R.
42. Mil. Gov. to FO, 29.6.48 (1224), (FO 371/70498).
43. Bullock, p. 579. Mil. Gov. to FO, 3.7.48 (1287), (FO 371/ 70499). See also B.H.R.'s comment: *Parl. Debates* (Lords), Vol. 296, 26.8.68, col. 540.
44. 'Secretary of State's Conversation with General Robertson', 27.7.48, (FO 371/70504).
45. Memorandum by Mil. Gov., 12.7.48, (FO 371/70501). Also printed in Steininger, pp. 60–64.
46. 'Economic Consequences of A New German Policy, 14.7.48', (FO 371/70501).
47. Eden to Bevin, 15.7.48, (FO 371/70504).
48. B.H.R. to Strang, (677) 16.7.48, (FO 371/70502).
49. *ibid.*
50. B.H.R. to Strang, 20.7.48, (FO 371/70504).
51. Secretary of State's Conversation with General Robertson, 27.7.48.
52. Steininger, pp. 72–75, (FO 371/70597).
53. Mil. Gov. to FO (1596), 10.8.48, (FO 800/467).
54. FO to Mil. Gov., 11.8.48, (18433), (FO 800/467).
55. FO to Mil Gov. (2061), 27.8.48, (FO 371/70510); Tusa, pp. 292–98.
56. B.H.R. to FO, 27.8.48 (1725), (FO 371/70511).
57. *ibid.*, FO to Mil. Gov (2102), 30.8.48.
58. B.H.R. to FO, 5.9.48 (1802), (FO 371/70512).
59. Francomb to FO (666), 30.9.49, (FO 1030/63).
60. The details of the statistics of flights and deliveries are in FO 1030/63. See also Tusa, Chapter 10.
61. See Mil. Gov. to Kirkpatrick (857), 25.10.48, (FO 371/70520) & B.H.R. to Strang, 20.11.24, (FO 371/70524).
62. B.H.R. to FO (2274), 8.12.48, (FO 371/70526).
63. Mil. Gov. to FO (124), 26.1.49, (FO 1030/63).
64. *ibid.*, and 'Record of Meeting in Strang's Office . . ., 30.12.48', (FO 371/76537).
65. Frankfurt to FO (779), 28.4.49, (FO 371 76586); Mil. Gov. to FO (598), 10.5.49, (FO 371 76589); Tusa pp. 419–474.
66. B.H.R.'s Memorandum (129/7/11/50), 15.3.50, (FO1030/253).
67. *ibid.*

68. Francomb to FO (0647), 1.7.48, (FO 1049/1151). For a precis of each document see 'Implementation of 6 Power Agreement', (IWM, Bishop Papers, Box 1/164).
69. Mil. Gov. to Regional Commissioners (5149), 4.7.48, (FO 371/70595).
70. 'Prospects of a Democratic Order in Germany with Special Reference to Education', 24.7.48, (FO 371/707160).
71. *ibid.*, B.H.R. to Strang, 6.8.48.
72. B.H.R. to Strang, 30.9.48, (FO 371/70599).
73. *ibid.*.
74. B.H.R. to Strang, 18.11.48, (FO 371/70603).
75. *ibid.*, Strang to B.H.R., 24.11.48.
76. Report of 1.1.49, (FO 1030/103).
77. B.H.R. to FO (2348), 7.3.49, (FO 371/76573).
78. B.H.R.'s weekly report to Bevin (727), 22.2.49, (FO 371/76651).
79. B.H.R. to FO, 8.3.49 (326), (FO 371/ 76573); Harvey to Kirkpatrick , 5.4.49. (FO 371/ 76580).
80. Frankfurt to FO (701), 14.4.49, (FO 371/76581); Berlin to FO (303), 3.3.49, (FO 371/76573); Bullock, pp. 690–91.
81. FO to B.H.R., 8.7.49, (FO 371/56753).
82. B.H.R.'s note to Kirkpatrick, 4.4.49, (FO 371/76579).
83. 'Relations with the German Federal Government', 13.7.49, (FO 371/76753).
84. 'Our Policy Towards Germany', Aug. 1949, (FO 1030/253).
85. B.H.R. to Kirkpatrick, 5.9.49, (FO 1030/253).
86. Bonn to FO (98), 28.10.49, (FO 371/76763). See also Ed. H.P. Schwarz, *Akten zur Auswärtigen politik der Bundesrepublik Deutschland, Vol. 1*, (Oldenbourg verlag, Munich, 1989), pp. 432–495 & docs. 1–13.
87. Annex to 'UK Record of Meeting at the Quai d'Orsay at 10.30 a.m. on 9.11.49 and Annex thereto', (FO 800/467).
88. C. Adenauer, *Memoirs, 1945–63*, (London, 1966) pp. 198–99.
89. Wahnerheide to FO (680), 2.5.50, (FO 371/85085).
90. *ibid.*, (356) 8.3.50.
91. *ibid.*
92. *ibid.*
93. See especially details in Wahnerheide to FO (430), 20.3.50, (FO 1030/237).
94. *Die Zeit*, 23.3.50.
95. 'Verbatim Record of 31 Meeting of the Council of Allied High Commission', 22.6.50, (FO 1023/313), and speech at the farewell dinner for General Robertson, 17.6.50, (B.H.R. Papers).

Chapter 8

1. Doris Humphreys to author, 27.5.92. Information on the polo from Lord Ronald Robertson to author, 21.12.95.
2. For an informative history of the base and the subsequent troubles with

the Egyptians see the unpublished manuscript by J. Reed, 'A History of the British Army in Egypt, 1950–56', (IWM, PP/Mor/117).

3. C. Barnett, *Britain and Her Army, 1509–1970*, (Penguin, 1970), p. 481.

4. 'British Defence Co-ordination Committee, Middle East. Working Party on Briefs For Defence Negotiations with Egypt. Paper no. 1. The British Base in Egypt, 18.3.53', p. 2, (FO 371/102802).

5. B.H.R. to Brownjohn, 22.8.50, (WO 216/349).

6. For the diplomatic background see E. Monroe, *Britain's Moment in the Middle East, 1914–56*, (Chatto, London, 1963); F.S. Northedge, *Descent from Power*, (Allen & Unwin, London, 1974); W.R. Louis, *The British Empire in the Middle East, 1945–51*, (OUP, Oxford, 1984).

7. COS (50) 157, 27.9.50, (DEFE 4/36).

8. Recorded memoirs of Stephen Anderson, June 1992.

9. B.H.R. to Brownjohn, 4.12.50, (WO 216/349).

10. *ibid.*

11. B.H.R. to Brownjohn, 16.5.51, (WO 216/734); Anderson memoirs.

12. 'Record of Discussion Held in the Iraqi Legation in Cairo . . ., 26.1.51', (FO 371/91657).

13. 'Record of Discussion Held at Air House, Habbaniya on 9.7.51', (WO 216/406).

14. B.H.R. to Brownjohn, 28.11.51, (WO 216/803).

15. COS (51) 133, 20.8.51, (DEFE 4/46).

16. Anderson.

17. Major Coverdale to author, 24.8.95.

18. B.H.R. to Brownjohn, 22.11.50, (WO 216/723).

19. B.H.R. to Brownjohn, 18.3 52, (WO 216/516).

20. *ibid.*, 21.4.52, (WO 216/536).

21. *ibid.*

22. B.H.R. to Brownjohn, 17.5.52, (WO 216/536).

23. *ibid.*

24. For a background to the crisis see J. Cable *Intervention at Abadan* (MacMillan, London, 1991), pp. 27–28.

25. Confidential Annex to COS (51) 100, 20.6.51, (DEFE 4/44).

26. *ibid.*, COS (51), 108, 29.6.51.

27. For the three 'phases' of BUCCANNEER see 'Current Plans for Ops. in Persia', (WO 216/400).

28. B.H.R. to Brownjohn, 4.7.51, (WO 216/400).

29. *Cable*, pp. 76–80.

30. Anderson.

31. COS (51) 134, 22.8.51, (DEFE 4/46).

32. 'Anglo-Egyptian Negotiations', 3.9.50, (FO 371/80454).

33. 'Memorandum by H.M. Ambassador, 30.9.50 & 'Comments by Cs.-in-C.M.E. . . .', Annexure 'A', (WO 216/356).

34. 'Anglo-Egyptian negotiations', 3.9.50.

35. 'Comments by Cs.-in-C. . . .'.

36. B.H.R. to Brownjohn, 29.11.50, (WO 216/722).

37. 'Record of a Conversation between the Sec. of State for Foreign Affairs and Chiefs of Staff, on 8.12.50, (FO 371/80457).
38. COS (50) 210, 19.12.50, (DEFE 4/38).
39. B.H.R. to Brownjohn, 22.11.50, (WO 216/723).
40. GHQ MELF (34294SDIA), 8.11.51, (FO 371/90119).
41. R.A. (Roger Allen), 15.3.52, (FO 371/96867).
42. Rapp, 'Canal Zone Situation Report, No. 3, Dec. 1–15', 16.12.51, (FO 371/90122).
43. Reed, p. 86.
44. Rapp, 'Canal Zone Situation Report . . ., No 5', 15.1.52, (FO 371/96860).
45. GHQ MELF to MOD (606/CCL), 16.1.52, (FO 371/96859).
46. *ibid.*, (613CCL), 23.1.52, (FO 371/96861).
47. Rapp to FO (82), 25.1.52, *ibid.*
48. GHQ MELF to WO (CIC 45617), 26.1.52, (WO 216/493). A. Eden, *Full Circle*, (Cassell, London, 1960), p. 232.
49. B.H.R. to Brownjohn, 12.2.52, (WO 216/754).
50. B.H.R. to CIGS, 21.11.51, (WO 216/798). See also B.H.R. to Brownjohn, 17.12.51, *ibid.*
51. GHQ to MOD, 16.12.51 (582CCL), *ibid.*
52. B.H.R. to Brownjohn, 12.2.52, (WO 216/754).
53. See Note 6 above.
54. 'Redeployment in the Middle East', 17.3.52, (WO 216/519). General Glubb's proposals for the Defence of the Middle East', Nov. '52, (WO 216/757).
55. 'Notes on a Talk between QMG and VCIGS and General Robertson, 27.12.51, (WO 216/469).
56. 'Note Prepared by War Office for ECAC Meeting, 29.2.52', (WO 216/519).
57. GHQ MELF to WO (CIC 87759), 5.11.52, (WO 216/811).
58. *ibid.*, (CIC 91985), 29.11.52, (WO 216/560).
59. Details in WO 216/851 & 852.
60. Slim to B.H.R., 14.2.51, and B.H.R. to Slim, 2.3.51 (B.H.R Papers).
61. Hamilton, (Vol.II), *Monty, 1944–76*, p. 819.
62. *ibid*.
63. *ibid.*, p. 817 and information from the Robertson family.
64. *ibid.*, p. 818.
65. *ibid.*
66. Slim to B.H.R., 8.5.52, (B.H.R. Papers).
67. B.H.R. to Harding, 13.5.52, *ibid.*
68. Piggott to B.H.R., 26.5.52, *ibid.* and 'Prime Minister's Personal Minutes' (WO 32/16213).
69. Minute by Roger Allen, 14.2.53, (FO 371/102796).
70. 'Defence Negotiations with Egypt', 13.4.53, (FO 371/102804).
71. Stevenson to FO, 1.5.53, (FO 371/12806); B.H.R. to Churchill, 12.5.53, (790), (FO 371/12808).

72. B.H.R. to Churchill, 12.5.53, (790).
73. COS (53) 72 9.6.53, (DEFE 4/63).
74. 'Anglo-Egyptian Defence Negotiations', (signed by Alexander), June 1953, (FO 371/102811).
75. B.H.R.'s minute on 'Mr. Hankey's letter of June 24 to Sir William Strang on Case A', 1.7.53, (FO 371/102812).
76. Strang's minute, 7.7.53, (FO 371/102817).
77. A draft is in FO 371/102817.
78. Note for Hankey by Allen, 10.7.53, (FO 371/102812) and Hankey to FO (1146) 5.8.53, (FO 371/102813).
79. B.H.R. to Bowker, 29.7.53, (FO 371/102813) and Allen to Hankey, 10.7.53, (FO 371/102812).
80. *ibid.*, (371/102813).
81. Churchill to B.H.R., 5.8.53, (1412 & 1418) (B.H.R. Papers).
82. Harding to B.H.R., 8.8.53, *ibid.*
83. Edith to B.H.R. – undated but probably about 8.8.53, *ibid.*
84. B.H.R. to Jenkins, 10.8.53, *ibid.*
85. *ibid.*, 'Egypt: Defence Negotiations', 14.9.53, (FO 371/102816).
86. B.H.R. to Allen, 17.10.53, (FO 371/102819).
87. B.H.R. to Allen, 17.10.53.
88. B.H.R. to Churchill, (790) 12.5.53, (FO 371/12808).
89. B.H.R. to Allen, 17.10.53.
90. Cairo to FO (1608), 19.11.53, (FO 371/102821).
91. *ibid.*
92. Eden to B.H.R., 30.7.54, (B.H.R. Papers).
93. Nasser to B.H.R., 29.7.54, *ibid.*
94. Head to B.H.R., 30.7.54, *ibid.*
95. B.H.R. to Head, 3.8.54, *ibid.*
96. Trevalyan to FO (1015), 12.6.56, (FO 371/118979).
97. *ibid.*, and FO to Cairo (1606), 14.6.56, (FO 371/118979).
98. Full details of the visit are in Trevalyan to FO (93), 23.6.56, and B.H.R. to Selwyn Lloyd, 9.7.56, *ibid.*

Chapter 9

1. Letters to B.H.R. from W.A. Gibson, 26.8.53, J.E. Edmonds, 5.8.53 and Konrad Adenauer,18.8.53, (B.H.R. Papers).
2. Ian Jacob to B.H.R., 17.8.53, *ibid.*
3. Lennox-Boyd to B.H.R., 14.8.53, *ibid.*
4. B.H.R. to Sir Robert Inglis, 31.8.53.
5. The manager was Charles Bird. Information given to author by Mr Michael Bonavia, (Interview), 24.9.94.
6. Interview with Miss Phyllis Rumbold, 31.1.92.
7. Bonavia, Interview, 24.9.94.
8. *ibid.*
9. M. Bonavia, *The Organisation of British Railways*, (Ian Allen, London,

1971), pp. 58–61. See also Gourvish, *British Railways, 1948–73*, (C.U.P., Cambridge, 1986), pp. 137–144. This book has been invaluable as a background for this chapter.

10. 'Draft letter for the Minister to send to Sir Brian Robertson', (MT 124/70).
11. B.H.R. to Lennox-Boyd, 15.4.54, *ibid*. See also Gourvish, p. 149.
12. 'Sir Brian Robertson's Memorandum' (115/6/4), MT 124/70; Minutes of Evidence taken before the Select Committee on Nationalised Industries, Reports and Committees, VII, 1959/60, 10.2.60, p. 38.
13. 'Draft letter . . .'.
14. Lennox–Boyd to B.H.R., 6.5.54, (MT 124/70).
15. B.H.R. to Jenkins, 16.7.54, *ibid*. Bonavia, *The Organisation*, p. 74.
16. Select Committee, 10.2.60, p. 36.
17. For both quotations see Gourvish, pp. 62 & 153; Bonavia, p. 75.
18. Select Committee, p. 37.
19. Interview with Sir Reginald Wilson, 28.10.94.
20. *Railway Gazette*, 10.12.54.
21. B.H.R., 'The British Transport System', *Journal of the Royal United Services Institute*, (hereafter RUSI), Vol. 101, Feb. 1956, p. 185.
22. Lord Falmouth to Lord Selkirk, 11.12.56, (MT 124/71). Gourvish, pp. 156–164.
23. M. Bonavia, *British Rail. The First 25 Years*, (Ian Allen, Newton Abbot, 1981), p. 89.
24. 'Reorganisation of the BTC', 10.6.60, Wansborough-Jones papers, Box 2, (BRB Record Centre). Interview with Sir Reginald Wilson.
25. Gourvish, p. 266.
26. Minutes of BTC (hereafter BTC), 19.8.54, 7/429, (AN 85/7).
27. Gourvish, p. 266.
28. Interview with Dame Alison Munro, 1.10.94.
29. BHR to Boyd Carpenter, 7.1.55, (MT 124/46).
30. *ibid*.
31. 'The Future of British Railways', Memo. by Minister of Transport and Civil Aviation, Jan. 1955, (MT 124/46).
32. 'Modernisation and Re-equipment of British Railways. Statement by Sir Brian Robertson . . . 24.1.55; copy in *ibid*.
33. Quoted in Gourvish, pp. 256–7.
34. This was the gist of a discussion he had with his ADC, Hugh Browne on nationalisation when they visited the Strasburg Fair in 1947. H. Browne to author, 31.10.95.
35. See Gourvish, pp. 217–245 for a detailed history of BR's industrial relations,1953–61, on which I have drawn heavily for this section. See also P.S. Bagwell, *The Railwaymen, I, The History of the National Union of Railwaymen*, (Allen and Unwin, London, 1963).
36. C.C. (53) 14.12. (CAB/128).
37. Gen. Secretary's (NUR) Report for 1954, Proceedings and Reports, 1954, Vol 2. (MS 127/ NU/1/1/56, Modern Records Centre, Warwick).

38. 'Note of a Meeting at 8, St. James Square, 6.1.55', (LAB 10/1319).
39. *Star*, 17.1.55. This was of course exaggerated. There were only three generals in the BTC and Brian Robertson had appointed only one. Indeed when in August, 1953, he was bombarded with requests by former military colleagues he was careful to turn them down. He told his friend Brigadier Belchem: 'I know that I shall have to be careful not to introduce too many soldiers into it. For these and other reasons, you should not rely on my ability to do anything.' (B.H.R to Brig. R.F.K. Belchem, 17.8.53, (B.H.R. Papers)).
40. *Sunday Chronicle*, 2.1.55.
41. *The Times*, 8.1.55.
42. K. Grand to Macmillan, 11.1.55. See also J.W. Watkins to B.H.R, 11.1.55, (B.H.R. Papers).
43. Rt. Rev. C. Bardsley to B.H.R., 20.1.55.
44. 'Note of a Meeting held at Min. of Labour . . . 27 & 28 April', 1955, (LAB 10/1390).
45. Jacob to Tewson, 9.6.55, (MS. 292, 253/41/3, Modern Records Centre, Warwick).
46. B.H.R. to Monckton, 7.6.55, (LAB 10/1390).
47. 'Notes of a Meeting . . . 9.6.55' and '. . . of 10.6.55', *ibid.*
48. *ibid.*, 11.6. 55.
49. Interview with Sir James Colyer-Ferguson, 17.1.92 and Miss P. Rumbold, 31.1.92. Mr. D. L. Stewart to author, 2.11. 91.
50. David Blee's notes on the Plenary Meeting of 31.1.57, (AN 6/56) & Hanks to B.H.R, 3.2.57, (B.H.R. Papers). The minutes of the meeting are in AN 85/10.
51. BTC., 30.6.55, 8/310, (AN 85/8).
52. B.H.R. to Marples, 24.1.61, (B.H.R. Papers).
53. R. Hardy, *Beeching. Champion of the Railway?*, (Ian Allan, London, 1989), pp. 35–6.
54. S. Hoskins to B.H.R., 2.7.55 and 13.7.55, (B.H.R. Papers).
55. Tel. conversation with Mr. Kentridge, formerly of the Watford Work Study Centre, May 1993.
56. BTC, 7.11.57 (10/463), (AN 85/11).
57. B.H.R. to Falmouth, 14.1.57, (MT 124/71).
58. *RUSI*, Vol. 101, p. 192.
59. BTC, 22.1.59 (12/47), (AN 85/12).
60. B.H.R. to G. Jenkins, 1.5.57, (T 124/12).
61. Elliot to B.H.R., 25.1.55, (AN 6/2).
62. 'Modernisation and Re-equipment of British Railways. Brief for the Minister', MT124/47. B.H.R. to den Hollander, 6.9.56, (Wansborough-Jones papers (hereafter W-J), Box/9, BRB Record Centre).
63. Sir Charles Goodeve, 'A Problem in Decision Making', *The Times*, 20.6.56
64. Gourvish, p. 291.
65. BTC, 30.1.58 (11/48), (AN 85/11).

66. Gourvish, p. 287.
67. Chairman's Conference On Modernisation, 26.4.57, (W-J/9).
68. 'Notes on a Visit to U.S. and Canada', p. 11, (AN 85/47).
69. R. Lamb, *The Macmillan Years*, (Murray, London, 1995), pp. 232–4.
70. 'Chairman's Conference . . .', 15.2.57, (W-J/9).
71. BTC, 15.3.56 (9/127), (AN 85/9).
72. Author's interview with Sir Reginald Wilson, 28.10.94.
73. 'Note of Meeting in Chairman's Room, 24 May 1956', (AN 6/53).
74. Gourvish, p. 297.
75. 'Memorandum', 13.3.58, (AN 6/56).
76. BTC, 30.10.58 (11/468), (AN 85/12).
77. *ibid.*, 25.9.58, (11/403).
78. Weir to B.H.R., 25.3.57, Hoskins to B.H.R., 26.3.57, (B.H.R. Papers.) (See also Gourvish, pp. 231–242).
79. Hanks to B.H.R., 20.1.60, *ibid.*
80. *RUSI*, p. 189.
81. See *Sunday Express*, 4.12.55, for example.
82. H. Edwards to B.H.R., 28.1.60, (B.H.R. Papers). Cassandra was William Connor.
83. 'The Generals Who Have Been Quiet'. (Enclosed in Edwards' letter.)
84. *RUSI*, p. 190.
85. BTC, 30.7.59 (12/316), (AN 85/13).
86. *Evening Standard*, 9.6.59.
87. BTC, 15.5.58 (11/195), (AN 85/11).
88. Information given to the author.
89. 'Note for the Record' 14.12.59, (PREM 3147).
90. BTC, 28.1.60 (13/44), (AN 85/15).
91. Select Committee, 18.2.60, p. 68.
92. C. Weir, to B.H.R., 29.7.60, (B.H.R. Papers).
93. 'Transport', Spring, 1960, (PREM 11/3147).
94. *ibid.*
95. BTC, 25.2.60 (13/75), (AN 85/15).
96. BTC Commission, 31.3.60, (13/138), (AN 85/15).
97. 'Note of Discussion between Minister and Sir Ivan Stedeford on 10 May', (MT 124/96).
98. B.H.R. to Stedeford, 3.6.60, (W-J/2).
99. *ibid.*, 20.7.60.
100. Wansborough-Jones to B.H.R., 27.5.60. (One of the more sympathetic Civil Servants was O.F. Gingell.)
101. *ibid.*
102. B.H.R to Stedeford, 30.8.60, (W-J/2).
103. Weir to B.H.R., 29.7.60, (B.H.R.Papers), Gourvish, pp. 302–304, 307–316.
104. 'Extract from the Minister of Transport's minute to the PM of 9.8.60, Rail', (PREM 11/3148).
105. Lamb. pp. 232–4. 'For the Record', 25.11.60 (PREM 11/3148),

22.12.60 (13/486) and 12.1.61 (14/8)), (AN 85/15 &16).

106. See C. Barnett ' A Dead Hand on Our Railways', *Time and Tide*, 20.2.60.

107. J. Betjeman to Macmillan, 1.6.60, (MT 124/88. This file contains the relevant material on the Euston debate).

108. *The Times*. 11.6.60. See also minute by R.M. Davis: 'The Doric Arch, Euston Station', 18.10.60, (MT 124/88).

109. Gourvish, p. 321.

110. B.H.R. to Marples, 24.1.61, (BHR Papers).

111. *ibid*.

112. Information given to the author by the Robertson family.

113. Weir to B.H.R., 29.7.60, (B.H.R. Papers).

114. Gourvish, p. 143. Telephone Conversation with Sir Reginald Wilson, 7.1.96.

Chapter 10

1. Information from the Robertson family and telephone conversation with Mr. J. Morris, 16.6.92.

2. Parliamentary Debates (Lords), 19.11.63, Vol. 253, col. 279.

3. Telephone conversation with Mr. Jim Thomas, 29.10.95.

4. For further details see the minutes of the Annual General Meetings of the Gloucestershire Association of Boys Clubs (G.A.B.C.), 1961–67.

5. *Sunday Times*, 7.11.65 & G.A.B.C. Executive Committee Minutes, 7.3.66. Conversation with Mr. Morris, 16.6.92.

6. Parl. Debates (Lords), 3.3.65 & 21.2.68, Vols. 263 & 289.

7. Vol. 263, col. 1142.

8. *ibid.*, 1138.

9. *ibid.*, 1148.

10. *ibid.*, 1147–48.

11. H. Barty-King, *The Salter's Company, 1394–1994*, (James & James, London, 1994), pp. 203–4.

12. Report of the Master to the General Court of the Livery on Election Day, 13.6.66, Court Minute Book (Rough), Vol. 14, Salters' Archives.

13. *ibid*.

14. Information from the Robertson family.

15. Parl Debates (Lords), Vol. 236, 18.12.61, col. 532.

16. *ibid.*, Vols. 255 & 297, 18.2.64 & 19.11.68.

17. *ibid.*, Vol. 265, 28.4.65, col. 669.

18. *ibid.*, Vol. 243, 1.8.62, col. 370.

19. *ibid.*, Vol. 247, 6.3.63, col. 446.

20. *ibid.*, Vol. 296, 26.8.68, cols. 539–542.

21. *ibid.*, Vol. 303, 25.3.70, cols. 1473–1476.

22. *ibid.*, Vol. 239, 12.4.62, cols. 603–4.

23. *ibid.*, col. 602.

24. *ibid.*, col. 604.

25. *ibid.*, Vol. 249, 1.5.63, col. 211.

26. *ibid.*, Vol. 250, 21.6.63, cols, 1514–18.

27. *ibid.*, Vol. 300, 18.3.69, cols. 739–742.

28. J. Straw, 'The Briton who put workers in the boardroom', *The Times*, 3.7.89.

29. There are several letters in the B.H.R. Papers which testify to the friendship of the two men. For instance on 6 Jan 1966 he wrote to Adenauer on the occasion of his 90th. birthday: 'My letter is late for which I apologize. We had the great pleasure of seeing you receive the congratulations of your own countrymen on television last night; we remarked to each other that you looked the youngest of all'. Adenauer wrote back on 14 January: 'I have not heard from you for such a long time that I assumed you had gone on a long journey . . . I am always very pleased to see you.' (translated from the German by the author).

30. Author's interview with Sir Frank Roberts, 1.8.92. In fact, Roberts recalls, the meeting never took place either because B.H.R cancelled his visit to Germany or Adenauer fell ill.

31. B.H.R. to Gen. Erskine, 29.9.64 & to Sir Harold Caccia, 20.1.65, (B.H.R. Papers), see Adenauer, p. 35.

32. Script is enclosed in G. Pieper to B.H.R., 4.7.69, (B.H.R. Papers).

33. B.H.R., 'A Miracle . . .?', p. 410.

34. Mrs. Bardsley to author, 11.4.92.

35. Mr. J. Morris' telephone conversation with author, 16.6.92.

36. After-dinner speech, 17.6.50, (B.H.R. Papers).

37. 'Service of Thanksgiving for the Life and Work of General the Lord Robertson . . ., 13.6.74'. This, together with a copy of Bardsley's address, is in the B.H.R. Papers.

LIST OF ABBREVIATIONS AND GLOSSARY

AAI	Allied Armies in Italy
ACC	Allied Control Commission
ADC	Aide-de-Camp
AFHQ	Allied Force Headquarters
AMGOT	Allied Military Government of Occupied Territories
AN	After Nationalisation
AQMG	Assistant Quarter Master General
A & Q	Administrative and Quarter Master General's Department
ASLEF	Associated Society of Locomotive Engineers and Firemen
BRB	British Railways Board
BTC	British Transport Commission
CAB	Cabinet Records
CAO	Chief Administrative Officer
CCG	Control Commission for Germany
CDU	Christian Democratic Union
CFM	Council of Foreign Ministries
C-in-C	Commander-in-Chief
CCG(BE)	Control Council Germany (British Element)
CGS	Chief of the General Staff
CIGS	Chief of the Imperial General Staff
DAQMG	Deputy Assistant Quarter Master General
DMO & I	Director of Military Operations and Intelligence
DSO	Distinguished Service Order
FBI	Federation of British Industries
FO	Foreign Office
GDR	German Democratic Republic
GFR	German Federal Republic
GOC	General Officer Commanding
GSO1,2 & 3	Staff Officer, First, Second & Third Grades
LHCMA	Liddell Hart Centre for Military Archives
L of C	Lines of Communication
MA	Military Assistant
MC	Military Cross

MELF	Middle East Land Forces
MT	Ministry of Transport
NATO	North Atlantic Treaty Organisation
NUR	National Union of Railwaymen
PAYE	Pay As You Earn
POW	Prisoner of War
PRO	Public Record Office
QMG	Quarter Master General
'Q'	All matters or personnel within the responsibility of the QMG
SHAEF	Supreme Headquarters Allied Expeditionary Force
SPD	German Social Democratic Party
TSSA	Transport and Salaried Staffs' Association
UK	United Kingdom
VCIGS	Vice Chief of the Imperial General Staff
WO	War Office

GLOSSARY OF GERMAN TERMS USED IN CHAPTERS 6 AND 7

Kreis	A district or unit of local government.
Land or, plural, *Länder*	German federal state(s).
Landtag	A local state parliament.
Schloss	Castle or manor house.

SELECT BIBLIOGRAPHY

PRINCIPAL ARCHIVAL SOURCES

Public Record Office, Kew
Cabinet papers: CAB 128; CAB 106; CAB 44. Chiefs of Staff meetings:
DEFE 4. Foreign Office and Control Commission: FO 371; FO 800; FO
938; FO 1010; FO 1014; FO 1030; FO 1049. Ministry of Labour: LAB 10;
Ministry of Transport: AN 85; MT 124. War Office: WO 32; WO 95; WO
169; WO 170; WO 204; WO 214; WO 216; WO 256.

Imperial War Musem, London
The Papers/Memoirs of: Major General W. Bishop, General Sir George
Erskine, Major General L.A. Hawes. Brigadier R. Lymer, Major General C.
Miller, Field Marshal Viscount Montgomery, J. Reed Esq., Lt. General Sir
Ronald Scobie, Major General G. Surtees, Lt. Col. K.F.B. Tower, Major
General D. Wimberley, Colonel H. Yeo.

Liddell Hart Centre for Military Archives
The Papers of Lt. General Sir Humphrey Gale; Major General W.R.C.
Penney.

The British Rail Board Record Centre
The Papers of Major-General L. Wansborough-Jones.

The National Army Museum, Chelsea, London
The Papers of Field Marshal Lord Harding of Petherton.

The Queens' College, Cambridge
The Papers of Major General A.C. Temperley.

Charterhouse School, Godalming
The School archive material for the years 1910–1913.

The Salters' Company
Records for the year of General Robertson's Mastership, 1965–66.

Young Gloucestershire, Gloucester
Minutes of the Gloucestershire Association of Boys Clubs, 1961–1970.

Private Papers:
The relatively small collection of the Papers of General the Lord Robertson of Oakridge and some personal correspondence of his father, Field Marshal Sir William Robertson, are with the present Lord Robertson.
The diaries of Michael Holland-Hibbert (Lord Knutsford), 1947–48.
The diaries of Lavinia Orde, 1944–45, *Better Late than Never.*
A. Albu, *Back Bench Technocrat,* an unpublished autobiography.

PRINTED SOURCES AND SECONDARY LITERATURE

K. Adenauer, *Memoirs,* (Weidenfeld and Nicolson, London, 1965)
P. Bagwell, *The Railwayman, I. The History of the National Railwaymen,* (George Allen and Unwin, London, 1963)
D. Bark and D. Gress, *A History of West Germany. Vol. 1, From Shadow To Substance, 1945–63,* (Blackwell, Oxford, 1993 (2nd edition))
C. Barnett, *Britain and Her Army, 1509–1970,* (Penguin, London, 1970)
H. Barty-King, *The Salter's Company, 1394–1994,* (James and James, London, 1994)
M. Bonavia, *The Organisation of British Railways,* (Ian Allen, 1971)
——, *British Rail. The First 25 Years,* (David and Charles, Newton Abbot, 1981)
B. Bond, *British Military Policy Between the Wars,* (OUP, Oxford, 1980)
V. Bonham-Carter, *Soldier True. The Life and Times of Field-Marshal Sir William Robertson, 1860–1933,* (Muller, London, 1963)
A. Bullock, *Ernest Bevin, Foreign Secretary, 1945–51,* (Heinemann, London 1983)
J. Cable, *Intervention at Abadan,* (Macmillan, London, 1991)
The Carthusian, (Charterhouse, Godalming, 1910–1914)
M. Carver, *El Alamein,* (Batsford, 1962)
L. Clay, *Decision in Germany,* (Heinemann. London, 1950)
Papers of, ed., J.E.Smith, Vols. 1 &2, (Bloomington and London, 1974)
H. Collins, *Mining Memories and Musings,* (Garden City Press, Letchworth, 1985).
A. Cowgill, T. Brimlow and C. Booker, *Repatriations From Austria In 1945, Cowgill Inquiry,* (Sinclair Stephenson, London, 1990)
——, *Report of an Inquiry,* (Sinclair Stephenson, London, 1990)
A. Deighton, 'Cold-War Diplomacy: British Policy Towards Germany's Role in Europe, 1945–9'. Ed. I. Turner, *Reconstruction in Post-War Germany,* (Berg, Oxford, 1989)
C. D'Este, *Fatal Decision. Anzio and the Battle for Rome,* (HarperCollins, London, 1991)
F. Donnison, *Civil Affairs and Military Government. North West Europe 1944–46,* (HMSO, London, 1961)
S. Douglas, *Years of Command,* (Collins, London, 1966)
Dunlop Gazette, 1934–40
A, Eden, *Full Circle,* (Cassell, London, 1960)

J. Edmonds & H. Davies, *Military Operations in Italy, 1915–19* (HMSO, 1949)

J. Elliot, *On and Off The Rails*, (George Allen and Unwin, London, 1982)

J. Farquharson, '"The Essential Division". Britain and the partition of Germany, 1945–49'. *German History*, 9 (1), 1991, pp. 23–45

A. Godwin-Austen, *The Staff and Staff College*, (Constable, London, 1927)

V. Gollancz, *In Darkest Germany*, (Gollancz, London, 1947)

T. Gourvish, *British Railways, 1948–73*, (CUP, Cambridge,1986)

N. Hamilton, *Monty: Master of the Battlefield*, (Hamish Hamilton, London, 1983)

——, *Monty: The Field Marshal, 1944–76*, (Hamish Hamilton, London, 1986)

R. Hardy, *Beeching. Champion of the Railways?*, (Ian Allan, London, 1989)

C. Harris, *Allied Administration in Italy*, (HMSO, 1957)

G. Jones, 'The growth and performance of British multinational firms before 1939: the case of Dunlop'. *Economic History Review*, 2nd. Ser., Vol. XXXVII, pp. 35–53)

A. Kramer, 'British Dismantling Politics, 1954–49: A Reassessment'. Ed. I. Turner, *Reconstruction in Post-War Germany*, pp. 125–153, (Berg, Oxford, 1989)

R. Lamb, *The Macmillan Years*, (Murray, London, 1995)

W. Louis, *The British Empire in the Middle East, 1945–51*, (OUP, Oxford, 1984)

H. Macmillan, *War Diaries. The Mediterranean 1943–45*, (Macmillan, London, 1984)

B. Marshall, 'German Attitudes To British Military Government, 1945–7'. *Journal of Contemporary History*, 15 (4), 1980, pp. 655–81

——, 'Democratic Rebirth Under British Control'. Ed. I. Turner in *Reconstruction of Post-War Germany*, (Berg, Oxford, 1989)

J. McMillan, *The Dunlop Story*, (Weidenfeld and Nicolson, London, 1989)

G.D. Martineau, *The Charterhouse We Knew*, ed. W.H. Holden, (British Technical and General Press, London, 1950)

C. Mather, *The Aftermath of War*, (Brassey's, London, 1992)

E. Monroe, *Britain's Moment in the Middle East, 1914–56*, (Chatto & Windus, London, 1963)

B. Montgomery, *Memoirs of Field Marshal the Viscount Montgomery of Alamein*, (Collins, London, 1958)

Natal Mercury, 1935–40, (Durban, South Africa)

N. Nicolson, *Alex. The Life of Field Marshal Earl Alexander of Tunis*, (Weidenfeld and Nicolson, London, 1973)

F.S. Northedge, *Descent From Power*, (Allen and Unwin, London, 1974)

The Official History of Operations on the North West Frontier of India, 1920–35, (Manager of Publications, Delhi, 1945)

N. Orpen, *South African Forces. World War II, Vol. I, East African and Abyssinian Campaigns*, (Purnell & Sons, Cape Town, 1968)

R. Overy, 'Hitler's War Plans and the German Economy', *Paths To War*, pp. 96–127. Ed. R. Boyce & E. Robertson, (Macmillan, London, 1989)

Owl Pie, (Staff College, Camberley, 1926–7)

F. Piggott, *Broken Thread*, (Gale and Polden, Aldershot, 1950)

B. Pitt, *The Crucible of War*, (Cape, London, 1980)

——, *The Year of Alamein*, 1942, (Cape, London, 1982)

E. Plischke, *History of The Allied High Commission For Germany* (Historical Division, US High Commission, Germany, 1951)

S. Playfair, C. Molony & W. Jackson, (The Official History), *The Mediterranean and the Middle East*, Vols I–VI, (HMSO, London,1954–87)

C. Richardson, *From Churchill's Secret Circle to the BBC*, (Brassey's, London, 1991)

U. Reusch, 'Das Porträt. Sir Brian Robertson', *Geschichte im Westen* 5, (1), 1990

B.H. Robertson, 'The British Transport System', *Journal of the Royal United Services Institution*, 101 (1), 1956, pp. 183–93

——, 'A Miracle? Potsdam 1945 – Western Germany, 1965', Royal Institute of International Affairs, 41 (3), 1965, pp. 401–410

W. Robertson, *From Private to Field-Marshal*, (Constable, London, 1921)

Royal Engineers Journal, (Chatham, 1920–26)

R. Ryder, *Oliver Leese*, (Hamish Hamilton, London, 1987)

Select Committee on Nationalised Industries, Reports and Committees, VII: B.R. 1959/60

A. Shepperd, *The Royal Military Academy, Sandhurst and its Predecessors*, (Country Life Books, London, 1980)

R. Steininger, 'Wie Die Teilung Deutschlands verhindert werden sollte. Der Robertson Plan aus dem Jahre 1948', *Militärgeschichtliche Mitteilungen* 33 (1), 1983, pp. 49–90

A. Temperley, *The Whispering Gallery of Europe*, (Collins, London, 1939)

N. Tolstoy, *The Minister and the Massacres*, (Hutchinson, London, 1986)

I. Turner, Great Britain and the Post-War Currency Reform'. *Historical Journal*, 30 (3), 1987, pp. 658–708

A. & J. Tusa, *The Berlin Blockade*, (Hodder and Stoughton, London, 1988)

D.C. Watt, *Britain Looks to Germany*, (Oswald Wolff, London, 1965)

A. Wavell, *Generals and Generalship*, Reprinted from *The Times*, Feb. 17, 18, 19, 1941

C. Weir, *Civilian Assignment*, (Methuen, London, 1953)

D. Williamson, *The British in Germany 1918–30*, (Berg, Oxford, 1991)

D. Woodward, *The Military Correspondence of Field Marshal, Sir William Robertson, 1915–18*, (Army Records Society, Bodley Head, London, 1989)

INDEX